Making Citizens in Africa

Making Citizens in Africa argues that citizenship creation and expansion is a pivotal part of political contestation in Africa today. Citizenship is a powerful analytical tool with which to approach political life in contemporary Africa because the institutional and structural reforms of the period since the 1990s have been inextricably linked with the battle over the "right to have rights." Professor Lahra Smith's work advances the notion of meaningful citizenship, which refers to the way in which rights are exercised, the effective practice of citizenship. Using data from Ethiopia and developing a historically informed study of language policy and ethnicity and gender, this book analyzes the contestation over citizenship that engages the state, social movements, and individuals in consequential ways. By combining original data on language policy with detailed historical study and an analytical focus on ethnicity, citizenship, and gender, this work brings a fresh approach not only to Ethiopian political development but also to contemporary citizenship concerns relevant to other parts of Africa.

Lahra Smith is assistant professor in the School of Foreign Service at Georgetown University. She has written extensively on ethnic identity, African elections, and gender and politics in Africa. Her research has been published in *The Journal of Modern African Studies, Democratization*, and policy briefs for organizations such as the United States Institute of Peace. She has received grants and fellowships from the National Science Foundation and the Fulbright-Hays program. In 2010 she was the Fulbright Visiting Research Chair in Ethnicity and Multicultural Citizenship at Queen's University (Kingston, Canada).

African Studies

The African Studies series, founded in 1968, is a prestigious series of monographs, general surveys, and textbooks on Africa covering history, political science, anthropology, economics, and ecological and environmental issues. The series seeks to publish work by senior scholars as well as the best new research.

A list of books in this series will be found at the end of this volume.

Making Citizens in Africa

Ethnicity, Gender, and National Identity in Ethiopia

LAHRA SMITH

Georgetown University

CAMBRIDGE
UNIVERSITY PRESS

CAMBRIDGE UNIVERSITY PRESS
Cambridge, New York, Melbourne, Madrid, Cape Town,
Singapore, São Paulo, Delhi, Mexico City

Cambridge University Press
32 Avenue of the Americas, New York, NY 10013-2473, USA

www.cambridge.org
Information on this title: www.cambridge.org/9781107610385

First published 2013

Printed in the United States of America

A catalog record for this publication is available from the British Library.

Library of Congress Cataloging in Publication data
Smith, Lahra, 1974–
Making citizens in Africa : ethnicity, gender, and national
identity in Ethiopia / Lahra Smith.
pages   cm. – (African studies ; 125)
Includes bibliographical references and index.
ISBN 978-1-107-03531-7 (hardback) – ISBN 978-1-107-61038-5 (paperback)
1. Citizenship – Social aspects–Ethiopia.   2. Political participation – Social
aspects – Ethiopia.   3. Language policy – Ethiopia.   4. Ethiopia – Politics and
government – 1991–   5. National characteristics, Ethiopian.   I. Title.
JQ3767.A2S65   2013
323.60963–dc23   2012033999

ISBN 978-1-107-03531-7 Hardback
ISBN 978-1-107-61038-5 Paperback

For Dawit, Abraham, and Milo
In memory of
Jotham Tezare Gebru
and
Emily Kathleen Arndt

Contents

Maps and Tables

Maps

Tables

Acknowledgments

One rainy afternoon in July 2003, I sat on a patio with my father-in-law, and he sang to me three different national anthems for Ethiopia. A man in his early seventies, he has lived through three major political regimes and three constitutions. He has been both a subject and a citizen: a subject of the imperial monarchy and a citizen of two other regimes. The implications of those three songs echoed through my research in Ethiopia. As many African states celebrate fifty years of independence, Ethiopia, a country with the distinction of never being colonized by European powers, constitutes a critical case of citizen making. My own understanding of how citizens are made anywhere, and especially in contemporary Ethiopia, has been shaped not only by my academic training and the formal research documented here but also by the personal relationships that have inspired and sustained my intellectual pursuits. I wish to acknowledge those individuals and their contributions here.

Perhaps the greatest intellectual and personal debt I have is to my mentor and friend, Dr. Edmond J. Keller. Ed has been a tireless critic and champion, sharing my enthusiasm for the complexities and uniqueness of Ethiopia, yet always pushing for thematic and disciplinary insights that could move beyond any one case. But most of all, he is a scholar of the utmost integrity and compassion and a true model of all that a teacher can be. My warmest thanks to you, Ed, for your guidance over the years and your tremendous leadership and vision with respect to African studies.

All errors and omissions are certainly my own, particularly errors of interpretation. Nonetheless, I have been guided by intellectual conversations before, during, and after graduate school. I would never have written this book or even gone on to graduate school were it not for the support of the Ronald E. McNair Scholars Program and my undergraduate mentor, Dr. Steve Reyna. Colleagues and mentors in my work at USAID also spurred me to further study, including my dear friend Annamaria Watrin, as well as Sheryl Pinnelli. I had several other excellent teachers at UCLA, including Richard Sklar, Raymond Rocco, Victor Wolfenstein, Brian Walker, Marc Sawyer, Daniel Posner, Carole Pateman, and Edith Mukudi. Colleagues at several institutions have contributed at various points to improving my analysis, including Susanna Wing, Amy Poteete, Wendy Belcher, Jennifer DeMaio, Robert Dowd, Jennifer Winther, Zachariah Mampilly, Hector Perla, Worku Nida, Pietro Toggia, Judith Stevenson, Matthew Hopper, and Bonnie Holcomb.

Special thanks to those who read all or parts of this manuscript, including especially Shobana Shankar, Scott Taylor, Grover Hudson, Ezekiel Gebissa, and Ruth Iyob. Your very different and often critical comments significantly strengthened the manuscript. Several colleagues at Georgetown University offered helpful advice, including John McNeill, Kathleen McNamara, Charles King, David Edelstein, Samantha Pinto, and Meredith McKittrick. A special thanks to Carole Sargent and the Office of Scholarly and Literary Publications for the support of this work at multiple stages. Two anonymous reviewers from Cambridge University Press provided insightful and challenging comments that greatly enhanced the conceptual development of meaningful citizenship presented in this book. I am most grateful for their contribution.

Thanks as well to Bruce Berman, John McGarry, and the faculty at Queen's University, Canada, for providing the setting to complete the writing of this book. Portions of the manuscript were presented to colleagues at Queen's University, UCLA, University of Victoria, Concordia University, and Haverford College, and comments were most appreciated. Gratitude goes to Grover Hudson, Solomon Addis Getahun, Shimelis G. Assefa, and, in Ethiopia, Mewael Sahel Selassie, for excellent Amharic language instruction. Research and translation assistance were provided by Shimelis Mulugeta, Azanaw Mengistu, Ahmed Ahmed, Hannah Hill, and Jescinta Izevbigie. I am also grateful for the assistance of local coordinators and regional program officers of World Learning, Inc., in Hawassa and the Southern region for their assistance in conducting fieldwork in the Gurage and Wolaitta zones, and the *woreda* and zonal coordinators who assisted in Bale, Siltie, Borena, Assosa, and elsewhere.

In Ethiopia, there are a few colleagues and friends whose influence cannot be overstated. First to Allehone and Allemmaya Mulugeta, both impressive intellectuals in their own right and people I am proud to call friends. Other friends and scholars of Ethiopia to whom I remain extremely grateful include Netsanet Demissie, Frehiwot Samuel, and Tsegaye Regassa, each of whom shared their diverse and wise perspectives on Ethiopian politics, law, and culture. Leonardo Arriola is both a dear friend and an incisive scholar of politics, and this book bears the mark of his intellectual influence in numerous ways. Finally, a sincere debt of gratitude to all the parents, teachers, and school directors in the Oromiya, Wolaitta, Siltie, Gurage, and Benishangul-Gumuz regions, as well as the administrators and regional and zonal educational officials with whom I worked. I have tremendous admiration for the dedication and professionalism of Ethiopia's teachers in particular, who are doing some of the most vital work in the country today, and under extremely challenging circumstances. A special thanks to those who worked with me on the 2003 Training of Trainers for the revised civics curriculum, including Ato Dagnaw, W/o Malkam, Mohammed Abdullahi, and other friends and colleagues.

Support for the fieldwork in Ethiopia in 2003 was provided by the U.S. Department of Education's Fulbright-Hays Doctoral Dissertation Research Abroad program. Writing support was given by UCLA's Graduate Division Dissertation Year Fellowship, as well as Georgetown University's Graduate School of Arts and Sciences Junior Faculty Research Fellowship. Final writing was done while serving as a Fulbright Visiting Research Chair in Ethnicity and Multicultural Citizenship at Queen's University in Kingston, Canada. During my time in Ethiopia, I was a Visiting Researcher with the Institute for Ethiopian Studies (IES) at Addis Ababa University (AAU). I continue to maintain my status as Visiting Researcher with IES and have also sustained a relationship with the Department of Political Science and International Relations (DPSIR) at Addis Ababa University. At Addis Ababa University, thanks particularly to now-retired University President Andreas Eshete, as well as Baye Yimam, former Director of IES, and Gebru Tareke, present Director of IES. I express my gratitude and sadness at the loss of Professor Assefa Medhane of DPSIR, who showed interest in this work early on. Others at AAU that offered support or guidance include Solomon Gofie, Kassahun Berhanu, Gemetchu Megerssa, Gideon Cohen, Merera Gudina, and Moges Yigezu. Thanks to Cambridge University Press and Sage Publications for permission to reprint portions of work previously published in *The Journal of Modern African Studies* and *Journal of Developing Societies*.

And last but not least, I thank friends and family. Those that have always supported this venture include dear friends Lindsay Reed and

Angelina Gagne. A warm thank you to my family in Ethiopia whose songs of old and new Ethiopia and warm love have made life so joyful. My family in the United States has long been invested in this work, especially my sisters who encouraged and sustained me through graduate school and beyond. I could never have done this without you.

I dedicate this book to the memory of two friends whose lives were lost far too young, but who live on in our memories, Dr. Emily Arndt and Jotham Tezare Gebru. We miss them so. And to the future as well, to Abraham and Milo especially, who are my deepest joy. May the citizenship of the future be even more equal and sustainable for you and future generations. Finally, to Dawit, in deep gratitude for an intellectually rich and gentle companionship through each and every stage of this project. Words cannot convey the depth of my appreciation for all that you are to my life.

Abbreviations

AAPO	All-Amhara People's Organization
AAU	Addis Ababa University
BPLM	Benishangul People's Liberation Movement
CCI	Council of Constitutional Inquiry
COR	Council of Representatives
CUD	Coalition for Unity and Democracy
ECSC	Ethiopian Civil Service College
EOC	Ethiopian Orthodox Church
EPDM	Ethiopian People's Democratic Movement
EPLF	Eritrean People's Liberation Front
EPRDF	Ethiopian People's Revolutionary Democratic Front
EPRP	Ethiopian People's Revolutionary Party
ESDP	Education Sector Development Program
ESM	Ethiopian Student Movement
EUS	Ethiopian University Service
EWLA	Ethiopian Women Lawyers Association
GPRDM	Gurage People's Revolutionary Democratic Movement
HOF	House of Federation
HPR	House of People's Representatives
ICDR	Institute for Curriculum Development and Research
ISEN	Institute for the Study of Ethiopian Nationalities
KMG	Kembatti Mentti Gezzimma (NGO)
MEISON	Amharic acronym for the All-Ethiopian Socialist Movement
MOE	Ministry of Education
MOI	Medium of instruction
MT	Mother tongue language (first language)
NDRP	Program of the National Democratic Revolution
NETP	National Education and Training Policy

NL	Nationality language
NLCCC	National Literacy Campaign Coordinating Committee
OFDM	Oromo Federalist Democratic Movement
OLF	Oromo Liberation Front
OPDO	Oromo People's Democratic Organization
PA	Peasant associations
PDO	People's Democratic Organization
PDRE	People's Democratic Republic of Ethiopia
PMAC	Provisional Military Administrative Council
REB	Regional Education Bureau
SEPDF	Southern Ethiopian People's Democratic Front
SNNPR	Southern Nations, Nationalities, and People's Region
SPDUP	Siltie Peoples Democratic Unity Party
TGE	Transitional Government of Ethiopia
TPLF	Tigray People's Liberation Front
TTC	Teacher Training College
TTI	Teacher Training Institute
TVET	Technical and Vocational Education and Training
UEDF	United Ethiopian Democratic Forces
WEO	Woreda Education Office
WPE	Worker's Party of Ethiopia
WSLF	Western Somali Liberation Front
ZEO	Zone Education Office

Glossary

Ateetee: Oromo deity that bestows upon women fertility, happiness, health, prosperity; ritual performed by women in the name of the deity (Oromo)

Balabbat: nobleman, chief (Amharic)

Beher: nation (Amharic)

Behereseb: nationality (Amharic)

Chaffee: grassy place where rituals and meetings are held among the Oromo; regional parliament for Oromiya regional state (Oromo)

Fidel: letter, alphabet, script, character (Amharic)

Gabbar: tenant farmer, serf, bondsman (Amharic)

Gadaa: age-grading socio-political system of the Oromo (Oromo)

Gult: land granted by a ruler to an individual or religious institution as an endowment; fief (Amharic)

Hanfala: belt worn by married women among the Arsi Oromo (Oromo)

Hebretesebawinnet: a kind of Ethiopian socialism espoused by the Derg regime, with principles such as equality, self-reliance, and unity (Amharic)

Hizb: people, community, public (plural: Hizboch) (Amharic)

Kebre Negast: lit. "glory of the kings," volume of biblical stories and legends as Ethiopian national epic

Ketema: town, city (Amharic)

Malkañña: local governor, owner of land and person to whom a gabbar owes tribute (Amharic)

Mannennet teyyaqe: "question of identity": legal term used in House of Federation rulings (Amharic)

Meserete timhirt: foundation of education; especially the educational campaign of the Derg period (Amharic)

Naft'añña: rifleman, especially a soldier of Emperor Menilek often given land in conquered territory (Amharic)

Odaa: Sycamore tree, now used as the symbol for the regional state of Oromiya (Oromo)

Qebelle: district, precinct (Amharic)

Qubee: Latinate Oromo writing system or letter of Qubee alphabet (Oromo)

Rest: inherited land or land-use rights (Amharic)

Resteñña: owner of rest land, landowner (Amharic)

Seera: traditional law (Oromo)

Siiqqee: decorated stick given to Arsi Oromo married women; used by women during ceremonies such as the Ateetee (Oromo)

Wayyuu: sacredness, sanctity; of person, place, or thing (Oromo)

Wereda: district, administrative subdivision (Amharic)

Yeluññeta: sensitivity to opinions of others, public spiritedness, sense of propriety (Amharic)

Zega: national, subject, citizen (Amharic)

Zegannet/Zegennet: nationality, citizenship (Amharic)

Zemeccha: campaign, especially the Derg regime's National Campaign for Development Through Cooperation (Amharic)

Notes

The meaning of words not listed in this Glossary is given in the text. The two primary dictionaries used were Kane (1990) and Tilahun (1989). Usage of others is cited where necessary.

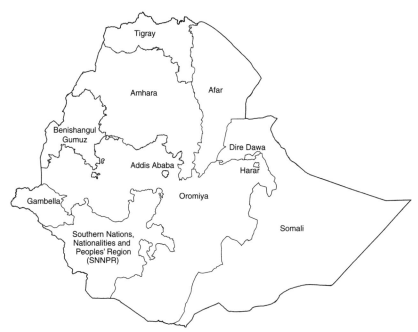

MAP 1. Regional States of Ethiopia.
Source: Leonardo Arriola

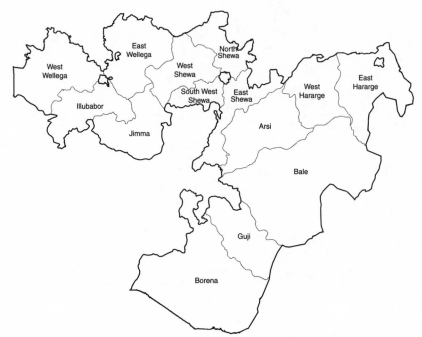

MAP 2. Oromiya Regional State Zonal Map.
Source: Leonardo Arriola

MAP 3. Southern Nations, Nationalities, and People's Regional State (SNNPR) Zonal Map.
Source: Leonardo Arriola

Introduction

In the Shola neighborhood of the Ethiopian capital, Addis Ababa, there is a bustling local market. Just a few decades ago, Shola formed the out-skirts of town, and much of its surrounding areas were open fields where children could play soccer and follow well-worn paths to school each morning. Now there are no fields for miles, and the edges of the city have moved out in all directions to new residential developments. Shola is now part of downtown Addis Ababa. It is also home to pockets of distinct ethnic communities, as are many of Addis Ababa's neighborhoods. I lived in Shola for a year, and I was repeatedly told that "a lot of Sudanese live in Shola." I did indeed observe many young men and some families who bore evidence of phenotypical difference from the Amhara, for instance, walking on the road near my home. In addition to crude phenotype differences such as skin color and stature, there were other cultural cues; for example, the women did not wear the *natalas* or *hijabs* more common among the Orthodox or Muslim women of my neighborhood.

Surely some of these individuals were Sudanese citizens – refugees, students, and residents – fleeing war in their country or seeking employment or educational opportunities in Ethiopia. In fact, I personally had a Sudanese friend who lived near Shola. He was a refugee and a student who struggled to make a living as a tutor to children of middle-class Ethiopian families interested in improving their children's English-language skills. It was impossible, however, for these Sudanese citizens to be visibly distinguished from Ethiopian citizens of similar ethnic groups. Short of stopping them on the street and asking what their citizenship was, I could not conclusively prove what proportion were Anywaa, Nuer, or other ethnic groups, probably from the western region of Gambella, and what proportion were Sudanese nationals or refugees. I would speculate that many of these families were Ethiopian citizens by birth and territory, if not by some elements of a shared culture, language, or, especially, history. Nevertheless, from the frequent reference to the "Sudanese" in Shola, I became quite aware of what unequal citizenship sounds like every day in Ethiopia. In fact, many Ethiopians of other ethnic groups are not quite sure that the Anywaa or Nuer – much like the Somali – really are Ethiopian, although of course the Oromo certainly are and must remain so. The potential of this dynamic to foster conditions for ethnic violence was highlighted quite dramatically in 2003, when ethnic clashes in Gambella regional state left some 1,100 people dead and thousands of others raped and wounded. Investigations into the violence demonstrate the role of both Ethiopian security forces and members of dominant ethnic groups (referred to as "highlanders" in Gambella) in the killing of local Anywaa citizens in particular.[1]

I think often of my Shola neighbors as I write about citizenship in Ethiopia, particularly because the participatory and meaningful notions of citizenship are denied to many people actually born within the borders of the country today. The contradiction between the passionate support for the "unity and territorial integrity of Ethiopia" and the refrains about diversity and culture in Ethiopia are multiple. Equal legal citizenship is a relatively new political identity for all Ethiopians. Even since the granting of legal citizenship in 1974, its content has been deeply contested, and meaningful citizenship is not yet fully realized. This book seeks to explore the nature of contemporary citizenship in Ethiopia in order to understand more fully the future trajectory of an emancipatory project begun by Ethiopians in the twentieth century and shared by citizens across the African continent and around the world.

But *why* citizenship? And *which* citizenship? Most studies of African politics today focus on elections, institutions, legal reform, and other elements of formal political arrangements. In this vein, the study of Ethiopian politics since the early 1990s has focused similarly on constitutional

---

[1] The term "highlander" has multiple meanings and contexts in Ethiopia. Local residents in Gambella identified at least some of the perpetrators as "highlanders," which in the frontier regions of the west and south of Ethiopia (now called the emerging regions) can refer to Amharas, Tigrayans, and Oromos, who are all considered outsiders from the highland regions of Ethiopia. In other places in the country, for instance, the Oromo refer to Amhara and others as "highlanders." This is partly a function of geography and partly an expression of historical and sociopolitical experiences. See Human Rights Watch 2005; Dereje 2006, 2008; Markakis 2011.

changes that introduced federalism, multiparty electoral contestation, and other changes in law and political structure within the country. This is partly because the study of politics is often the study of those in power, and also perhaps because of optimism that institutional reform could dramatically alter the socioeconomic conditions of the millions in places such as Ethiopia and elsewhere in Africa – people who had spent much of the postcolonial period living under authoritarian regimes.

All this political reform is centrally about the making *of* and the making *by* citizens. Although there are many definitions of citizenship, surely a citizen is one who makes the laws by which he or she lives, whereas a subject has no such claim or ability. Citizens are more than just those who make laws, and citizenship is most definitely more than a status. Citizenship is also a practice, an activity, a thing that is done, reflected in the choices people make and the sets of choices they perceive they have.[2] Although the very concept of a citizen implies a noncitizen, it is never as simple as the "insiders/citizens" and the "outsiders/noncitizens." The contestation of citizenship engages the state, social movements, and individuals in meaningful ways. It is also often a matter of prioritization. This is why citizenship is such a powerful analytical tool with which to approach political life in Africa at this very moment – because the institutional and structural reforms of recent years that have swept across the continent have been inextricably linked up with the battle over the "right to have rights."[3] Groups that were left out of the political reforms of the newly independent African states of the 1960s have since clamored for greater access to the "goods" of citizenship, to distinctly more than the status of citizen in an independent state, aspiring ultimately to the meaningful application of citizenship in the form of participation and accountability of leaders. Citizenship has also become, at least in some parts of Africa, about the kind of quality-of-life and development initiatives one could or should expect.

The citizenship of this book is not the kind you get from birth, in a geographic place or from one or both parents. It is not the kind of citizenship that is represented by a passport that grants access to some places and not others. These are surely powerful statuses, particularly in the modern state system and in the context of global economic inequalities.[4] Legal citizenship has a particular and specific relevance to the majority of African

[2] Tilly 1995.
[3] Arendt 1951, 296.
[4] Shachar 2009; see also Geschiere 2009.

contexts where colonialism produced political boundaries demarcating which groups were inside a given colonial territory and which were not. The ramifications for postcolonial politics, particularly after the period of political reform in the 1990s that ushered in multiparty politics, have been stark. Political elites have battled over citizenship as a specific tool to restrict the scope of contestation and render powerful opponents illegitimate by virtue of noncitizen status. At the grassroots level, too, we have seen legal citizenship as a tool of violence and an expression of generalized political dissatisfaction, as in the case of xenophobic attacks against other Africans in South Africa, calls for "indigenization" in Tanzania and Sierra Leone, and other related movements or episodes. Manby summarizes these well by noting that all involve the "manipulation of citizenship laws" either through "raw violence ... [or] the apparently dry detail of the rules for obtaining papers [that] can hide an ocean of discrimination and denial of rights."[5] In this focus, one must look to the specific historical process of border delineation, citizenship law, settler pattern, and so on in any particular African colonial case.

The present work is not a study of legal citizenship per se. The citizenship of this book is the kind that labels an ethnically Anywaa woman "Sudanese" even if she carries (or could carry) an Ethiopian passport, even if she was born in Addis Ababa or a village hamlet of Gambella, and even if she speaks the Ethiopian national language, Amharic. Although it is not a book specifically about the Anywaa as a distinct ethnocultural or linguistic group, it is about how the Anywaa, who make up about 27 percent of the population of Gambella regional state but only a very small part of the total population of Ethiopia, are integrated in and enact meaningful citizenship inside the modern state of Ethiopia.[6]

Meaningful citizenship refers to the way in which rights are exercised, or the effective practice of citizenship. It is concerned with the ability and environment for realization of rights and discharging of duties within a polity in ways that have practical implications for all citizens' lives. Meaningful citizenship is an extension of an idea about democratization that could both explain a stalled or aborted democratization exercise, and suggest what citizens are doing in that instance. Citizens are, of course, still practicing some sort of citizenship across all of postcolonial Africa regardless of where they rank on a scale of democracy or freedom or any other quantitative or qualitative index of political outcomes. In

[5] Manby 2009, 2.
[6] Dereje 2008.

this framework, Ethiopia provides an excellent and not entirely unique context for considering what citizens do to create and expand citizenship both during periods of democratic reform and in the intervening periods when authoritarian traditions and structures are resurgent.

This book is also about the citizenship of that Anywaa woman as a *woman*. Ethiopia's expanding citizenship trajectories are multiple, contested, and contradictory. The emancipatory projects of the past fifty years have dramatically challenged some categories of unequal citizenship and left other projects as yet mostly unfulfilled. This is strikingly the case when considering questions of the equality of women, both legal and actual, as contrasted with the equality of at least some members of ethnic communities. In part this suggests that although there is exciting potential for expanded citizenship across the developing world, where there are competing emancipatory projects, trade-offs may be made that too frequently privilege one form of equality over another. In Ethiopia, opportunities for expanded citizenship gains for women, and the attendant benefits to their families and communities, have been mostly missed in recent decades. Although a vibrant and productive – albeit acrimonious – debate in Ethiopia and abroad has radically altered the nature of ethnic group relations in the country, discussions of the democratization of the home, the family, and the neighborhood remain muted, particularly at the level of national discourse.

Writing specifically about the political process of elections, journalist and longtime observer of Ethiopian civic life René Lefort insinuates that citizenship in Ethiopia is a revolutionary idea with limited daily relevance to most of the citizens for whom it is intended. Lefort argues, with regard to the 2010 landslide victory of the ruling regime and the utter failure of all political opposition, that the vast majority of Ethiopians, residing as they do in isolated, rural communities, "have a vision of the world where absolutely everything is determined by divine will, including who is in power. They feel they have no right to choose."[7] Implicit here is an observation on the state of the citizenship project in this country. It lies at the heart of this book, too – that citizenship in Ethiopia is incomplete and so contested as to be a project of construction. Although I take a decidedly more optimistic view of Ethiopian citizens' present understandings of what their social and political potential is, I share an interest in excavating the state of the citizen in contemporary Ethiopia, as a window into political and social development in the country and for its potential

[7] Lefort 2010.

to shed light on broader concerns of conflict, underdevelopment, and inequality in Africa and across the globe.

Ethiopian Citizen Creation and Citizenship Expansion

Ethiopia is the focus of this study because there is arguably no better case of the dynamic and contradictory processes of citizen creation and contestation than this diverse and divided country in the Horn of Africa. Nevertheless, citizenship has been generally understudied in the African context. Democratization in Ethiopia has been neither an obvious nor linear process. Nor has it been only an elite-led or western-imposed process. It has always been driven by a variety of diverse social groupings in pursuit of precisely the goods of meaningful citizenship that are the focus of this study: recognition, participation, and, centrally, equality of lived experience. At the same time, the three political regimes of post–World War II Ethiopia have each introduced successive packages of institutional reforms meant at least in part to address grassroots quests for citizenship. The history of modern Ethiopia is a complicated web of citizens, subjects, partial citizens, and rights legally granted but not fully realized. Still, Ethiopia has become a state through the difficult task of expanding its community of members, and in a sense each generation – as well as each regime – has played its part. Contemporary federalism is only the latest iteration of a modern project of expanding equality in a developing country. What the current political arrangement addresses – and does not address – is all part of the story of Ethiopian citizenship.

But what is unique about Ethiopia today that makes it such an ideal context for this study? After decades of a nation-building strategy that emphasized centralization and assimilation, the country embarked in the early 1990s on an experiment with federalism and decentralization that was explicitly organized along ethnic lines. Ethiopia's constitutional and institutional reforms were wide-ranging and controversial, both within the country and internationally. Radical social reforms were made – most prominently the granting of self-determination rights, including the right to secession – for members of ethnic communities as groups, or "Nations." The preamble to the constitution vests power in ethnic groups by opening with these words: "We, the Nations, Nationalities and Peoples of Ethiopia." Ethiopia is home to at least 75 ethnolinguistic groups in a total population of at least 85 million people, the second most populous country in Africa.

Federalism in Ethiopia is yet another institutional and social project toward citizen creation and citizenship expansion in the country.[8] Each political regime in the modern period in fact reformed and expanded citizenship in Ethiopia in meaningful ways. This has never been without controversy, in large part because the very notions of public and private life inherent in a citizenship model are antithetical to some historical traditions of hierarchy and social order that have framed core elements of Ethiopian society. Nonetheless, citizenship has been created and expanded through the reforms of each of these modern political regimes in Ethiopia, constituting a vibrant, contentious, and fundamentally hopeful national conversation on social, political, and economic life. It has been the persistent fact of ethnic conflict and the content of institutional reform that has captured most analytical and political attention in prior studies. The addition of a study of citizenship to the existing debates about political developments in Ethiopia sheds new light on accomplishments and future challenges, not only for Ethiopia but also for similarly diverse, divided, and democratizing countries in Africa.

One of the reasons that Ethiopia is often seen as an outlier in Africa is that it was not colonized by a European power. Yet despite the lack of effective European colonization, Ethiopia is similar to the rest of the African continent in critical ways. Its borders were defined by the processes of colonization occurring in the late nineteenth and early twentieth centuries, both externally and internally. The political complexity of simultaneously pursuing empire expansion and a blend of treaties and wars to keep European powers at bay, as well as the impact of Italian occupation, pushed Ethiopian monarchs at the turn of and well into the twentieth century to focus on rhetoric and actions that fostered a "dualistic nationalism"[9] more like its long-standing rival, Egypt. In the Ethiopian case, this was staunchly anticolonial in the international arena and a "unique case of African imperialism"[10] at home, within the borders of an expanding state. The development of an Ethiopian national identity was created through practices, policies, and beliefs about ethnic and

---

[8] Federalism in Ethiopia was referred to as "ethnic federalism" for some time, denoting the distinct priority given to ethnic communities in the federal arrangement created by the 1995 Constitution. An ethnofederal state is a federal state in which "at least one constituent territorial governance unit is intentionally associated with a specific ethnic category" (Hale 2004, 167). Clearly, Ethiopia's federal arrangement is ethnically structured, but I tend not to use this now-controversial term despite my more neutral meaning.

[9] Powell 2003, 6.

[10] Keller 1988, 45.

gendered groups within that expanding empire. Ethiopia's lack of effective European colonization does not mean that it does not share interesting tensions over the nature and extent of meaningful citizenship along the lines of most of the other postcolonial African societies. Even its historical particularity does not diminish the essentially "liberatory"[11] nature of contentious citizenship struggles in Ethiopia, such as those for formerly marginalized ethnic communities and women, as this book considers.

Ethiopia's diverse ethnolinguistic and religious composition, which is mirrored across Africa, makes its attempts to establish and consolidate a national identity contentious, as has been the case in other postcolonial states. Despite successive political regimes that aimed to undermine and even eliminate its potency, the persistence of ethnic identification, both in formal political and social organization and in its symbolic power, suggests that it is a deeply felt identity. What makes the argument about meaningful citizenship – empirically tested in Ethiopia – relevant to postcolonial Africa is the way in which certain kinds of claims, such as ethnic and gendered claims by citizens, can be read as liberatory and democratizing rather than atavistic or primordial, as both the western media and dominant political regimes would have us conclude. Meaningful citizenship expands our lens on democratization by focusing on what citizens do in the intervening years – outside of elections or running for political office – on how and why they send their children to school or join community associations, or, especially, challenge hierarchies and inequalities in the home, village, and community.

There is one point that should be made unequivocally at the outset. As it will be clear to the reader who finishes this text, this is not a laudatory study of the present Ethiopian political system. I do not conclude that Ethiopia has achieved or is even aspiring to be a liberal democracy. Nor is it a polity approaching so-called participatory democracy. This project is not intended to assess the level of democratization achieved through a federal model or under the current ruling regime. Evidence suggests that after a relatively brief period of political opening in the late 1990s and the early part of the twenty-first century, the regime has returned to somewhat familiar patterns of political and social control. This is in line with the cautionary note of one recent study of postcolonial citizenship in Africa in which the authors point out that "new identities and struggles emerge from a complex web of new and old power relations....

---

[11] I draw the term "liberatory" from the idea of "Africa's second liberation" in Osaghae 2004; see also Zuern 2009.

The nature of citizen participation may as often be patterned by existing relationships rather than conforming to the more abstract democratic promise of these new institutions."[12]

Ethiopia is a deeply hierarchical and traditional society, one in which complex and generally rigid relations of authority structure nearly every exchange, making political transformations slow and nonlinear. The legacy of authoritarian political institutions and leadership styles will take some time to be effectively altered, in large part because the sources of authority and power are created at the family and community levels. These sources of power are generally understood as hierarchical and male and are persistently dominated by elites from specific ethnic communities and parts of the geographic space called Ethiopia. I consider the general state of politics in Ethiopia in the Conclusion. Although it is doubtless true that the topics, methods, and locations I studied in 2001 and 2003[13] can no longer be studied at this time, the fact that they were so transparently and cogently explored then has much to say about Ethiopian citizenship expansion in the modern period.

What I do assert in this study of citizenship is that, despite political and economic contradictions and asymmetries, Ethiopia has seen an exciting and unprecedented project of citizenship expansion. That these changes have occurred in a country that is relatively diverse and economically underdeveloped and that has a strong tradition of hierarchical authority is both hopeful and instructive to a community of states aspiring to improved quality of life for all. This argument hinges on much more than the legal citizenship that arrived late to Ethiopia and is arguably still denied in practice if not in law to many. First, however, it is important to distinguish among the citizenship meanings in this text and in Ethiopia particularly.

In contemporary Ethiopia, there are a number of citizenship categories that overlap and even compete for prominence with respect to the kinds of citizenship this book discusses. There is a *zega*, a citizen in the legal and formal sense; that is, a person who holds membership in a state, with the attendant rights and responsibilities. The very fact that the contemporary word for a citizen derives from a word that only ninety or so years ago referred to one who was "subdued" or "subject" is highly informative. There is in a sense a direct link from subjecthood in early modern political development to the present-day citizen, female or male, Oromo,

[12] Robins et al. 2008, 1073.
[13] L. Smith 2005.

Amhara, or Anywaa. It suggests much about how historical trajectories of
citizen creation and citizenship expansion were developed and on which
contemporary social movements must build. Anthropologist Donald
Donham (and others) has argued that the idea of a fixed territory in
which all were counted as citizens did not exist in Abyssinia historically
and only came to be gradually understood to be foundational to political
life in the modern period. He says:

> Abyssinians, that is, those who spoke Semitic languages and who were Orthodox
> Christians, lived in a certain territory – what I have called the core. But Abyssinian
> power, and during the twentieth century, Shewan power in particular, was never
> thought to be limited to that sphere. Rather, it radiated out from the centre. The
> people who happened to reside in the far peripheries were not Abyssinians....
> This whole history appears to be encapsulated in the word that came eventu-
> ally to mean citizen, *zega*, "subdued," "subject," "obedient." Gradually, *zega* came
> to be applied to anyone within the boundaries of the modern state, under the
> dominion of the nation.[14]

In addition to this expanding legal category of citizenship, there is
another crucial type of citizenship implicit in this historical understanding and reflected in the constitutional designation under the present political arrangement of *beher, behereseboch, ina hizboch*, generally translated
as the "Nations, Nationalities, and Peoples" of Ethiopia. The 1995
Constitution and present political dispensation identify these groupings
as the bearers of rights that would grant meaningful citizenship as I refer
to it here.

This book really is about the *behereseboch*, the "nationalities," and *hizboch*, the "peoples," as well as the *setoch*, the women, of Ethiopia, more
than the *zeganet*, or legal citizenship of these individuals. It is precisely
the tension, however, and even the contradiction between social models
of conformity and hierarchy and the normative aspirations of meaningful
citizenship, that make the Ethiopia case fascinating and instructive for
a study of citizenship. What I demonstrate empirically through the case
studies in language policy, self-determination claims, and gendered and
ethnically based social and political movements is that even in contexts
where power is shaped differently from western liberal contexts, meaningful citizenship is nonetheless a project of the aspiring citizens as much
as state agents and political elites. Not only may clientelist or paternalistic

---

[14] Donham and James 2002, 43. In the footnote, Donham notes the shift in definition in
linguistic dictionaries as indicative of this, from the 1920s when *zega* was translated as
"dependent subject," to the 1970s when "citizen" was given as one of its meanings. Still,
it is striking that in Leslau (1976), *zega* is both subject and citizen.

relationships persist but aspiring citizens in these contexts are actively shaping the content of meaningful citizenship. What emerges is a hybrid and contentious citizenship, one that is often mostly only locally meaningful but often part of a national conversation about expanded and meaningful citizenship. Although it may be a highly imperfect democracy, it is a citizen-creation and citizenship-expansion project, and citizenship itself "is a vital democratic or democratizing institution."[15]

This book situates Ethiopia's dramatic institutional and constitutional reforms of the mid-1990s within a modern history of contentious and expanding national citizenship. In the context of a new constitution and reformed political institutions created by political leaders, citizens and social movements have also contributed to this national discourse on citizenship. In Ethiopia some of these movements are ethnonationalist movements, others decidedly nonethnic but nationalist. They generally operate sporadically. There are periods of energy and the possibility of social transformation as well as episodes of localized violence, conflict, and even war (national, regional, and local). This view of citizen participation in citizenship expansion better explains the tremendous accomplishments in Ethiopia in particular windows of time, followed by periods of relative political closing. In order to make this argument, this book assesses specific ethnic movements with divergent outcomes related to citizenship in Ethiopia, particularly the Oromo and Siltie communities, and includes not only ethnic movements and citizenship-expansion projects, but also women and the so-called emerging regions or border areas such as Benishangul-Gumuz in the west, and groups in southern Ethiopia such as the Gurage and Wolaitta.

A focus on specific communities is instructive because each has used different means to contest the reality of unequal citizenship in Ethiopia, and each has experienced different outcomes. The Siltie have used federalism to advance their claims to recognition and inclusion, while other Ethiopians, including groups in the Southern region, have been far less effective in this effort. Those in the emerging regions, such as Gambella and Benishangul-Gumuz, have also benefited under federalism, but starting from a place of staggering inequality. Finally, the critical case of the Oromo people, the majority ethnic group in Ethiopia but long marginalized and suppressed, is more mixed. Vital Oromo claims, such as the use of their language and cultural development, have been realized to a far greater extent under present-day federalism. Nevertheless, human

---

[15] Isin and Turner 2008, 16.

rights violations and political control continue to limit the full exercise of citizenship rights in many parts of the Oromiya region. Both the state and politicized social movements are perhaps indispensable to the outcome that is evident: slow but steady progress toward a more inclusive citizenship.

This book also considers the unique nature of Ethiopian women's aspirations for meaningful citizenship in a country that is striking for its deep-rooted and seemingly intractable gender inequality. In fact, the kinds of competing and contested citizenship identities distinguished notably by ethnic and linguistic (and sometimes religious) difference are the subject of considerably more attention by Ethiopians and scholars of the country alike. The intersectional features of gender when related to ethnic identity put Ethiopian women in the distinct position of attempting to achieve meaningful citizenship at the meeting point of multiple inequalities. Like women globally, gender identity in Ethiopia functions as both a resource and a challenge for women and their families, particularly as it overlaps with other inequalities. The exciting possibilities for women's ethnic, religious, and regional communities to be resources for their social and economic participation under federalism in Ethiopia have been underexplored by scholars to date. In general, scholarship in Africa and the developing world has tended to see ethnocultural communities as always and only a hindrance to equal citizenship for women, even as a more nuanced approach has emerged in the west. One is prompted to ask: Are robust constitutional protections for members of Ethiopia's "Nations, Nationalities and Peoples" obstacles to the achievement of gender equality, or a repository of meaningful citizenship for women *and* ethnic communities?

Outline of the Book

Therefore, this book seeks to move beyond entrenched views on politics in Ethiopia, particularly those focused on electoral processes or elite leadership. Considering Ethiopian history through the lens of expanding and meaningful citizenship provides a distinctive perspective on some of the more controversial elements of the present federal arrangement. In what follows, I outline the general history of modern Ethiopia by identifying critical moments for citizenship creation and expansion, analyzing these chronologically, spatially, and conceptually. This status as subject is one way in which Ethiopia is strikingly similar to the rest of colonized sub-Saharan Africa, where "people related as subjects and clients, rather than citizens, to an authoritarian and paternalistic state."[16] One of several analytical contributions of a citizenship study is to place Ethiopia's experience within African citizenship history.

In each period of modern Ethiopian history, there were conflicting positions on citizenship. Of these, a dominant political practice emerged, shaping significantly the conceptual terrain on which contemporary citizenship exists and is contested. Competing citizenship visions have developed out of the historical struggles over inclusion and participation in Ethiopia. These competing visions have their roots in historical practice, but this fact is rarely acknowledged in Ethiopian political discourse today. At the same time, a national conversation was begun and advanced by citizens and political elites alike during these primary periods and continues today. Ethiopia's social and political future is shaped in profound ways by these past expansions of citizenship.

While national and even continental in theoretical scope, the empirical data in this work is primarily informed by a local and ethnic group perspective on the topics. The concern with citizenship reflected in this text is a novel lens through which to view ethnolinguistic conflict and historical relations between and among ethnic groups, as well as expanding women's rights, which, it is hoped, will open up new intellectual terrain in discussing ethnicity and gender politics in Ethiopia and much of sub-Saharan Africa. Primary fieldwork in 2001 and 2003 on language policy, and in particular the educational sector, took me to schools and villages across mainly Oromiya and the Southern region, but also to Tigray and Benishangul-Gumuz. This has been followed by nearly annual trips to different parts of Ethiopia. I discuss the methodological approach and include interview questions in the various appendixes to this text.

Part I of the book seeks to connect the challenges of ethnic conflict and gendered inequality in the democratizing states of sub-Saharan Africa with the normative literature on diversity and citizenship globally, and to link this with an analysis of Ethiopian citizenship creation. Chapter 1 focuses on the connection between our empirical and conceptual understanding of what democratization means in Africa and the forms of citizenship debates that have arisen. This requires an attention to much more than formal political processes or institutions. African citizens have in many ways defined the success or failures of democracy in terms of participation, equality, and accountability. Therefore, the importance of meaningful citizenship as a conceptual approach must be connected with

[16] Berman et al. 2004, 8.

how democratization pressures and processes are initiated, sustained, and contested by states and particularly by citizens themselves. Chapter 2 links those understandings of citizenship and inequality with modern Ethiopian history, offering a spatial, temporal, and conceptual reading of citizenship creation, expansion, and contestation in Ethiopia that is a variant way to think about its contemporary political history, as well as provide the context for the discussion that follows. Ethiopia emerges in these two chapters as historically and structurally distinct from other parts of postcolonial Africa but also sharing a critical aspiration – for meaningful citizenship in a democratizing state.

Part II of the book then considers specific instances or examples of citizen creation and contestation in Ethiopia, linking them back to the theoretical and historical trends previously noted. Chapter 3 presents the institutional changes related to language policy in Ethiopia as indicative of the efforts of both the Ethiopian state and the members of formerly marginalized ethnolinguistic communities in ensuring better access to the political goods of communication, recognition, and autonomy that language policy structures. Perhaps more than any other policy sector, the language policy of the EPRDF, since at least the early 1990s, reflects a substantive and observable intervention directly linked to specific ethnic communities and therefore a critical test of the possibilities of the ethnic rights provided for by federalism and the constitutional project in Ethiopia. Language policy is controversial, particularly among certain groups within the country. It carries tremendous financial and administrative burdens for the Ethiopian state and local communities, but it is arguably an avenue where the regime has gone further than any other in changing the material reality with respect to ethnic inequality.

Chapters 4 and 5 present micro-level studies of particular ethnic groups in Ethiopia, exploring the specific trajectory of citizenship formation and expansion. Chapter 4 focuses on a common criticism of any institutionalization of ethnicity, even in the context of deep-seated historical inequality, that suggests it will harden or deepen existing ethnic identities, rendering identities that we understand to be fluid, situational, and constructed as absolute and final. I analyze this claim by looking at the unique case of a referendum to identify and delineate the boundaries of one ethnic community, the Siltie, as distinct from another ethnic group, the Gurage. Because of the political, economic, and symbolic value associated with ethnic group recognition under Ethiopian federalism, identification as a separate ethnic group has immediate financial and political benefits and the potential to lead to innumerable conflicts at the local level. Although it may be the exception to the rule in many ways, the case of the Siltie referendum is highly instructive for the more general question of *how* citizenship formation in the context of ethnic diversity can be accomplished.

Chapter 5 considers the experience of the Oromo, the single largest ethnic group in Ethiopia, whose citizens have also been systematically excluded from the highest levels of political and economic life. The argument here is that Oromo aspirations for full and meaningful citizenship are at the heart of the "unity" versus "fragmentation" discourse that is central to the contestation over the very nature and shape of the Ethiopian state, especially as it relates to the present-day political dispensation of federalism. Provisions in the 1995 Constitution providing for ethnic self-determination up to secession remain the most controversial elements of the contemporary political framework, and yet it is not at all clear that secession is a widespread or deeply valued political goal of Oromo citizens. Anxieties over secession and self-determination remain central to the "Oromo question," both for Oromo citizens' understanding of what meaningful citizenship is and other ethnic communities' articulation of these values. Yet ongoing human rights violations and political control undermine ethnic self-determination provisions in substantial ways.

Chapter 6 shifts the attention from the micro-level questions of ethnicity, as central as they are to contemporary citizenship debates in Ethiopia, to a form of unequal citizenship rarely analyzed in tandem with identity markers such as ethnicity. The relationship between one set of emancipatory concerns, those of ethnic groups, and the dramatic structural inequalities for Ethiopian women is analyzed. Why and how does one set of inequalities reach the level of national attention and become the site of institutional and procedural interventions, while another category of unequal citizens remains muted? I consider the general question of women's equality in Ethiopia, particularly in the context of the multiculturalist provisions of the 1995 Constitution, as well as subsequent legal reforms. I then consider the critical relevance of feminist concerns for women's rights in the face of ethnic and communal group rights that have emerged most generally in the case of minority groups in western democracies. The argument is that the challenges of balancing women's rights and ethnic groups is distinct in Ethiopia, and we should not immediately or completely transpose important normative debates over women's citizenship in the context of migration and minority status in the west onto the unique landscapes of national debates. In fact, there are important cases where cultural norms and practices are better designed and equipped to manage the concerns of women and their families than western-style interventions, giving serious pause to western feminist concerns over multiculturalism, particularly in a universal application.

Meaningful citizenship is an exciting project of liberation that is not entirely emancipatory at any particular moment or, especially, under any particular political regime. It cannot be captured in a specific constitutional or legal provision or set thereof. It cannot be scored or evaluated along any quantitative or qualitative index. It is not even something that might be identified or assessed by citizens themselves in a public opinion poll, were one ever to be conducted in a country such as Ethiopia. It does signify, however, a deepening of the social language of equality and is absolutely pivotal to any subsequent attempts at actual legal and political reform. So the Anywaa woman of the Shola market in the capital city of Addis Ababa may still be seen as "other" in some way by her neighbors, but now she conceivably has available to her a repertoire to contest these perceptions and practices of exclusion. Of course, she may not know of these tools – particularly the legal protections, which may not be applied in practice in any event. That must come, of course. But first this language of equality, of "liberation" must be formed and debated and incorporated into the public domain. There is little doubt this is happening in Ethiopia today, and it is at least as pivotal to future aspirations to democratic outcomes as any constitutional reform or political election.

THE CHALLENGE: UNEQUAL CITIZENSHIP

I

Comparative Perspectives on Citizen Creation in Africa

The study of citizenship is as old as the ancient Greek philosophers, but we have seen a resurgence of focus on citizenship in western democracies as new challenges confront relatively stable and institutionalized democratic states. Key among these are globalization and migration, the power of markets in shaping political and economic life, and a constellation of security threats, both real and perceived – as well as the various actors implicated in each of these, including the state, groupings of citizens, and noncitizens residing within the state. This scholarship provides a rich and nuanced terrain on which to consider the modern manifestations of citizenship and the contestations over its expansion. Somewhat surprisingly, however, the analytical lens of citizenship has rarely been deployed in many parts of the developing world. This is problematic for a number of reasons, not the least of which being that challenges of citizenship in postcolonial contexts such as sub-Saharan Africa are distinct from those in the western liberal democracies with relatively defined political boundaries, developed capitalist economies, and political and social traditions of individualism and autonomy. It has also resulted in the primary focus on formal politics that are of limited usefulness in explaining contemporary political and social dynamics in Africa.

That does not mean that the discourse on citizenship in the west has no relevance to places such as Ethiopia or other parts of Africa, which are the focus of this study. Based on its relatively recent decolonization, its distinct cultural traditions, and its persistent authoritarian political traditions, the political, historical, and social context for African citizenship may be divergent from the west. But the framing of citizenship as a "set of mutual, contested claims between agents of states and members of socially-constructed categories"[1] has tremendous explanatory power in analyzing some of the most intractable and critical moral and political debates on the African continent. Thus I seek here to apply conceptual models of citizenship created from the landscape of western possibilities and western realities to African contexts – with the goal of reinterpreting widely pathologized ethnic identities and understudied inequalities, such as those relating to women in social and political life in Africa, to provide evidence of their emancipatory potential. Understanding the extent of citizenship expansion underway in sub-Saharan Africa is key to this work.

This exercise will require us to answer a few questions: Where does modern African citizenship fit within theoretical paradigms of citizenship in diverse states, particularly in relation to liberal citizenship forms? How was African citizenship constructed in the modern historical period and contested in contemporary sociopolitical life? On what moral and cultural foundations are African citizenships based and what evidence do we have that they are the basis of an invigorated political context? Finally, in the creation and expansion of citizenship, what kinds of citizenship identities are prioritized, why, and with what effect? An intersectional analysis of citizenship in Ethiopia underscores the multiplicity of citizen-creation projects, and the distinct trajectories of each.

Nowhere in the world are the boundaries of citizenship unambiguous. Although formal legal citizenship may be clearly defined in western democracies, contestations at the edges of those definitions are ubiquitous. Questions of English-language use in the United States in the context of growing numbers of Spanish-language immigrants from Latin America, for instance, signal a contested citizenship category in a bureaucratized state with standardized citizenship rules. A 2008 court ruling denying French citizenship to a Moroccan woman who chose to wear the *niqab*, a form of Muslim head covering, similarly suggests a sharpening of the boundaries in the delineation of citizenship in that country. Even where legal citizenship is not at stake, full rights and privileges of citizenship are sometimes denied to individuals within states based on various identities, behaviors, or other assumptions, as illustrated by recurrent themes in secular Turkey relating to the right to wear religious attire such as the veil, and a proposal to require the Roma of Italy to carry special identity cards. In each of these cases, the membership and content of citizenship emerge as contentious, even in states with well-defined borders and relatively long traditions of constitutionally guaranteed citizenship.

---

[1] Tilly 1995, 6.

In the developing world, these sorts of contestations take on even greater salience, as the actual legal, political, and social meaning of citizenship is actively under construction. The legacy of European colonization is not only a patchwork of illogical state borders but has created deep and persistent structural inequalities within those same states. Colonial laws, institutions, and practice created in most of Africa a legacy of unequal citizenship based on some combination of ethnicity, region, religion, and gender. In addition, the geography and politics of the greater colonial project led to states that have persistent border disputes with neighbors, spillover of domestic conflicts across national boundaries, and human refugee and migration flows. State borders in many parts of sub-Saharan Africa "have remained porous and often undefended."[2] These porous borders, histories of labor migration, and communities fleeing violent conflicts have created states in Africa that have diverse citizenship constituencies, and few have escaped confronting questions of the status of these communities within their borders. The 2007–2008 election-related violence in Kenya, xenophobic attacks against regional migrants in some cities of South Africa, the series of civil wars in eastern sections of the Democratic Republic of the Congo (DRC) since the late 1990s, and the civil war that rocked Cote d'Ivoire are just the most prominent examples of these phenomena.

Many African states went through a period of democratic transition in the early and mid-1990s. In addition to reform of the state structures, which were mainly inherited from colonialism, rooted in autocracy and riddled with corruption, the substantive project of many of these democratization exercises also focused on histories of inequality, exclusion, and discrimination along communal lines. Old inequalities and structural hierarchies came under attack as the language and intent of democracy were embraced in surprising and creative ways by members of disparate social movements. Women, ethnic minorities and disadvantaged groups, youths, and others joined movements for democratic reform in part because democratization offered them the chance to assert claims to inclusion that had been previously denied.

Although formal legal citizenship had been assured in most countries of sub-Saharan Africa at independence, meaningful citizenship has remained elusive for individuals who are members of particular groups. Because of these pressures for inclusion and meaningful citizenship, the tendency for democratization processes to lead to conflict is obvious. In most parts

---

[2] Larémont 2005, 2; Englebert 2009.

of sub-Saharan Africa, these conflicts have taken an ethnic character.[3] In a fascinating study of autochthony and citizenship in Cameroon and the Netherlands, Geschiere argues that a debate over autochthony or "belonging" in Africa is rooted at least partially in the impact of global pressures to democratize and decentralize.[4] There is, therefore, a real need to consider the relationship between democracy as a project of building a better life for people and the types of conflict that occur. Centrally, even if citizenship is not immediately emancipatory, it is a step in the direction of inclusion. Because of that, the struggles for meaningful citizenship are at least as important in the context of democratic transitions as elections, constitutions, and political institutions.

Implicit in this proposition is an argument that political institutions provide the necessary but insufficient conditions for democratization outcomes. They must be accompanied by new forms of inclusive and meaningful citizenship to contribute to genuine democracy. I use the term "meaningful citizenship" throughout this book, a term that I describe in relation to formal and legal theories of citizenship. Meaningful citizenship refers to more than the legal status as possessing a nationality or associated rights within a particular polity. It signifies the effective *practice* of citizenship, the ability and environment for exercising the various rights of citizenship and discharging the associated duties in a way that has practical and lived implications in one's life, both on an individual and community level. The process of citizenship construction is iterative and episodic, fitful and contentious. It is shaped by domestic political elites and influenced by international actors such as donors, activists, and even social scientists, but always only meaningfully realized by the citizens who themselves vest power in those leaders and institutions. Meaningful citizenship is the social citizenship that "makes citizens," not in the finality of conferring legal citizenship on a subject (or alien) but iteratively, repeatedly, and through expansion and contestation. Otherwise, democratic reforms can be undermined or even abandoned by citizens who find little usefulness in their provisions. Without meaningful citizenship some groups within the political community, notably women, may be left out of the national conversation about the realization of citizenship gains, and families and communities may be unreformed, even while dynamic changes are occurring in formal political realms.

---

[3] Osaghae 2004; Ekeh 2004.
[4] Geschiere 2009, 6; see also Manby 2009.

A Legacy of Unequal Citizenship in Africa

Successive political regimes in Africa have dealt with the particular challenges of multiethnic societies through diverse institutional models, most of them highly centralized and emphasizing national unity over communal identities. A classic example of this is Kenya. All of the post-independence political regimes in Kenya have explicitly downplayed any formal role for members of the forty or so ethnic communities in the country, preferring instead to emphasize a unified, national Kenyan identity – and Kenyans do generally value their national identity as Kenyans. Yet this has done little to diminish the potency of these ethnic identities, both in the positive form of ethnic and cultural nationalism, and in the negative, especially manifest as interethnic conflict. This was painfully borne out by Kenya's 2007 elections and the ethnic violence that followed, when at least 1,100 Kenyans were killed and 350,000 displaced. As one Kenyan intellectual noted, what is needed is a "consti-tution that names and recognizes the tribal nations within our nation," as the postindependence project of eradicating "tribalism" has miserably failed.[5] Another recent assessment of Kenya's prospects strikes a mark-edly hopeful tone, suggesting that the postelection crisis is not evidence that Kenya "is just another lost African cause" but that the violence occurred at least in part because of a "broad democratic awakening that has occurred to different degrees in other African countries and other regions."[6]

There is a distinctly optimistic tone to these two accounts coming out of Kenya in the wake of what was surely a horrific episode of ethnic violence and displacement. What reason do we have for this optimism about the prospects for African democracy, particularly in the face of the persistence of conflicts in places such as Kenya? Social science theories offer us relatively little cause for hope. Existing studies of ethnic con-flict in Africa have tended to focus on the limitations to peace, security, and democracy posed by the fact of diversity. Although it is true that ethnic, religious, and kin-based identities continue to be important to African citizens and sometimes contribute to conflict and violence, there is also evidence that these identities do not themselves prevent the devel-opment of national identities, even if there is more of a coexistence of

---

[5] Wainaina 2008.
[6] Gershman and Kiai, 2009, 7.

national and subnational (ethnic) identity than a replacement.[7] Much of the scholarship on ethnicity and conflict in Africa takes a rather narrow institutional approach, to the neglect of the meaning-producing nature of how citizens themselves respond to state-led interventions. Political institutions do indeed have tremendous influence on political outcomes, including the potential for conflict. In fact, it is the changing form and content of these institutions that creates the context for expanding and contested citizenship, and as a result, we should expect more conflict during periods of institutional change, and this conflict will likely be ethnic in nature. We must, however, look beyond the simple fact of ethnic conflict to evaluate the implications of these debates. They form, in many places, what I call a national conversation about citizenship. The corrective of meaningful citizenship contributes to a more thorough accounting of the agency of all actors in a democratization project – the state, political and economic elites, foreign donors, and hegemonic powers – but also those vested with and actively demanding these various citizenship powers – the people.

At the same time that scholarship on Africa has been focused on elections and political institutions, a rich and diverse literature in the study of citizenship, multiculturalism, and racial and ethnic politics has developed in the west. Much of this literature is at least normatively committed to finding political solutions to the kinds of conflicts that arise in conditions of sociocultural diversity in contemporary states. But most of the prominent work in this field has been based on empirical studies in western states. There is a need to bring this literature into the diverse and divided societies of places such as sub-Saharan Africa. Theories of citizenship and multiculturalism have tremendous relevance to nonwestern contexts, to places such as Ethiopia, Nigeria, South Africa, and Kenya. Although the historical, economic, and political contexts may vary substantially, the normative framing of claims to inclusion, recognition, and participation are strikingly similar, and a study of multiculturalism can yield rich insights not only into democratizing reforms in Africa but also to the meaning of identity-based politics in the context of citizen creation, expansion, and contestation.

Using data from Ethiopia, this book demonstrates that a theory of citizenship can facilitate the identification of critical citizenship questions

---

[7] The findings of multicountry public opinion surveys, including the Afrobarometer project, point to this, as well as the conclusion of Mattes 2004; Bratton, Mattes, and Gyimah-Boadi 2005. See similar single-country surveys in Larémont 2006.

relevant to contemporary African democratization challenges. Such a study must extend beyond formal legal or constitutional provisions relating to citizenship and into the realm of citizenship creation, what some call "acts of citizenship,"[8] especially as they are locally understood. In particular, this is because a legacy of unequal citizenship is often the primary political challenge of new social groupings in democratizing societies. Institutional structures such as decentralization and federalism influence the social and political traditions by which citizens and members of ethnic communities navigate, access, and contest their own political agency. They become new sources of legitimacy and frame the national conversation on unequal citizenship.

Democratization in Africa

The social and political environment in which modern citizenship is defined, contested, and expanded has been shaped by both historical and contemporary factors. Critical among these is the global rise of democracy as the dominant political model. Perhaps the most important political story of the period since the early 1990s was the wave of democratic "transitions" that swept across the globe, and in this Africa was no exception. This included electoral and institutional reform and often, constitution revision or creation. For instance, in the period from 1989 to 1994, twenty-nine African countries held multiparty elections, largely in response to a rising groundswell of opposition to the persistent authoritarianism of Africa's postindependence regimes.[9] Since 1989, more than fifty-seven new constitutions have been adopted in forty-one African countries.[10]

The study of democratization in contemporary Africa has typically focused on formal political institutions, such as the design of electoral rules, the choice of presidentialism versus parliamentarianism, a unitary versus federal state system, the structure of party systems, and executive-legislative relations. Much of this literature has argued for the potential positive impact that institutional engineering and institutional choice can have in creating the enabling conditions for democracy in societies characterized by high levels of ethnolinguistic diversity.

[8] Isin and Nielsen 2008.
[9] Bratton and van de Walle 1997.
[10] Wing 2008, 1.

This emphasis arises in part due to the recognition that political institutions are foundational to political processes and outcomes. Institutions are argued to "structure incentives in human exchange, whether political, social or economic."[11] Because institutions limit the choice set for citizens, they "act as filters that selectively favor particular interpretations either of the goals toward which political actors strive or of the best means to achieve these ends."[12] It is precisely because of the formalized nature of institutions that they have emerged as favored targets of policy intervention, particularly in contexts where democracy has failed to take root. Lipset makes this point well by stating that "cultural factors deriving from varying histories are extraordinarily difficult to manipulate. Political institutions – including electoral systems and constitutional arrangements – are more easily changed. Hence, those concerned with enhancing the possibilities for stable democratic government focus on them."[13] Quite simply, the view is that "to craft democracies is to craft institutions."[14]

Nowhere is the "crafting" of democracy seen as more vital and more potentially fruitful than in the failed or weak democracies of the developing world. The faltering and even failing of democracy in the many parts of the developing world – particularly in Africa, parts of Asia, Latin America, and the Middle East – have added impetus to the search for better institutions, while at the same time opening up exciting opportunities for experimentation and comparative study. Contemporary scholarship builds on the earlier theories of institutional design and has led to their application in new contexts. The authors of a recent volume, aptly entitled *The Architecture of Democracy*, assert that "it is probably in divided societies that institutional arrangements have the greatest impact."[15]

But institutional reforms rarely produced the expected optimistic outcomes, particularly hoped-for outcomes such as ending conflict and war. For instance, multiparty electoral contests, the clarion call of the early 1990s, only occasionally led to consolidated democratic regimes anywhere in the world. More typical are successive elections marked by charges of vote fraud, continued ruling party dominance, and episodic (or sustained) political violence. Constitutional reforms have also been fairly easily thwarted or stalled. Civil liberties such as rights of expression and

---

[11] North 1990, 3.
[12] Immergut 1998, 20.
[13] Lipset, in Diamond and Plattner 1996, 153.
[14] Scarritt and Mozaffar 1999, 3.
[15] Reynolds 2002, 3.

association, as well as rule of law, while improving, continue to be more aspirational than actual in much of sub-Saharan Africa. The excitement of the initial phase of the political transitions in the 1990s has given way to cautious assessments of the democratic content and outcomes of these transitional periods.[16] Some political transitions were stalled, incomplete, or reversed, while few have led to vibrant multiparty political orders, with functioning parliaments and judiciaries, a free press, an active civil society, and so on. Typologies and explanations abound. Most are now considered "defective democracies," "partial democracies," or "electoral authoritarian regimes."[17] More recently, a "democratic recession" has been noted.[18]

Despite the obvious challenges of dramatic institutional reform in a relatively short period of time, these political transitions did lead to sometimes significant procedural and institutional changes with the potential to dramatically alter social status and equality. Multiparty electoral competition was introduced, or reintroduced, in many countries of sub-Saharan Africa, providing the space for competition at the national level. Lindberg's conclusion that multiple sequences of elections have beneficial outcomes over time is plausible in the ways he proposes, and his general conclusion that "movement from dictatorial rule to a competitive electoral regime tends to lead to further democratization and, eventually, democracy"[19] is hopeful and supported in at least a few instances. Certainly, subsequent legal and constitutional reforms often involved changes to citizenship laws, revised legal frameworks relating to equality – particularly with regard to women, minorities, and religious and ethnic communities – sometimes decentralization and even federalism, and a host of similar reforms that represented what are radical new approaches to political and social life.

Even if the experience thus far on the continent suggests that these changes have had only a marginal impact on electoral competition, the

---

[16] There are several approaches to measuring the progress of democratization in Africa. One standard measure of democracy is provided by Freedom House's worldwide annual ranking system. By this measure, at least three-quarters of the countries in sub-Saharan Africa are "not free" or "partly free." while only nine countries are considered "free" (http://www.freedomhouse.org/). The 2009 Freedom House report says Africa is the region that saw the greatest declines in freedom. See also Bratton et al. 2005; Doorenspleet 2003; Manning 2005; Barkan 2002.

[17] Bratton et al. 2005; Manning 2005; Osaghae 2004; Harbeson 1999; Aalen and Tronvoll 2009; Merkel 2004.

[18] Mo Ibrahim Press Release 2010.

[19] Lindberg 2006, 3.

composition and effectiveness of parliaments or the strengthening of nonexecutive powers such as the judiciary, these reconfigurations represent the "reformulating [of] new social contracts, which outline new limits, rights and obligations. It is a process that also seeks to renegotiate the nature of the state and the public sphere and the nature of the nation (who belongs and who does not)."[20] Democratic transitions were initiated in large part as a response to demands by ordinary Africans for meaningful citizenship. This is centrally then a matter of citizenship, not only of who is included in the state (citizenship as status) but what practices are tolerated and even required (citizenship as rights/duties).

The challenge of building democracies in multiethnic states has long been a point of meaningful debate among scholars and political leaders of Africa. The imperatives of nation-building and national integration were almost universally understood to mean a shift from subnational, ethnic, or communal loyalties to state loyalties.[21] The dominance of one-party states across Africa was frequently justified on the grounds that it discouraged ethnic politics. It has also been convincingly demonstrated that time and again the formal or official policy and practice of delegitimizing of ethnicity facilitated their manipulation and deployment by savvy powerful ethnic actors in the political realm.[22] The postindependence African leadership frequently engaged in what has been called ethnic politics, including consolidating political and economic power in the hands of their own ethnic group. However, the explicit and formal practice has been almost entirely nonethnic from independence up to the present.

Central to the political imperative to build democratic institutions in the divided societies of the world is the extent to which ethnic and communal diversity has led to political instability, ethnic violence, and even civil and regional wars. Accommodating and including diverse populations in the modern state remains a primary task of western and nonwestern polities alike, but the political costs of failing to do so are perhaps greater in the developing world, where ethnic conflict tends to lead to violence and warfare. This explains, in large part, the sheer volume of research currently available on ethnic conflict in parts of the developing world, such as sub-Saharan Africa.[23]

---

[20] Ndegwa 2001, 12.
[21] Elaigwu 1993.
[22] Berman et al. 2004; Ndegwa 1997; Ottaway 1999; Olukoshi and Laakso 1996.
[23] Larémont 2005; Collier 2003; C. Young 1993; Horowitz 1991, 1985; Wamwere 2003; Joseph 1999; Lake and Rothchild 1998; Glickman 1995.

Decentralization – from limited decentralization to a full federal model – is one of the possible institutional solutions to address high levels of social polarization and elite hegemony present in unitary and centralized states.[24] Federalism in particular is increasingly a favored political prescriptive in multiethnic and postconflict societies. Although by definition a democratic government involves some division of power, "federalism means a constitutionally guaranteed division of power between the central government and the governments of the member units or component units of the federation. [And] it is usually accompanied by decentralization, that is substantial autonomy for the members of the federation."[25] Federal systems are generally thought to be better suited to deliver democratic outcomes, as they institutionalize the types of power sharing that make democracy more likely to develop and be strengthened. Similarly, elements of self-government for subnational units are believed to reduce incentives for conflict by members of ethnic and communal groups.[26] For instance, in assessing the state of democracy in Africa, political scientist Joel Barkan counts among the more optimistic outcomes the fact that there have been "new experiments with federalism ... to enhance governmental accountability to the public and defuse the potential for ethnic conflict."[27] While there is some evidence that institutional arrangements such as federalism and other forms of power sharing and decentralization can foster cooperation, particularly among political elites, it is increasingly clear that institutions are context bound, and the results of contemporary institution-building exercises can be said to be quite mixed.[28]

So a central political question in contemporary Africa is the relevance of democracy in the context of ethnic diversity and the persistence of communal conflict. The authors of a recent edited volume reinforce this concern, stating, "Relations between population groups in the continent have had a significant impact on both democracy and democratization.... Democratization is expected to enhance management of diversity in the continent."[29] This statement about the expectations for democracy is supported by recent multicountry public opinion surveys, which reveal that democracy is a political ideal of great value to most African citizens, but

[24] Crawford and Hartmann 2008.
[25] Lijphart 1984, 169.
[26] Roeder and Rothchild 2005; Horowitz 1985; Lijphart 1977; Berman et al. 2004.
[27] Barkan 2002, 74.
[28] Rothchild and Roeder 2005; LaPonce and Saint-Jacques 1997.
[29] Ihonvbere and Mbaku 2003, 9; see also Berman et al. 2004.

respondents also report there are conflicts between ethnic groups and trust among groups is low.[30]

Interestingly, the same set of public opinion surveys demonstrate an ongoing attachment to ethnic and other group identities, despite fifty or more years of unitary nation-building projects in most postcolonial African states. Yet there is a curious relationship between communal or ethnic identities and what we might term a "national identity." In their summary, the authors concluded that, despite variation between countries, "overwhelmingly, people express pride in their self-defined group identity and do not consider that it conflicts with national identity."[31] Similarly, in a focused consideration of the results of the same survey in South Africa, the authors note three interesting conclusions that can be drawn from the data, relevant to this study:

South Africa has achieved what is perhaps the irreducible prerequisite of political stability and democratic consolidation: that is, a near consensual agreement among citizens that the legally defined political community is the appropriate one, that they are indeed members of that community, and that they are proud of that membership.... Second, race and ethnicity remain an important source of social identity, but this tendency may be decreasing.... Third, high levels of national identity and loyalty can coexist with equally high levels of identification with sub-national social identity groups. In other words, to the extent that there has been a nation-building project since 1994, it has succeeded, not in transforming group identities into national identity (or of transferring loyalty from one to the other), but creating a *transcendent national identity* that overarches but coexists with group identities.[32]

This idea of a "transcendent national identity" seems to surprise the analysts of the Afrobarometer, but this is only a surprising finding if one takes the traditional view toward ethnicity as fundamentally negative. This perspective, grounded in western assimilationist and majoritarian models of citizenship, cannot accommodate the complex and nuanced ways that citizens of diverse backgrounds in postcolonial Africa experience and articulate their understanding of their communal identities and an often growing sense of national identity. Therefore, it sees nationalist projects of citizenship and integration as fundamentally at odds with particularistic or communally based identities, whereas citizens see ethnicity as a core part of realizing a meaningful citizenship in the contemporary state. The view from the ground often sees dynamism and change within

---

[30] Bratton et al. 2005.
[31] Afrobarometer.org 2002, 4.
[32] Mattes 2004, 13, emphasis added.

ethnic communities, and their relationship to state and national political institutions, but nowhere have we seen the rejection of ethnicity or other communal identities entirely.

Clearly, ordinary African citizens do not share this oppositional and mutually exclusive view, and a theory of citizen formation and expansion helps link these local understandings of communal identities such as ethnicity and gender with the emancipatory and liberatory hopes of democratization. The lacuna in the institutional engineering literature to date has been in failing to account for the role of citizens. Agency here lies with a bureaucratized state, and perhaps some institutional architects, in the form of social scientists and international funding agencies. Those for whom the institutional reforms are created are merely waiting to be "acted on," to be told what the new rules of the game will be and to react as they will. In this vision of democratization, it is difficult to call these individuals and groups citizens in any meaningful sense. Although they may, for instance, have a right to vote in the new institutional dispensation, the content of what they are voting on has already been predetermined by processes controlled by ruling regimes.

Citizenship Theory

Because democratization exercises, whether successful, stalled, or thwarted entirely, are intimately connected with citizenship struggles, we must consider the relationship between these two dynamics more explicitly. Once this is done, it is obvious that even imperfect democracies are often alive with vibrant and contentious citizenship debates. Citizenship is a critical corrective to the overreliance on formal democratization measures, providing leverage for considering transformed social and political landscapes continent-wide. It also gives us cause for optimism about future trajectories of political life, regardless of any individual country's ranking as a democracy, or the outcome of any particular election and the like.

At a minimum, citizenship is a legal and formal position based in law. It is the ultimate expression of a state's sovereignty, in that it alone has the right to define who is and who is not a citizen.[33] Citizenship is generally linked with a particular national community, as distinct from personhood, for instance, which "evokes the rights and dignity of individuals independent of status."[34] Citizenship is also central to the democratic

[33] Heater 1999, 80.
[34] Bosniak 2010, 9.

principle of self-rule, and the distinction between citizens and subjects. Subjects of a state have no "voice in the way in which political power is exercised," but citizens make laws and subject themselves to those laws through their own participation.[35] Pocock provides a vital historical lens for this by pointing out that a citizen is both ruler and the ruled, meaning "among other things that he was a participant in determining the laws by which he was bound," whereas a subject could appeal to the laws of the ruler (say Paul appealing to Caesar as a subject of Rome), but "he might have no hand whatever in making that law or in determining what it was to be."[36]

Citizenship also encompasses a set of rights and duties enjoyed by individuals by virtue of their belonging to a particular national community. For some, "citizenship requires ... a direct sense of community membership based on loyalty to a civilization which is a common possession," as opposed to kinship and sentiment.[37] The concept of citizenship captures the essence of belonging to an organized political community to which one feels an allegiance.[38] Therefore, in modern times, citizenship has been equated with national identity, whereas in the global and postmodern world, scholars increasingly emphasize citizenship understood as participatory, and less related to a national community or a juridical link to a particular state.[39]

Political theorist James Tully has noted that the liberal view of citizenship as only a set of rights and duties is limiting, and that citizenship is better seen as "an identity that members acquire through exchanging reasons in public dialogues and negotiations over how and by whom political power is exercised."[40] Tully's view of citizenship as the "intersubjective and dialogical" engagement in the "institutions of self-rule of a free people" points to the importance of recognition and participation by members of diverse citizen groups in the practice of politics.[41] This view privileges the struggles over recognition rather than a particular end goal of achieving a sense of belonging. Similarly, Charles Tilly points to the fact that "scholars have come to think of citizenship as a set of mutual, contested claims

---

[35] Tully 2000, 213.
[36] Pocock 1995, 39.
[37] Marshall and Bottomore 1991, 40.
[38] Beiner 1995.
[39] Benhabib 1999; Martiniello 2002.
[40] Tully 2000, 215.
[41] Tully 2000, 214.

between agents of states and members of socially-constructed categories: genders, races, nationalities and others."[42]

The classical ideal of liberal citizenship has been "that there should be only one status of citizen (no estates or castes), so that everybody enjoys the same legal and political rights. These rights should be assigned to individual citizens."[43] Although western liberalism assumes an autonomous individual,[44] rights-based struggles – even in the west – have often confronted the denial of basic human and political rights collectively. It has been argued, for instance, that the American civil rights movement was not about the protection of individual rights in the strict western liberal sense, but rather the pursuit of collective rights for all members of racial groups. Social movement activists have made the claim that rights were denied to all members of the group, as a group. Therefore, the legal and social changes were sought for the entire group, so that individual members could benefit as they were able and willing. Similar arguments have been advanced for women as a group.

The debate over the appropriateness of group-based rights protection in western liberal democracies has very little resonance in much of sub-Saharan Africa.[45] Scholars as distinguished as the late Claude Ake emphasize that communalism in Africa "defines the people's perception of self-interest, their freedom and their location in the social whole."[46] Others assert that in Africa "group and community rights are both deeply embedded in the cultures of the peoples ... and that individual rights of citizens within the state must be addressed in the context of group rights."[47] Whether one conceives of this as a strategic or practical reaction to weak, corrupt, or ineffective governments,[48] or because of a certain moral weight to community norms and commitments that are absent

---

[42] Tilly 1995, 6.

[43] Barry 2001, 7.

[44] A brief definition of liberalism is in order here. There are perhaps four common elements to the definition of liberalism, which include its focus on individualism "in that it asserts the moral primacy of the person against the claims of any social collectivity," as well as its focus on egalitarianism, universalism, and meliorism, or the affirmation of the "improvability of all social institutions and political arrangements." Gray 1995, xiii).

[45] Barry 2001; Kymlicka 1995, 2001; Song 2007; I. Young 1990; Tully 1995.

[46] Ake 2000, 31.

[47] Mutua 2008, 35.

[48] Ekeh's (2004) argument about kin groups and security dilemmas in Nigeria is a good example of this, as is Habiyaramana et al.'s 2009 study of coethnicity and public service provision in Uganda.

from more liberal "civic commitments,"[49] liberal individualism has very little purchase in the social contexts of most of Africa.

Meaningful citizenship is conceptually tied up with equality, inclusion, representation, and participation in democratic states. These elements of citizenship constitute perhaps the greatest democratic challenges for the multicultural, multiethnic, and multiracial societies of the west, and a great deal of scholarly attention has been directed to these topics in recent years. Because of the types of groups and group conflicts in western states, this has led some to call for "differentiated citizenship," "special representation rights," and other legal and institutional provisions recognizing group-based rights.[50]

Mamdani's work on colonialism and citizenship in South Africa is instructive here. He points to the ways that various colonial forms, direct and indirect, rural and urban, impacted citizenship creation, arguing that these forms signified despotism, albeit of distinct natures. His central claim is that colonialism created a bifurcated state with "two forms of power under a single hegemonic authority. Urban power spoke the language of civil society and civil rights, rural power of community and culture. Civil power claimed to protect rights, customary power pledged to enforce tradition."[51] This perspective centrally sees customary power as illegitimate, unyielding, and, in a sense, primordial, just as civil power is hegemonic, but equally delegitimized and unyielding. The so-called native authority was distinctly tribalized and essentialized in Mamdani's characterization in ways that transcend colonial forms or divergent ethnocultural or social contextualization.

The problem with Mamdani's theoretical analysis is not the uses to which he puts it: to explain the failures of democratization in the context of a historical trajectory related to colonial structures. In fact, it is a conclusion many find quite compelling, particularly for the country contexts he focuses on, such as Uganda and South Africa. Rather, Mamdani's typologies cannot explain the reasons why and the extent to which "tribalized" identities and groupings, to use his terminology, have become liberatory movements in Africa's second liberation period. Similarly, it fails to give us a useful perspective on the path of citizen

---

[49] A variant of Peter Ekeh's classic "two publics" argument (1975), or the more recent "moral ethnicity" of Berman and Lonsdale (2004).

[50] Kymlicka 1995; I. Young 1990. This debate over citizenship as inclusion and recognition in the west is extensive; illustrative perspectives are offered by Barry 2001; Huntington 2004; Tully 1995.

[51] Mamdani 1996, 18.

creation and expansion in Ethiopia, where no colonial superstructures descended rapidly and authoritatively to simultaneously create racialized urban/civil power or tribalized rural/customary power. Ethiopian experiences with persistent communally based inequalities (ethnic, gendered) point to the historical specificity associated with these groupings, which defy essentialization, even if they often use the language of essentialism in their daily social and political narrative.[52] The modernizing and expanding Ethiopian state of Emperors Menilek and Haile Selassie sought to reduce native authority in most cases, and the persistence of ethnic identities is testament to not only the monarchy's abuse of power but the salience of those identity groupings.

One way to bridge the gap between the forms of liberalism dominant in the western context and the importance of communalism in parts of sub-Saharan Africa has been the work of scholars who emphasize that citizens are members of, and often active participants in, two substantively different political communities, which are not able to extract similar obligations from or grant similar rights to their members. This view, referred to as "dual citizenship" or the "two publics" by Africanist scholars, is related to the more general theoretical distinction between two conceptions of citizenship.[53] The first, the liberal form of citizenship, focuses on citizenship as status, and holds that rights exist outside and prior to community and are held by individuals because they are "both logically and morally prior to the society and the state."[54] In contrast, the civic-republican form of citizenship tends to emphasize duties over status, and considers rights not as inherent but as acquired through civic practice and upholding obligations to the community. Because the community is primary, this view of citizenship associates the fulfillment of citizenship duties with the very identification as citizens.

It is generally agreed that in the west, these two conceptions of citizenship have competed for prominence at different historical periods, or through the intellectual and political activity of scholars and political elites. Some argue that liberal individualism is ascendant in the west, although communitarians and others wish to reverse this trend because they point to a lack of social solidarity and social cohesion that is created

---

[52] Richard Sklar (1999) takes a distinct approach to the mixture of formal state power and customary or traditional power, focusing on the positive democratic potential of traditional authority in his concept of "mixed government."

[53] Ekeh 1975; Ndegwa 1997.

[54] Oldfield 1990, 179. The paradigmatic statement of contemporary liberal theory is Rawls 1971.

when citizenship is understood as merely or even primarily as status.[55] There are also distinct historical and geopolitical reasons why citizenship has developed differently throughout the world.

The nature of contested citizenship in sub-Saharan Africa, however, is distinct from that of the west, both politically and historically. Rather than these two forms of citizenship – the liberal and the civic-republican – clashing and competing in the social and political realm at any given time, those writing about dual citizenship have argued that they operate simultaneously and compete within the individual and larger social community in the modern period. In this view, African citizens are members of two types of political community in the same temporal and spatial world. The first is their civic-republican community, which is most often their ethnic or communal group. This community demands participation and fulfillment of duties to the collectivity.[56] At the same time, however, these individuals are citizens of a modern state, guided by a liberal conception of citizenship as status and a focus on rights rather than duties. Modern constitutions and formal political practice vest citizens with a variety of rights that are individual and inherent rather than collective or earned.[57]

The clash of identities represented by these two forms of citizenship is unresolved in modern political and social life. In his study of Kenyan politics, Ndegwa concludes that central to the failed transition to democracy throughout the postcolonial period is that liberal and majoritarian institutions' "presumption of autonomous individual actors is at odds with the reality of individuals fulfilling republican obligations to their subnational community."[58] Therefore, citizens may be most engaged in their civic-republican community, which, by its exclusion from formal political practice, is unable then to transform these community goods into public goods for advancing democracy. Put simply, dual citizenship is not supporting democratization processes.

The framework of dual citizenship has been usefully deployed to explain a vast array of political dysfunctions that impede democratic consolidation in sub-Saharan Africa, such as political despotism,

---

[55] Etzioni et al. 2004; MacIntyre 1981; Oldfield 1990; Sandel 1982; Taylor 1995; Walzer 1983.

[56] C.R.D. Halisi's (1999) study of South Africa is by far the most important assessment of the liberal-republican distinction and its relevance to African political thought and political development.

[57] Heater 1999.

[58] Ndegwa 1997: 613.

corruption, ethnic voting, and even ethnic violence. Study of formal citizenship laws points to the critical contribution of legal and institutional structures to democratization processes.[59] In the wake of political liberalization, African leaders have sought to invoke nationalist sentiments, using citizenship laws to narrow the realm of political competition.[60] Englebert argues that the dominant nationalism in Africa, what he calls "sovereignty-derived nationalism," is that which "lacks a nation." In fact, he goes so far as to call it "unemancipatory and divisive," particularly in the way it divides and excludes groups within the state, and he provides critical analysis of some of the most prominent instances of this divisive strain of nationalism.[61] With respect to dual citizenship, Africanist scholars have also used the citizenship lens to explain stalled or failed democratic transitions.[62] Others have used dual citizenship identities to theorize the persistence of racial, class, and ethnic identities despite the "ascendancy of liberal constitutionalism" in these contexts.[63] However, as the guest editors to a special volume on citizenship in Africa note, "The tendency to overemphasize liberal citizenship with emphasis on legal-rational factors while ignoring populist and communitarian conceptions of citizenship" in sub-Saharan Africa is problematic, in part because it obscures the distinct ways in which citizenship is conceptualized in Africa, owing to the vagaries of history, culture, and contemporary political practice.[64]

With respect to ethnic identity in particular, Osaghae goes so far as to claim that in the context of ethnic domination, ethnicity "functions as a liberationist ideology, providing aggrieved groups a pedestal for seeking redress and state reconfiguration."[65] Similarly, Lonsdale in his normatively rich discussion of Kenyan politics, points to the paradoxes of ethnicity and politics in Africa, concluding that for Kenyans, "their imaginations of ethnicity, too often destructive, can nonetheless be among their most fruitful sources of nationally active citizenship."[66] Increasingly, the view of longtime African and Africanist scholars alike is that the study of ethnicity must be approached in radically new ways to account for

---

[59] Herbst 1999.
[60] Aminzade 2003; Manby 2009; Whitaker 2005; Woods 2003.
[61] Englebert 2009, 214.
[62] Mamdani 1996; Ndegwa 1997.
[63] Halisi et al. 1998, 423.
[64] Halisi et al. 1998, 342.
[65] Osaghae 2004, 229.
[66] Lonsdale 2004, 75.

its democratic potential. It would seem that a theory of meaningful citizenship could facilitate the identification of critical citizenship questions relevant to contemporary African democratization challenges. This must extend beyond formal legal or constitutional provisions relating to citizenship, and into local ways citizenship is created, enacted, expanded, and contested.

Citizenship provides a means to reframe ethnicity as positively experienced and as having potential for expanding and deepening democracy in parts of sub-Saharan Africa. In fact, ethnic creativity is evident across sub-Saharan Africa, sometimes peaceful and democracy promoting, sometimes conflict driven. In both cases, however, it is concerned with meaningful citizenship when it seeks to redress the inequalities created, ignored, or perpetuated by the institutions of the state. Citizenship also introduces questions of social solidarity that can be useful in explaining the failure of institutional reform packages to create the enabling conditions for democratic consolidation.

Citizenship is both a legal status and a practice, created by the actors: states and citizens. The notion of contentious and engaged citizenship is almost entirely lacking in political analyses of African politics today. Although there are certainly important cases in which formal citizenship laws play an increasingly important role in restricting political participation by citizens, there are other countries on the continent where the competing notions of citizenship within and between groups and the state constitute barriers to democratization efforts.

What scholars of diversity and multiculturalism theory in the west offer is a dynamic and optimistic view of the role of identity politics in supporting democratization. Adopting and modifying this theoretical approach would radically change the pessimistic and defeatist tone of what is typically studied as "ethnic politics" in the African context. It will, I argue, go a long way toward explaining the persistence of ethnic and communal identities in Africa far better than we have done to date, in line with the admonitions of scholars such as Osaghae to "mainstream" ethnic politics in studies of transitional democracies.[67] One of the most important linkages between ethnic identity and political outcomes in democratizing states is citizenship.

---

[67] Osaghae 2004. I am not, however, saying that ethnic groups are inherently or intrinsically egalitarian or more democratic. It is widely noted that they are often hierarchical, conservative, and socially traditional. This has important ramifications for women and other groups within the group. See Berman et al. 2004; Shachar 2001.

Gendered Citizenship

A substantial literature on the gendered implications of state citizenship and the intersectional nature of women's multiple identities has deepened our understanding of how inequalities are created, sustained, and experienced by different groups of citizens – especially women and subgroups of women. Patriarchal laws, institutions, and cultural norms often collude to impose distinct and gendered burdens on women in economic, social, and political life. Some of the most trenchant critiques of multiculturalism as a normative project have come from feminist theorists, in large part because so many of the concerns for feminists and activists regarding women's status are justified or defended on "cultural" grounds, whether of the majority or minority culture. Focusing on women allows for considering citizen creation in ways that attend to matters of fairness and justice, but it is also linked to the very practical and urgent effort to improve the daily lives of women and their families.

The shift to citizenship provides a whole new lens through which to consider what it means to be an Ethiopian citizen in the case under consideration. A new question emerges: Is an Ethiopian citizen a man? The formal Ethiopian constitutional provisions are staunchly pro-women, and subsequent legal reforms, particularly the Revised Marriage and Family Code of 2000, are impressive. But in sorting through data on development indicators for Ethiopian women, such as age of marriage, maternal mortality, and so on, one finds evidence of staggering inequality, both compared to men and compared to other women in Africa. Elite women have seen relative advances throughout this period, but what of the rest of women in Ethiopia? It is striking how little has been accomplished for Ethiopian women as equal, participating citizens in the democratization and development of their society and to consider what the implications of this are not only for their own lives but for their families and communities. Very little space is given to the gendered implications of full and equal citizenship for Ethiopian women, particularly those from formerly oppressed and marginalized communities. This suggests that citizenship and feminist approaches may provide useful correctives.

There are a number of ways to approach the sets of questions that emerge from thinking about gendered citizenship in Ethiopia and its implications for the democratizing potential of citizenship creation and expansion. Is gender inequality in Ethiopia to be addressed through the institutional structures of federalism? And how do the strong constitutional and legal protections and affirmative rights for ethnic communities impact women in particular? These two questions are rooted in two distinct constellations of empirical data: one related to women in Ethiopia in particular and the other arising from global experiences with gender and multiculturalist concerns. An interesting corollary to the attention to ethnic claims, even if consistently framed as ethnic conflict, is to consider the ways in which being ethnic (Oromo, Tigrayan, or Siltie, for instance) presents a challenge to national identity in a way that being gendered (a woman) not does. Is a gendered approach to Ethiopian politics also a challenge to the essential foundations of Ethiopian-ness? If not, why?

Although a poor country, there is little doubt that poverty is structurally distinct for Ethiopian women as a group. Women in Ethiopia experience bias in the provision of services and the protection of law. They remain underrepresented in formal political and social life. The immense poverty at the national level affects women disproportionately. While urban and elite women may have particular tools at their disposal to cope with domestic demands (usually the labor of younger women and girls), most Ethiopian women spend significant portions of their time attending to the basic needs of their family. This often includes collecting water, grinding grains, and preparing meals and caring for their children as well as sick or elderly family members.

Both the formal legal system and the reliance on various customary laws have left the vast majority of women with little protection from discrimination, including in land and property, in marriage and family, and in the informal market and access to resources.[68] In particular, certain cultural traditions distinctly impact women and girls in Ethiopia. Because most of these practices are not evenly distributed among the ethnic groups of Ethiopia, but are structurally tied to ethnic community identity and boundary formation and boundary policing, any legal changes in these practices might reasonably be interpreted by women and men in these communities as related to their community identity as least as much as their gendered identity.

Notwithstanding the tremendous challenges to implementing these progressive provisions for women and girls, the 1995 Constitution and the Revised Family Law of 2000 do suggest a major tension inherent in Ethiopian federalism. What happens when members of an ethnic community (or their political leadership) determine that a particular practice relating to women is a constitutionally protected aspect of their national right to self-rule and cultural development? How are these two sets of

---

[68] Vaughan and Tronvoll 2003.

rights to be adjudicated? Somewhat surprisingly, very few cases have arisen, even fewer than those relating to ethnic rights, as discussed in Chapter 6 of this book. This suggests the relative importance of ethnic rights over women's rights in the current discourse about citizenship in Ethiopia and the challenges of expanded citizenship for women and girls in the country. Some have argued that the legal and constitutional rhetoric notwithstanding, "state actions continue to focus on the 'woman question,' taking the lead in a paternalistic form of welfarism and suspiciously muting any call for the genuine empowerment of women."[69] Nuancing the study of Ethiopian citizenship by introducing women as a distinct category of citizen highlights the challenge of balancing multiple citizenship claims in diverse and divided societies. Generations of ethnic inequality compete in some sense with centuries of gendered inequality in contemporary Ethiopia. This intersectional approach, which sees a multiplicity of overlapping identities and the linkages of these to institutional and policy reforms in the context of a democratic transition, provides both a normative and a practical dimension to the study of politics.

Much of the liberal attack on the "illiberal cultures" of the nonwestern world would strip women of the cultural context within which their identities as women and as citizens have been shaped. It is hard to imagine what women or men would be able to accomplish without these cultural tools, or why this would be preferable for them. As has been noted, shifting from studying women or ethnic communities as bounded and monolithic groups, from "asking what cultures *are* to what cultural affiliations *do*"[70] carries with it the possibility to see how cultural group identity and gendered identity not only structure inequality but create opportunities and resources. It is also a highly paternalistic approach to assume that some women are incapable of reforming their culture to attain their full rights, while women in the west have of course managed to do this at least in some respects. Joseph Raz reminds us that "we do not reject our culture when we find it replete with oppression and the violation of rights; we try to reform it."[71] Surely women in all cultures are capable of this kind of reform, and, in this book, I provide examples from Ethiopia and elsewhere.

There is very much the possibility of reconciling ethnocultural rights with women's rights. Because Ethiopia's federal system is explicitly formed

---

[69] Biseswar 2008, 141.
[70] Song 2007, 8, emphasis in original.
[71] Raz, in Okin 1999, 97.

around ethnic and language group identities, it provides a unique and crucial case to consider in the context of a global concern with justice. Are women oppressed internal minorities within ethnocultural groups in Ethiopia? Or do these group-based norms and rules provide women with unique resources to confront the economic and social challenges they face, both as women and as multicultural citizens in democratizing states? How do formal legal and institutional reforms for women compare to cultural traditions when it comes to application, legitimacy, and effectiveness? I cannot answer these questions decisively, but I am confident that even asking these sets of questions can open new possibilities for Ethiopians – women and men alike. And the examples from Ethiopia suggest that ethnocultural diversity and the attendant resources of group-based identities not only provide women today with critical resources in confronting their gendered inequality but are possible resources for a nationwide structuring of uniquely Ethiopian citizenship.

Conclusion

It is clear that a citizenship lens on political processes in Africa reveals dynamic and contentious struggles for recognition, inclusion, and participation – all cornerstones of meaningful and expanded citizenship. Across all layers of the African social landscape, conversations about citizenship continue to reverberate, sometimes trickling up to elite levels, with impacts on policy and politics. Many are happening at the family and village level, however, rarely captured in electoral contests, party politics, or even legal or institutional change. They are about the best ways to obtain the participation of all members of society. These conversations and resultant changes in local family and community life reflect a sea change in terms of life prospects, in terms of the realization of each individual's potential in many of the countries of Africa. Each is essential to any democracy-promoting initiatives.

All of this is of course happening in particular historical and social contexts, and the meaning of these practices of making citizens is shaped by the trajectories and narratives of the societies they inhabit. Shifting now to Ethiopia provides a dynamic and complex terrain on which to explore how this is occurring and why. Never colonized by European powers and home to rich cultural, linguistic, and religious diversity, with a rapidly growing population and an emotive if deeply contentious nationalist project, Ethiopia is just the right terrain for thinking about meaningful citizenship, ethnic groups and women, and the making of a national identity. In the quest for a more meaningful citizenship, Ethiopians, despite important differences in how their political and social life has been organized, are actually quite similar to other postcolonial Africans.

2

The Historical Context for Modern Ethiopian Citizenship

In a 2003 revision to the civics curriculum in Ethiopia, middle and high school students are introduced to a radical reordering of Ethiopian history and social life. In the second chapter entitled "The Rule of Law," students are told that "before 1974, the political system in Ethiopia was set up on the basis of the divine right of kings. Monarchs claimed to be elects of God. Such belief helped the monarchs establish absolute power over their subjects by monopolizing legislative, executive and judiciary powers." In the next chapter, students are taught that, because of the change of government in the early 1990s and the subsequent revision of the constitution,

the Constitution of the Federal Democratic Republic of Ethiopia (FDRE) became the first charter of equality in Ethiopian history.... The major purpose of the FDRE government is to secure the peaceful co-existence of Nations, Nationalities and Peoples who consented to live together on the basis of equality and other principles of democracy. These principles and values ... are designed to protect not only individual members but also the rights of all Nations, Nationalities and Peoples of Ethiopia as a whole.[1]

The Ethiopian Constitution of 1995 is a dramatic departure from modern Ethiopian political practice in its explicit and extensive attention to group-based rights provisions, especially those of ethnic communities. It builds on several decades of citizenship creation and expansion but takes the contentious contours of that citizenship to new realms of political administration and cultural policy. It is argued to be innovative by some, divisive and destructive by others, and therefore, extremely controversial

[1] Civic and Ethical Educational Student's Textbook, Grade 9, 25, 37.

both inside Ethiopia and abroad. It also includes a number of individual rights provisions, including those that guarantee equality between men and women. These latter constitutional provisions paved the way for dramatic revisions to existing penal law so as to provide the context in which women and girls could realize these rights. Why did Ethiopia need to reorder social and political life so dramatically? Or put another way, how does this reordering of citizenship expand the contours of opportunity for the Anywaa woman of the Shola market?

In Ethiopia, the legal structure of citizenship has been altered, and yet the content and nature of these meanings remain deeply contested by individuals and members of particular communities. Communal conflicts, often ethnic in nature and form, ignite periodically or simmer at local levels for long periods of time. More importantly, several decades of political conflict in the country have been shaped by both the aspirations for full and meaningful citizenship and the particular forms that these aspirations have taken. Ethiopians became legal citizens of their state in the mid-1970s when the country's military dictatorship took power from the imperial regime, under which Ethiopians had been subjects and not citizens. If citizenship is the "right to have rights," the 1970s marked the beginning of a national conversation within Ethiopia of what those rights would be and how they would be realized. For various historical and social reasons, that conversation has often focused on the centrality of ethnic and communal identities and the social, political, and economic rights that had been denied. To a lesser extent, this has also involved some reordering of women's place within the Ethiopian social and political realm but often at the intersection with ethnic identity, rather than as a marker of political and social inequality on its own.

The discussion here, then, turns to *when* and *how* the Ethiopian Anywaa woman of the Shola market became a citizen of Ethiopia, and what that citizenship *means*. For our purposes here, she must be Ethiopian, not an Anywaa refugee or citizen of Sudan. Since there at least 85,000 Anywaa in Ethiopia, she must be part of that community of identity. And of course, she must be a woman, and a resident in that capital city, living in an ethnic neighborhood as so many citizens do. What does meaningful citizenship entail, but particularly, how is her citizenship different from that of her parents and grandparents?

Contemporary citizenship law and practice in Ethiopia have evolved out of a complex and contested mix of imperial and dictatorial decree, sociocultural practice and tradition, and public protest and opposition. Throughout the modern period, particularly beginning with Emperor

Menilek's military incorporation of the southern regions of present-day Ethiopia, the delimitation of who was an Ethiopian citizen and what the rights and duties of citizenship were stand out as prominent, if not explicit, political imperatives. Menilek consolidated the geographic boundaries of the modern state, but his campaigns surely did not resolve the contentious matter of the terms of inclusion for newly incorporated peoples, nor for those groups such as the Oromo or Anywaa who, although already physically part of the Ethiopian state, were by no means included in political, social, or economic life on equal terms. Similarly, the citizenship status of marginalized and oppressed peoples, particularly on the borders, is an as yet unfinished political project. Those ethnic groups on the western borders – what are more recently referred to as the emerging regions, – are illustrative of the incomplete extension of citizenship in Ethiopia, as are Ethiopian Somalis, who can be argued to be the most precariously placed group when it comes to formal citizenship status. The contemporary Ethiopian state uses the lack of formalized citizenship status along the relatively fluid border of Somali regional state and its neighbors to manipulate and dominate Ethiopian Somali politics.[2] Finally, although each of these more contemporary regimes introduced dramatic reforms for women, this has largely been a top-down process rather than one initiated by communities or families, or even women themselves. Legal and structural reforms seem to have yielded few tangible improvements for Ethiopian women, while cultural traditions continue in at least some cases to provide women with resources for expanded citizenship.

Ethiopian Citizenship in the Highlands

The borders and political practices and policies that emerged within the borders of the Ethiopian state evolved through the same complex mix of internal and external influences as in other African states, but in Ethiopia the domestic and internal influences were always far greater than the outside ones, owing to the lack of effective colonization by a European power. Although influenced by international and regional imperatives and evolving global norms, as well as military and political responses to imperial encroachments by European powers, the impact of these on citizenship creation and expansion in the past 150 years or so of history was relatively minimal. Nonetheless, as the Abyssinian state expanded,

[2] Samatar 2004; Interview #42.

citizenship practices were created and expanded.[3] Because these historical trajectories are pivotal to major restructurings since 1974, I briefly consider here the question of earlier regimes in the modern period.

However, rather than consider these developments in chronological form, this chapter will proceed geographically, considering citizenship creation and expansion in the northern Abyssinian highlands first, and then moving south, west, and east to consider how citizenship was conceived, obstructed, and quite slowly expanded to communities that were absorbed into the modern Ethiopian state. This is a view suggested by a growing body of Ethiopian historiography that critiques the ahistorical nature of so-called Great Tradition scholarship, which had generally assumed a particular inevitability about the creation of the Ethiopian state. In this telling of history, Ethiopia always existed throughout the centuries, but some people, "notably those who speak Amharic and Tigrinya, *are* Ethiopia, whereas other peoples merely *become part of* Ethiopia."[4] Rather, some argue that the history of Ethiopia as a state really does not make sense, as the state expanded and contracted over the centuries. Clapham, for instance, argues that a more appropriate approach would be a history of the Horn of Africa as a region.[5] Richard Reid would have us focus on "frontiers of violence" across the subregion, an intervention I find equally thought provoking.[6] This would not privilege any people over others and would make geography, not culture or conquest, the unifying theme. Of course, we generally do study Ethiopia as a state, and I will follow that convention here, although my purpose is to point out how newly incorporated groups came to receive grants of first legal, then expanded meaningful citizenship over the modern period.

Even before questions of place (highlands/lowlands, core/periphery), however, what of questions of time, of when modern Ethiopia is born? Across nearly all of sub-Saharan Africa, the "modern" state is the one

---

[3] Abyssinia refers to the geographical area of northern Ethiopia that includes what are today the Amhara and Tigray regional states, as well as highland Eritrea, which shared a "commonality of polity, land tenure, culture and religion" (Gebru 1991, 230). It also denotes the ethnic Tigrean-Amhara hegemony that can be traced back to the ancient kingdom of Axum (Donham 2002, 34). Gebru points out that although Abyssinians tended to identify by region in relation to each other, they "regarded themselves as belonging to a supra-region, supra-ethnic community which they called *Habesha*," which was defined by *Geez* (historical language), the Orthodox Church, and the *Kebre Negast* (Gebru 1991, 27, 36; Mekuria 2002, 12–13).

[4] Clapham 2002, 40, 41(emphasis in original).

[5] Clapham 2002.

[6] Reid 2011.

that takes shape after independence. But what is the modern state of Ethiopia? As Teshale Tibebu notes, Ethiopian history is "as old as one wants it to be."[7] Historians of the "3,000 Years" persuasion start their accounting of Ethiopia in antiquity, with greater historical details available starting with the Aksumite kingdom of the fourth century A.D. and the mythical visit of the Queen of Sheba to King Solomon in the tenth century B.C., the result of which produced Menilek, the first Ethiopian king in the Solomonic dynasty. Those of the "150 Years" school prefer to begin with the so-called modern history of Ethiopia, dated at 1855 with the rise of Emperor Tewodros II and the end of the Zamana Masafent, the so-called Era of the Princes. This term refers to a period of general decline in imperial rule from about the second half of the eighteenth century until the rise of Emperor Tewodros II. Tewodros II (1855–1868), and Emperor Yohannes IV (1872–1889), set in motion events in which political power and authority were restored, and external and internal challenges to central authority were met with military force.[8] Bahru summarizes the competing visions that led up to Menilek's reign:

Since the middle of the nineteenth century, the unification of Ethiopia had been a matter of utmost priority.... For Tewodros, it meant the creation of a centralized unitary state. For Yohannes it signified the establishment of a loosely united Ethiopia, with autonomous regional rulers under an emperor exercising benevolent political suzerainty. By 1889, it had become clear that both approaches had failed to produce the desired result.... It was to be Menilek's main claim to historical distinction that he presided over the realization of an idea that had first been kindled in the fiery mind of Tewodros.[9]

The Christian highland kingdom of historic Ethiopia had a number of distinct features that relate to the development of citizenship, particularly as its expansion and contestation emerged in the early and middle parts of the twentieth century. First is the centrality of land to relations between what we could call the state, which refers to the administrative, political, and legal functions, performed on behalf of a larger collectivity, and those who occupied territories controlled by that state(s). Second is the system of tax or tribute. I discuss these two here briefly, as a foundation to understanding the expansion of the imperial state in the so-called modern period. They are linked, as historian Donald Crummey notes, in that "the main, ongoing way in which, through the centuries, the Ethiopian state and rulers affected the lives of ordinary people ... was through its system

[7] Teshale 1995, xi.
[8] Bahru 1991, 42.
[9] Bahru 1991, 60.

of taxation and tribute, known by the term *gult*, an institution of land tenure which brought together producers and privilege, farmers and rulers and provided the means whereby the former supported the latter."[10] At its most basic level, *gult* was a grant of land or a "fief." *Gult*, then, is "all rights by groups or individuals to collect tribute," and it was not restricted in this sense to periods of conquest, such as the Menilek expansion into the south, east and west.[11]

Critically, there were other forms of land and labor in the highland plateau, including *rest*, or inherited land. *Rest*, unlike *gult*, was a birthright, and Crummey argues that "Christian Ethiopians apply the term quite broadly.... When it came to land, they also used it in a general sense to refer to any inherited right, but more narrowly it referred to the inalienable right of farming people to inherit the land which they till. This was a right held equally by men and women."[12] Crummey's work challenges the idea that most Christian farmers of the pre-twentieth-century Ethiopia were exclusively or primarily *restanna*, or holders of *rest* land. He points to the "ambiguous" evidence suggesting important examples of landlords, or *malkañña* in Ankobar, northern Shewa, and perhaps in wider use. In fact, Crummey argues that "even those farmers who were *restanna* were also at the same time *gabbar*, or tributaries." Put another way, "*Rest* and *gult*, as property rights, formed the basis for distinct classes. The Ethiopian ruling class, then, consisted of *gult*-holders. Their primary interest was the subordination of others and the extraction of wealth from them.... The class which stood against the *gult*-holders consisted of farmers with inherited rights to land on which they paid tribute. In this sense, the farmers were *restanna*."[13]

The importance of this rather specific historical argument will be apparent below, when considering the extension of extractive and coercive political and economic relations into western and southern Ethiopia since the late 19th century. But it is worth pausing to consider the implications of these relations. Crummey concludes that "by the nineteenth century, the status of serf and tenant was probably less widespread in Christian Ethiopia than it had been in the sixteenth, although in most other respects, the relations between rulers and ruled remained similar."[14]

---

[10] Crummey 2000, 5.

[11] Crummey 2000, 11.

[12] Crummey 2000, 9.

[13] Crummey 2000, 12.

[14] Crummey 2000, 67. The complexities of Ethiopian feudal land relations are beyond the scope of this work. General descriptions can be found in Bahru 1991; Marcus

These social, economic, and fundamentally political relations, however transformed they may have been in terms of land ownership and tenancy in the northern highlands, were the basis of citizenship as the Ethiopian state expanded rapidly at the turn of the twentieth century.

Another important study of Ethiopia, by sociologist Donald Levine, attempted to develop the essential internal characteristics of Ethiopian society that could explain its success in resisting European colonial occupation. Levine argues for the notion of a civilizational area called Greater Ethiopia, based primarily on cultural and political contributions from Tigreans, Amharas, and Oromos in Ethiopia. Although Levine's work was an interesting attempt to grapple with the social and psychological features of ethnic identities in Ethiopia and how these groups interacted with each other, their geographical and political environments, and other outside groups, his arguments about the foundations of unity and cultural sharing among Ethiopia's ethnic groups were simplistic and flawed. He focused particularly on the *Kebre Negast*, which is the narrative of the Solomonic dynasty written by Tigrean scribes and completed somewhere in the fourteenth century. It details the story of Solomon and Sheba's encounter and the birth of Menilek, as well as the events that led to the Ark of the Covenant being brought from Jerusalem to Axum in northern Ethiopia. While the historical accuracy of the *Kebre Negast* is debatable, just as controversial is the role of the narrative in shaping Ethiopian political identity. Levine claims that it serves as the national script, giving legitimacy to the Ethiopian (Amhara) monarchy and cementing connections between Tigreans and Amharas. In the preface to the 2000 edition of the book, Levine himself notes that the *Kebre Negast* and the Solomonic ideology "could no longer serve as a script for the Ethiopian nation, both because of its sacralization of imperial authority and because its linkage with the Christian tradition rendered the inclusion of non-Christian groups increasingly difficult."[15]

What are we to make of this highland history? It is crucial to frame the context of economic, social, and political life in the core of the Ethiopian state at the time of expansion. The demands of land and tribute that was the reform of the *gult* system formed a critical impetus for citizen creation in the northern core of the Ethiopian state and were later also

1994; Keller 1988; Gebru 1991. Somewhat more detailed study of these topics can be found in McCann 1987, 1995; A. Hoben 1973; R. Pankhurst 1969; Crummey 1980; Brietzke 1975.
[15] Levine 2000, xvii.

part of the demands for citizenship expansion in these new peripheries of the empire.

Territorial Expansion and Citizenship Denied

Emperor Menilek realized the dreams of unification and territorial expansion that were envisioned by his predecessors, Tewodros and Yohannes. His rule was marked by the perceived imperative to create internal unity and prevent external invasion, particularly from the Italians but increasingly from the Mahdists. Menilek's rule was also significant for a number of important modernizing initiatives, including those in trade, military development, external relations with Europeans, infrastructural development, and educational advancements. By 1896, with the Ethiopian defeat of the Italians at the historic battle of Adwa, Menilek had successfully resisted the most significant of the external threats to his reign as well, although at the expense of losing the territory of what is now Eritrea. Menilek's success at Adwa earned him greater stature in the international community, allowing him to secure on Ethiopia's behalf a number of agreements with the surrounding colonial powers, including French Somaliland (now Djibouti), British Somaliland (now part of Somalia), British East Africa (now Kenya), and Italian Eritrea.[16] These were the agreements that for the most part came to delineate the modern-day boundaries of the state of Ethiopia.

In addition to Menilek's military successes, both with foreign powers and in incorporating new lands in the southern and western regions, he made the important political contribution of creating a Council of Ministers, which some have argued helped pave the way for the bureaucratizing reforms of Haile Selassie.[17] His establishment of a ministerial system in 1907 appears to have been directly related to Menilek's awareness of the problem of succession, which eventually came to define the period 1908–1930.[18] Although most members were old palace nobles, and their portfolios and powers did little to change the tasks they had performed under the traditional administrative mode, the creation of the Council of Ministers was the first attempt to create an institutional basis to political authority in Ethiopia, and it had enduring implications for the modern state.

---

[16] Bahru 1991, 110–114.
[17] Carmichael 2001, 240.
[18] Bahru 1991, 114.

Internally, through a combination of military defeats and negotiated peace treaties, Menilek subjugated southern rulers, and he extended the Ethiopian state to its present size. After the Battle of Embabo in June 1882, most of the Oromo states submitted to Menilek.[19] The northern Gurage (the Kestane) peacefully submitted to Menilek, but the western Gurage were subdued after fierce fighting. Menilek's forces also waged a successful military campaign against the emirate of Harar, the powerful commercial city in eastern Ethiopia, achieving victory on January 6, 1887. The conquests of the Wolaitta and Kafa were particularly bloody and were followed by conquests on the western frontiers, including Bela Shangul (Benishangul), Aqoldi (Asossa), and Khomosha.[20]

Menilek's southern conquests also had important administrative implications. Perham notes that "the land was regarded in most parts as confiscated to the crown, a varying portion being allotted to the conquered chiefs and people, and the rest used to reward or maintain Amhara, and especially Shoan, soldiers, officials and notables."[21] This created land scarcity and concentrations, leading to various forms of absentee landlordism by Amhara nobles over southern lands and ethnic nationalities, which created tremendous resentment against northern rule. Northern and highland Ethiopian social and economic relations were transposed to southern lands where they were foreign. Lands that had resisted Menilek's invading armies were subjected to various foreign social and economic relations, including those of *gabbar*, or tribute labor, as well as surplus labor, usually on the state or governor's land. Peasants were also forced to provide goods and services for overlords, known as *malkañña* or *shalaqa*, several times a year. Those lands that had not resisted Menilek's armies were spared imposition of the *gabbar-malkañña* relations, but all were subject to a fixed annual tribute (*qurt geber*), collected by the governors of the regions.[22] Crummey notes that "each settler, normally a male head of household, received a set number of individuals, each one of whom became his gabbar.... Each gabbar, again normally a male head of household, owed his lord labor service and material tribute ... the obligations it entailed were extensive and onerous."[23]

The southern regions also saw the appropriation of large areas of land. Among the land that was not state property, it was divided three

[19] Bahru 1991, 60–62; Mohammed 1990.
[20] Bahru 1991, 60–66.
[21] Perham 1969, 295.
[22] Bahru 1991, 87; Keller 1988, 59; Marcus 1975.
[23] Crummey 2000, 223.

ways: Some land was given to the local ruler or *balabbat*, some land was retained by peasants, subject to payment of tribute and rendering of labor services, and the Ethiopian Orthodox Church was given land (*samon*). *Naftagna*, or northern soldier-settlers, took the place of *malkañña*, the northern overlords.[24] In the *ketemas*, or garrison towns erected throughout the country but particularly important in the administration of the southern regions, settlers, soldiers, and their families lived removed from the realities of tribute obligations and forced labor required of the indigenous populations, and many, like Keller, argue that "this in large measure inhibited the development of a sense of national identification with the Ethiopian state" among these peoples.[25] The *ketemas*, and the northern administrators and soldiers who lived in them, came to be the source of assimilation and acculturation that accelerated later under Haile Selassie. A number of scholars, particularly Levine in his 2000 introduction to *Greater Ethiopia*, point out the oppressive nature of northern highland social relations for Amhara (and, by implication, Tigrayan) peasants. This fact is not disputed here. The critical point being made is the transfer of these foreign relations and the striking severity of their impact, particularly on conquered areas that had resisted Menilek's imposition of central authority and the role that the *naftagna* and *balabbats* played in this.[26]

The nature of social and political arrangements under Menilek influenced the patterns of inclusion. Most ethnonationalist historians of Ethiopia refer to this period of territorial expansion and consolidation of imperial control as an African form of internal colonization. Greenfield wrote in his 1965 history of Ethiopia that "members of minority groups even within Ethiopia have not been unknown to use privately the term 'colonialism' when discussing Menilek's expansionist achievements," although Greenfield himself seems to take the official stance as fact, that these conquered regions had been ruled in earlier times.[27] Marcus portrays the general view of the *naftagna* toward the indigenous inhabitants as scornful and paternalistic. Social assimilation was typically required of *balabbats* and *qoros* (their assistants), and others as well. It generally included conversion to Orthodox Christianity, changing one's name, mastery of the Amharic language, and even adjustments in dress and eating habits.[28]

[24] Bahru 1991, 90–92; Marcus 1994, 105.
[25] Keller 1988, 39.
[26] Marcus 1994, 105; Marcus 1975, 192–195.
[27] Greenfield 1965, 109.
[28] Marcus 1975, 194.

More recent scholarship, however, suggests the diversity of experiences wrought by the extension of northern Christian highlander control and increasing centralization of authority under the state. Like other prominent contemporary historians of Ethiopia, such as Bahru Zewde, Donham and James argue persuasively for a middle-ground interpretation of Ethiopian history, a "story of the *political interaction* between the expanding imperial state on the one hand, the peoples of its new southern frontiers on the other."[29] In doing this, Donham interrogates the idea that Abyssinian cultural identity was homogenous, arguing instead that regional identities typically associated with local elites probably tended to dominate. In particular, scholars note that Abyssinian identity was fragmented into regional identities associated with local elites, and that "it was only in relation to the permanent periphery of Shankilla slaves and Muslim Afar that Abyssinians saw themselves as members of a more inclusive category: Habesha (both Tigrinnya- and Amharic-speaking peoples)."[30] Much earlier, in his discussion of the use of northern settlers in expanding Menilek's empire, Marcus argued a similar point: "In their isolation from the homeland, the settlers felt more common cultural identity than ever before."[31] In a short but groundbreaking article on the subject, Russian historian Sevir Chernetsov also focuses on the evolution of the Amhara identity through the transformation of a military class seeking access to land via military service to the imperial throne into a "regular Ethiopian people" known for particular cultural habits and speaking the Amharic language.[32]

That the Amhara ethnic group has a distinct ethnogenesis should not surprise us. In fact, work like Chernetsov's and the scholars he cites suggest the origins of the traditions of hierarchy, discipline, and deference that are crucial to political developments today. Equally as important is to focus on the forms that state expansion took at the turn of the twentieth century. In fact, newly conquered regions were not uniformly or even similarly assimilated into the expanding imperial state. Donham develops a typology of three main paths for how peripheral areas were linked to the center of the empire-state: (1) semi-independent enclaves, which were made tributary to the crown; (2) *gabbar* areas, where northern

---

[29] Donham and James 2002, xv (emphasis in original).
[30] Donham 2002, 23.
[31] Marcus 1975, 194.
[32] Chernetsov 1993, 102. Chernetsov relies on some excellent original sources, and cites prominently the work of Allen Hoben (1973).

governors were appointed and local peoples made into near serfs; and (3) fringe peripheries, mainly the lowlands occupied by hunters and pastoralists.[33] A similar point is made by Gebru in his study of peasant revolts in Ethiopia, who notes that although Abyssinian conquest was similar in its overall impact – it was "dispossessive, extortionist and very repressive" – it was, nonetheless, accompanied by regional differences. From his view, northern peasants had "affiliative relations and long-standing shared traditions" that protected them from the most excessive abuse from local authorities. By contrast, southerners were subjected to brute force at the hands of settlers and landlords, with no legal or traditional recourse.[34]

Relatedly, the western and eastern regions of the country – what are now referred to as the emerging regions of Gambella, Benishangul-Gumuz, Somali, and Afar regions – each saw periods of economic, political, and especially military encroachment by the expanding highland state. In these regions the Ethiopian highland encroachment was complicated by the presence of European colonial powers. For instance, in what is today Gambella, the turn of the century saw both the British and Ethiopian states competing for prominence, which local ethnic groups such as the Anywaa sought to use to their competitive advantage. This initially meant cooperation with the imperial state, and turned to conflict and even rebellion at various points.[35]

However varied the experience of imperial incorporation was, because colonial policy emphasized political and economic control, and because most of these peoples were ethnically, culturally, linguistically, and religiously different from the Amhara-Tigre ruling class, this led to a "class structure with distinctive ethnic undertones."[36] While Menilek's reign was a time of tremendous military and territorial change in modern Ethiopia, the social implications of his economic and political policies were far-reaching. The establishment of *ketemas* and the practice of encouraging Amhara settlement in formerly conquered areas not only introduced foreign landholding patterns and burdensome external labor and taxation obligations but also set in motion increasingly unequal class relations and conflict among ethnic groups. This facilitated a process

---

[33] Donham 2002, 37.

[34] Gebru 1991, 20. A fascinating example of the complex overlay of imperial conquest, cultural creativity, and resilience and individual ability and acumen is given in the story of a female Gamo balabat (local ruler) in the 1970s (see Olmstead 1997).

[35] Dereje 2008; see also Markakis 2011; J. Young 1999.

[36] Keller 1988, 45.

whereby not only northern Amharas coalesced around a newly significant common identity, but also southern kin groups began to see themselves in common as ethnic groups. Although disputing the idea that we can read ethnicity back into earlier periods of Ethiopian highland history, Crummey does concur that "the combined result of *gabbar* status and of the seizure of land was the creation in large parts of southern Ethiopia of a social system which combined subordination, poverty and cultural alienation. Associated with and supported by the state were immigrants who brought with them a complete culture – Amharic speech, Christian religion.... Subject to them, whether as individual tributaries or as renters of land, were peoples of diverse speech, Islamic or traditional faith and distinctive customs and legal traditions."[37] The changes brought by Menilek and Haile Selassie meant increasing identification with ethnic groups as we know them today, pointing to both the historical role of the state in citizen creation and the dynamic and diverse nodes of ethnic identity formation. This occurred in both the historical highlands and the newly conquered and incorporated lands of Ethiopia.

Still, there were no citizens under Menilek's rule. It was the political and social policies of assimilation under Menilek that laid the foundations for contemporary citizenship identities in Ethiopia. He led political, military, and diplomatic efforts that came to delineate the Ethiopian nation not just by its territorial boundaries but attempted to also define it by a particular cultural, religious, and linguistic identity. During Menilek's rule, particularly through the pivotal role played by northern settlers and soldiers, and the imposition of the *gabbar-naftagna* social and economic relations, incorporated subjects found that their participation in the dominant political and economic structures required tremendous leaps of acculturation and learning.[38] In an infamous quote, Emperor Menilek was purported to have boasted after his occupation of Harar in 1887, "This is not a Muslim country, as everyone knows."[39] It was this emerging and distinctly nationalist image of a "modern" highland Christian kingdom that established the basis of modern citizenship forms in Ethiopia – the history that Ethiopians from those conquered regions contest today as they seek the rights and responsibilities of a meaningful citizenship in modern Ethiopia.

[37] Crummey 2000, 225.
[38] Marcus 1975, 2, 65.
[39] Quoted in Laitin and Samatar 1987, 12. A fascinating parallel came in the present regime's framing of the reasons for the 2006 invasion of Somalia by the Ethiopian military, where the trope was again restated by the prime minister.

From Expansion to Consolidation

Menilek suffered a series of strokes beginning in 1906, and for nearly the full seven years until his death, a brutal power struggle ensued over succession to the throne. For parts of this period (1906–1913), Menilek's wife, the capable but disliked Empress Taitu, was the de facto head of state. After her forced departure from political matters, the recently appointed cabinet ministers ruled the country.

From 1909 to 1916, Menilek's grandson and appointed heir, Iyasu, ruled, if de facto, from 1911 through the death of Menilek in 1913. He was hounded by opponents from the outset, and his own political views and perhaps personal choices contributed to the fate that befell him. Iyasu had radical notions of an Ethiopian society without religious or ethnic inequalities, celebrating those distinct identity groups. His dealings with diverse Ethiopian communities and neighboring Somali Muslims in particular raised the ire of both the political leadership in the capital and the leaders of the Ethiopian Orthodox Church. Historian Harold Marcus notes that the governors of the southern provinces opposed Iyasu, "as their economic interests required a servile population to exploit."[40] Bahru also points to the role that European colonial powers in the region played in the overthrow of Iyasu.[41]

In light of more recent citizenship-expansion processes since the 1970s, it is perhaps time to reassess Iyasu's brief reign. His downfall at the hands of church and business elites was ostensibly to protect Shawan power politics, and the fall of Iyasu and rise of Ras Tafari signaled the triumph of the latter. Iyasu almost immediately came into conflict with the aristocracy and with foreign colonial powers in the region. He "supported some of the claims of subject peoples and nationalities against the social order established by his grandfather," Emperor Menilek.[42] Some have argued it is time to reconsider what might have happened to Ethiopia if Iyasu's brand of multiculturalism had been allowed to take hold. In a reinterpretation of Iyasu's political vision for the empire, Mekuria argues that "Iyasu was determined from the very beginning of his rule to dismantle the empire's rigidly hierarchical social and political order in favour of a united and equitable society."[43] Teshale asserts that "emperor Iyasu, despite being

[40] Marcus 1994, 117.
[41] Bahru 1991, 127.
[42] Crummey 2000, 229.
[43] Mekuria, 2002, 161.

a Christian, acted and behaved in a manner appropriate of a leader of a multi-religious and multi-ethnic country like Ethiopia."[44] Tibebe also notes that "he saw the need to develop a more inclusive vision of the Ethiopian nation by putting greater focus upon the neglected peripheral parts of the country."[45]

The seeming "inevitability" argument about Ethiopian history, that the arc of history bends in only one direction and was destined to be that way, is particularly challenged by the Iyasu period. One could at least imagine a more inclusive, multiethnic, multireligious national identity forged in the early modern period had such a ruler been left to carry forward this kind of political project. Instead, Iyasu's attempts to integrate Muslims into the administration made it relatively easy for the church and allied aristocrats and international actors to allege his conversion to Islam and excommunicate him, making him ineligible for the throne.[46] In particular, Tibebe's conclusion is prescient, that "perhaps there is something in the political culture of Ethiopia that does not tolerate the creation of a new mold of leadership.... [And] in his quest for a new venue in which to practice the religious toleration and personal social egalitarianism that came naturally to him," he alienated local notables and powerful international elites simultaneously.[47] Tibebe's presentation of how political culture may have influenced the complex responses of nobles and religious elites to the incorporation of new communities, new religions, new power dynamics in Ethiopia evokes Chernetsov's depiction of the roots of Amhara ethnic identity.

Iyasu's brief rule was followed by the rule of Empress Zawditu, Menilek's daughter, who was crowned empress in 1916. Dajjach Tafari Makonnen was made Zawditu's regent and heir to the throne. This was a period of turmoil, with Tafari increasingly ruling the country and consolidating his power against opponents of various motivations.[48] The death of Empress Zawditu in 1930 opened the way for Ras Tafari, crowned Haile Selassie I, to assume his place as the Negusa Nagast (King of Kings) of Ethiopia. Haile Selassie's reign was pivotal in Ethiopian history for consolidating the territorial and political gains of earlier military campaigns, particularly those of Menilek. Emperor Haile Selassie embarked on a project of national integration, using

[44] Teshale 1997, 228.
[45] Tibebe 1998, 165.
[46] Bahru 1991; Marcus 1994.
[47] Tibebe 1998, 179.
[48] Bahru 1991, 128–137.

distinct methods for accomplishing this, which make this historical period crucial in the history of citizen creation and citizenship expansion in Ethiopia.

Prior to the Italian occupation of Ethiopia (1936–1941), the most significant reform enacted by the emperor was the 1931 Constitution, which set up the juridical framework of Haile Selassie's absolutism and attempted to craft a compromise between the forces of centralism and regionalism. Article 1 made all territory and all "natives of Ethiopia subjects of the Empire" and as such, "subject to the Government of His Majesty the Emperor."[49] Supreme power rested in the hands of Haile Selassie, whose hereditary line, according to Article 3, "descends without interruption from the dynasty of Menilek I, son of King Solomon of Jerusalem and the Queen of Ethiopia, known as the Queen of Sheba." Chapter 3, entitled "The Rights Recognized by the Emperor as Belonging to the Nation, and the Duties Incumbent on the Nation," began with the statement that "the Law specifies the conditions required for the status of Ethiopian subjects."[50] There was only "the Nation," singular, as well as the emperor and his subjects.

In the published version of a speech given by Haile Selassie on the occasion of his signing the 1931 Constitution, he stated that the principal provisions of the constitution were that "Ethiopia must remain united and undivided like the members of a family.... The strength of this accord must be based upon community of interests, in such a way that the individual, while renouncing every ambition of a personal character contrary to the common weal, may understand the power of the union."[51] The imperative placed on unity and the analogy of a family as a community of interests is instructive. Yet Haile Selassie did little to develop the sense of Ethiopia as a "community of interests," and this failure has had tremendous implications for the development of a social consensus over citizenship. And in fact, because the Ethiopian family has historically been quite hierarchical and patriarchal, the implications for social relations among Ethiopia's disparate and highly unequal ethnolinguistic and religious communities is compounded when one considers the gendered nature of a family-based analogy. Surely, the emperor did not include the vast majority of Ethiopian women in a meaningful engagement with the "common weal."

[49] 1931 Constitution, reprinted in Perham 1969, 426.
[50] Perham 1969, 428.
[51] Perham, 1969, 424.

In the end, the constitution not only legalized the emperor's absolute rule, but also sounded the political death knell of the regional nobility. A bicameral Parliament was established with a Senate and a Chamber of Deputies. The Senate was composed of *masafent* (hereditary nobility) and *makwanent* (recently appointed nobles).[52] The Chamber of Deputies was selected through indirect elections of landed gentry. Not only were these not elected positions, the members of the Parliament had extremely limited powers, primarily the power to communicate ideas to the emperor through the president of the Parliament and to deliberate on such matters that the emperor thought worthy.[53] All ministers were appointed by the emperor himself. Although certainly not a democratic political system, the constitution did establish the parameters for the increasing exercise of central government authority by Haile Selassie, and most consequently, the reduced power of the regional nobility.

In addition to the important symbolic and administrative implications of the emperor's promulgation of the 1931 Constitution, he was at the same time quite busy consolidating the territorial and political authority of the imperial state in more direct ways. With the arrest of the rebellious Gojjame leader Haylu Takla-Haymanot, and the end of Jimma's autonomous status in 1932, the state of Ethiopia came under full imperial control.[54] During this time the emperor undertook a variety of international agreements to purchase arms, secure foreign assistance, and complete some significant development projects, such as construction of roads, schools, hospitals, and creation of public services.[55] Ever concerned with Ethiopia's international reputation, Haile Selassie also undertook the official abolition of slavery and the organization of local police forces and administration.[56]

The Italians had long harbored imperial ambitions toward Ethiopia, particularly since the humiliating defeats at Dogali and the Battle of Adwa. Armed conflict with the Italian Fascist government of Mussolini followed several years of increasingly strained relations. After the Italian invasion of Ethiopia in October 1935, the emperor led the nation in resistance before eventually fleeing Ethiopia on May 2, 1936, for exile

[52] A good glossary of Amharic nobility and historical terms is Bahru 1991. See also Leslau 1976.
[53] Markakis and Asmelash 1967, 200; see also Clapham 1969.
[54] Bahru 1991, 144–146.
[55] Marcus 1994, 137.
[56] Although, as Edwards notes, on the slavery issue the emperor's motivations were complex and the enforcement provisions quite lackluster for some time (Edwards 1982, 7).

in England.[57] The Italians occupied Ethiopia from 1936 to 1941, with Ethiopian patriots continuing to resist Italian rule. In 1941 the emperor returned to a country little changed by Italian rule, federated with the former Italian colony of Eritrea and under the provisional administration of the British government. But Haile Selassie quickly acted to restore imperial power and diversified Ethiopia's external support structure by seeking American advisors and arms. In all, the Italians had managed to facilitate changes in the economy and infrastructure that the restored Ethiopian rulers exploited after 1941, but they had very little impact outside of the capital city and a few provincial centers.[58]

After his return to Ethiopia, in addition to consolidating the federation of Eritrea with Ethiopia and pursuing external funding and military assistance, the emperor embarked on a number of development initiatives.[59] These included investments in financial institutions, internal security, public works, education, and social services.[60] One of his early acts was to redraw provincial boundaries, creating 14 new *taqlay gezats* (provinces), 103 *awrajas* (subprovinces), 505 *woredas* (districts), and 949 *miktel woredas* (subdistricts). The new boundaries broke up previously heterogeneous regions, expanded the size of some regions and reduced the size of others, and put the emperor's two sons in charge of the strategically important provinces of Wallo and Harar.[61] The political implications were reduced power for traditional nobility and consolidation of the power of the emperor. Subsequent proclamations were targeted at further reducing absentee administration of the provinces and the ability of regional governors to negotiate or sign treaties with neighbors. These provisions were all aimed at centralization; the emperor's vision was for a truly integrated state.

At this time, Haile Selassie also oversaw the rapid acceleration of land privatization. Northern settlers who had acquired rights over southern *gabbar* were given rights to these lands outright, while land given to those in government service was converted to freehold, and the government took over rights to most land. This government land was in turn given primarily to loyalists who had fought against the Italians. *Rest* land was

---

[57] The Italian occupation was both the realization of Italian imperial aspirations in Ethiopia begun long before and the result of continental European politics. The complexities of these issues are discussed thoroughly by both Marcus (1994) and Bahru (1991).

[58] Bahru 1991, 164: Marcus 1994; Clapham 1969; Teshale 1995.

[59] See Woodward and Forsyth 1994; Tsegaye 2010, 81; Iyob 1995.

[60] Marcus 1994, 164.

[61] Perham 1969, 345; Teshale 1995, 115.

converted to private land, and the extension of the first absolute private ownership rights to land led to a period of tremendous growth in land sales.[62]

Increasing tax burdens also led to a significant rise in tenancy. Bahru argues that despite the administrative benefits of the rationalization of the tax system and the progressive nature of the new tax schedule, the cumulative effect was to polarize rural society into landlords and tenants, particularly in the south.[63] Crummey similarly concludes that "little in the succession of decrees which had started in 1935 lessened rural inequality in the country. Some of them intensified it.... In short, the government's concern had been to eliminate the *political* power of the *gult*-holding nobility, not its social influence or its economic wealth."[64] As early as 1961, a committee on land reform was established, leading to the creation of the Ministry of Land Reform and Administration in 1966.[65] Famines in Tigre in 1958, Wallo in 1967, and the infamous Wallo Famine of 1973 revealed the inability of the imperial government – in part because of the entrenched interests of the landowners in Parliament – to resolve the fundamental contradictions in the land tenure and taxation systems, a foreshadowing of events that led to the 1974 Revolution.

Ministerial government had been restored by the emperor relatively soon after the Italians' departure.[66] In 1955, on the occasion of the twenty-fifth anniversary of his coronation, the emperor promulgated a revised constitution. Although the constitution consolidated and affirmed the absolute power of the monarchy, greater powers of taxation and oversight of ministers and imperial decrees were given to members of Parliament. Significantly, the lower house of Parliament was to be popularly elected, universal adult suffrage was introduced, and nominal provisions for an independent judiciary, a doctrine of the separation of powers, and some human rights were incorporated in this constitution.[67] Not insignificantly, the revised constitution reaffirmed the assertion of the Solomonic roots of Haile Selassie's reign, the rightfulness of that bloodline, and also formally established the Ethiopian Orthodox Church as the "Established Church of the Empire and ... as such, supported by the

---

[62] Bahru 1991, 190–192.
[63] Bahru 1991.
[64] Crummey 2000, 241.
[65] Bahru 1991, 195.
[66] Bahru 1991, 203.
[67] Marcus 1994, 166; Bahru 1991, 206.

State. The Emperor shall always profess the Ethiopian Orthodox Faith. The name of the Emperor shall be mentioned in all religious services."[68]

In terms of citizenship, little had changed from the 1931 to the 1955 Constitution. Ethiopian people were subjects, not citizens. The emperor was "inviolable," his person "sacred," and his power "indisputable."[69] Sovereignty was vested in the emperor, not the people. These conditions were stipulated in Article 1 and Article 26 but contradicted somewhat in Article 39, which included the provision for determining "Ethiopian nationality and Ethiopian citizenship" by law. Clearly, this did not mean citizenship in the sense of full rights or inclusion on the grounds of equality. Article 64 further stated that Ethiopian subjects owed their loyalty and exercise of certain duties to the emperor and the empire "when called upon to do so."[70] Interestingly, the new constitution outlined for the first time that only males could ascend to the throne, "thus excluding the possibility of another reigning empress like Zawditu."[71]

Generally it is believed that Haile Selassie introduced the new constitution to enhance Ethiopia's international image, particularly in light of the more democratic political systems in newly independent African countries, to deal with the inconsistencies between the Eritrean and Ethiopian Constitutions, and to address the subtle pressures for democratization being pushed by newly educated Ethiopian elites. After the Italians lost their African territories with their defeat in World War II, Eritrea was federated with Ethiopia but allowed powers of self-governance in certain affairs. The Eritrean Constitution was considered more modern and democratic than Ethiopia's.[72] Still, most scholars take the view that the practical significance of most of the provisions of the 1955 Constitution was minimal.

But what of meaningful citizenship for Ethiopians under the imperial regimes of Menilek and Haile Selassie? Although there was increasing northern Shoan Amhara domination throughout these years, it was through the modernizing and centralizing policies of Haile Selassie that the roots of ethnic conflict were sown.[73] Although the practices might have been understood immediately as less related to ethnic group than

---

[68] 1955 Constitution, reprinted in Perham 1969, 461.
[69] 1955 Constitution, reprinted in Perham 1969, 435.
[70] 1955 Constitution, reprinted in Perham 1969, 448.
[71] Clapham 1969, 38.
[72] Markakis and Asmelash 1967, 205; Clapham 1969.
[73] Levine is one of many scholars who point to the distinctly Shoan character of the Menilek and Haile Selassie regimes, to the neglect of other Amhara areas such as Gojjam, Begemidir, and Menz (Levine 2000, xix). Clapham (1969) makes a similar argument for Haile Selassie's reign.

as conquered peoples, descendants of these communities have come to see themselves as ethnic communities and understand Ethiopian history through this lens today. Most members of the newly incorporated ethnic groups in the state-expansion phase (1890–1913) suffered greater oppression through the imposition of the foreign and exploitative *gabbar* system and the various requirements of tribute and labor services. Conversion to the Orthodox religion, knowledge of the Amharic language, and various behavioral and cultural changes were requirements of mobility under Menilek's expanding empire, as noted above, but with the prospects for upward mobility limited to very few individuals. In fact, with educational and economic prospects so slim, most peasants in the north and the south alike suffered more from economic conditions linked to class and the relationship of the peasant to land and labor.

Historians, scholars, and some Ethiopian citizens may prefer to read back to Haile Selassie a greater concern for equality than was in evidence from any policy or practice of his regime. In terms of national cultural policy, it was under Haile Selassie that Amharization as a pervasive social policy came into being. Perham noted in 1969 that

the Ethiopian Government, as regards a large proportion of its lands and subjects, is itself in the position of an imperial power differing in race or religion from its subject peoples. All the arguments used in British Africa against ironing out the cultural identity and traditional loyalties of subject peoples under an imposed uniformity and those supporting the rights of even small groups to cultural self-determination might seem to apply to these parts of Ethiopia.[74]

Perham justifies this by pointing out that the emperor might be excused for the lengths he must go to in the attempt to rapidly modernize and create a sense of national unity. It was this quest for national integration that dogged Haile Selassie much more than his predecessors. And it was his failure to create a coherent and just national integration program that led not only to the demise of the emperor himself, but generated the contested citizenship claims that challenge economic and political developments in the country. It is instructive to remember again that his immediate predecessor, Lij Iyasu, had already recognized some decades earlier that the incorporation of new communities into the Ethiopian polity might require reconciliation, toleration, and a new national ethos. That Haile Selassie, and his allies, rejected such tactics created the context for the challenges of recognition and accommodation in subsequent regimes.

[74] Perham 1969, 376.

What are we to understand by the process of Amharization? Generally, we can say that it refers to the espoused or encouraged policies of assimilation, including the imposition of Amharic language, the formal political establishment of the Ethiopian Orthodox Church and its distinct theology as the national religious identity of the state, and the dominance of Amhara cultural and political symbols in political life. Keller suggests that it involved "the selective incorporation of ethnic elites into the ruling class" through elevation of Amhara culture and religion and the denigration of other cultures and religions.[75] Although it is true that there were a few members of other ethnicities in the imperial regime – mainly educated Oromos – they were those who had become totally assimilated. Donham goes further by connecting Abyssinianization (Amharization) with the expansion of the *rest* land tenure system, as well as the forced imposition of Amharic and conversion to Orthodox Christianity.[76]

The importance of these specific practices of Amharization becomes clear in light of the so-called elasticity of Amhara identity. Much has been made of the assimilatory qualities of Amhara identity, but the cultural and psychological costs of this assimilation – not to mention the economic, political, and spiritual ones – were tremendous for those who were able to choose the path of "becoming Amhara." The ability to "become" Amhara was limited not just by the ability and willingness to learn Amharic to the level of native fluency, fully convert to the Orthodox Church, and realize other identity changes such as a name change; there are clear racial characteristics to Amhara identity as well that are often ignored by writers emphasizing the "flexible" path of assimilation. For instance, they could not be notably negroid in racial features, and Young also points out the racializing of "red" or "Shankilla" peoples.[77] The best example of this is the pejorative of *barya* (slave), used often to racially identify someone as too dark to be Amhara and most famously applied to General Mengistu Haile Mariam to signify his inappropriateness to be ruler of Ethiopia.[78] The fact that both Haile Selassie and Mengistu may have had Oromo ancestry does little to diminish the political potency of citizenship restrictions on these communities.

Amharization was also a political attempt to transform distinct ethnic symbols into national symbols – making symbols of northern highland

---

[75] Keller 1988, 150.
[76] Donham 2002, 11.
[77] Donham 2002, 12; see John Young 1999
[78] Teshale 1995; Mekuria 2002; Clapham 1988, 21.

culture the symbols of the modern state of Ethiopia. In a famous statement of the "question of the nationalities in Ethiopia," Walleligne Makonnen wrote in a student publication in 1969:

Ask anybody what Ethiopian culture is? Ask anybody what Ethiopian language is? Ask anybody what Ethiopian music is? Ask anybody what Ethiopian religion is? Ask anybody what the national dress is? It is either Amhara or Amhara-Tigre!! To be a "genuine Ethiopian" one has to speak Amharic, to listen to Amharic music, to accept the Amhara-Tigre religion, Orthodox Christianity, and to wear the Amhara-Tigre *shamma* in international conferences. In some cases to be an "Ethiopian" you will even have to change your name. In short, to be an Ethiopian, you will have to wear an Amhara mask.[79]

Walleligne and other Ethiopian high school and university students at the time debated the issues of ethnic diversity, inequality, class exploitation, and the host of other political explanations for Ethiopia's tremendous poverty and unequal ethnic relations. They attacked the core tenets of Amharization by identifying the nationalist project as assimilationist and undemocratic.

But the imperial government's effort at defining Ethiopian national identity gained ground with foreigners in particular. One finds numerous references in early scholarship in which elements of Amhara culture and practice are presented as national, when in fact they are not. It is not at all clear, however, that other ethnic groups in Ethiopia ever truly assimilated even the symbols of national identity as their own. Cities and town were renamed under Haile Selassie, but local people continued to use the older (often ethnic) name. Recently, cities such as Addis Ababa, Debre Zeit, and Nazareth have been renamed by the Oromiya regional state government back to their traditional Oromo names: Finfinnee, Bishoftu, and Adama. In fact, because they were given these Amhara names very recently, their Oromo names were never forgotten and remained widely in use, although nationalists in Addis Ababa and the diaspora generally refuse to use the legally designated original Oromo names today. Islam flourished in some parts of the country, despite the official promotion of the Orthodox religion, as did Protestant groups, particularly in the conquered territories.[80]

---

[79] Quoted in Balsvik 1985, 277.

[80] The 1994 census counted Muslims as 33%, Orthodox Christians as 51%, and Protestants as 10% of the country (1994 Census). See Trimingham (1965) for a classic account of Islam in Ethiopia; Terje Østebø (2012) for a thorough and updated review of the literature on Islam, as well as a thoughtful study of Islam in one part of Oromiya, Bale. See Mekuria (2002) and Eide (1996) for greater detail on the work of Protestants in Ethiopia.

During the ethnic revival movements of the 1960s and onward, Oromos and others took back their ethnic names, shedding their Amhara names.

Assimilation and domination were outmoded political ideals, even as far back as the 1930s and 1940s. Haile Selassie never successfully created a consensus about the proposed national symbols of Ethiopia. Amharization was not an uncontested political process at any point. There is little doubt that the roots of the question of nationalities, which emerged primarily during the Ethiopian Student Movement (ESM) and led in turn to the demise of the imperial and the socialist regimes, lay directly in the attempted imposition of cultural and political identities that did not resonate with the newly conquered peoples. Amharization created such deep resentment and alienation on the part of these ethnic groups that they rose up to topple the imperial government. In fact, Amharization created the conditions of its own ruin, because by denying people's access to their distinct linguistic, religious, and cultural identities and foisting a foreign identity onto them, it compounded the degradations of the political and economic relations that were oppressive enough.

Despite the attempts by some historians and sociologists to dismiss any talk of regional or ethnic disparities based on the assertion that "there are downtrodden peasants or herdsmen enough in every religious and racial grouping and in every province,"[81] the fact remains that most Ethiopian peasants in the newly incorporated areas increasingly came to identify with fellow ethnics. Whether they initially located their oppression in economic and class-based origins, or based on cultural and religious domination, the vigorously enforced initiatives of centralization and cultural assimilation pursued by Haile Selassie surely encouraged ethnic identification, without the attendant attention to building a sense of Ethiopian-ness. Dereje's work on the Anywaa of Gambella provides an excellent example of this historiography, which is only one extreme example of how integration into the Ethiopian state at the turn of the century has dramatically accelerated the precarious situation for one ethnic community.[82]

---

[81] Greenfield 1965, 110; Donald Levine, in the preface to his 2000 edition of the 1974 classic *Greater Ethiopia* similarly takes issue with the image of the "wicked Amhara" oppressor in part because "ninety-five percent of the Amhara people have lived under such oppressive political and economic conditions that it is hard to say who was most oppressed" (Levine 2000, xix). Teshale too notes that "the overwhelming majority of the Amhara have not benefitted in the form of economic, political or psychological advantage ... [although] on the regional level, however, the very expression 'Amhara domination' can be applied to the South" (Teshale 1995, 179–180).

[82] Dereje 2008.

This was most practically experienced through language policy. Teshale notes that "the only singular reference to the national question in Ethiopia is the question of language."[83] Although there surely was no inevitability of the importance of ethnolinguistic identities to how recently incorporated communities contested the citizen creation and citizenship-expansion project of the modernizing Ethiopian state, it was the specific project of Amharization that facilitated the ethnic nature of that citizenship trajectory. Class or regional grouping or some other marker of inequality might have been central to individual and even collective identity at some point, but by the mid-twentieth century, groups in the marginalized regions of the Ethiopian state were in the process of an ethnogenesis. This is owed in large part to the specific policies and practices of Menilek and, especially, Haile Selassie. It is a legacy with which each Ethiopian today lives.

Perhaps most significant of Haile Selassie's achievements were the rapid improvements in formal education. Traditionally, education had been provided in various culturally specific forums – home, community, church or mosque, and so on. The first state school, Menilek II School, was opened in 1908, named after its benefactor, Emperor Menilek. Haile Selassie opened the Tafari Makonnen School in Addis Ababa in 1925, and Empress Menen opened the first girls' school in 1931. Additionally, there were some mission schools throughout the country. Primary schools in regional towns followed, and by the early 1930s, the imperial regime had begun plans to build the first university in the country.[84] As much as this creation of an elite cadre of male administrators and civil servants was a hallmark of Haile Selassie's regime, however, it was this educated class that led the intellectual and political opposition to the emperor.

Whereas the administrative and diplomatic achievements of Haile Selassie's rule stand out as notable efforts at state-building, his accomplishments in nation-building were considerably more limited.[85] Greenfield concluded his discussion of constitutional reforms in the early 1960s by noting that "the neglect over the years of the promotion of a positive program of nationality unity throughout the empire" was beginning to be in evidence.[86] Along the same lines, Keller argued that Haile Selassie "almost completely ignored the need to build a sense of genuine

---

[83] Teshale 1995, 180.
[84] Bahru 2002.
[85] Gebru 1991, 28–29.
[86] Greenfield 1965, 312, 457.

Ethiopian national identity" among the non-Amhara and non-Tigrayan ethnic group.[87] Presciently, Clapham noted in his 1969 study of the imperial government of Haile Selassie, after outlining rather starkly the dramatic Shoan Amhara domination of the government, that "the risk of division along ethnic or tribal lines is with little doubt the greatest danger that Ethiopia will have to face.... And there are signs that such consciousness is slowly being aroused in Ethiopia today."[88] It was on the questions of land and the nationalities that historical patterns of citizenship become particularly contentious.

By 1965 the imperial regime faced threats from Eritrea, Harar, Bale, Sidamo, and the Ogaden. The attempted coup d'état in 1960 was a turning point in that it signaled a kind of opposition to central rule different from that of previous eras. Bahru argues that "before the coup, opposition tended to be conspiratorial and elitist; after it opposition was more open and mass-based.... Peasants rebelled against increasing demands on their produce. Nationalities rose for self-determination."[89] In particular, the ESM, led by urban educated students, consolidated and sustained pressure on the imperial regime for meaningful social and economic reform. It began as a cultural and intellectual grouping of newly educated elites, many having been educated abroad, and grew into a mass revolutionary movement in the late 1960s and early 1970s.

Several factors led to the "steady radicalization" of the students, including the presence of larger numbers of students from other African countries, the demonstration effect of the 1960 coup attempt, and, particularly, the Ethiopian University Service program begun in 1964. Under this program, university students spent a year in the countryside, usually teaching in secondary schools. For many, this provided a stark learning experience about the conditions of the peasant under Ethiopian feudalism.[90] While the late 1960s saw student support for land reform programs under the slogan "Land to the Tiller," the student movement came eventually to tackle the controversial issues of the nationalities question. The relationship between the two was intimately connected to the dispossession of southern lands under Abyssinian expansion and conquest but was also a reaction to unequal land relations in general.[91]

---

[87] Keller 2005, 59.
[88] Clapham 1969, 80.
[89] Bahru 1991, 209.
[90] Bahru 1991, 222. See also Balsvik 2007, 21.
[91] Gebru 1991, 22.

Even while he was able to avert an attempted coup d'état in 1960 and successfully put down rebellions in Bale and Gojjam in the mid-1960s, the emperor was unable to address the two issues that had been quietly growing into major political contradictions: the issue of land and the question of the nationalities. Legal scholar Paul Brietzke noted in 1975 the connections between land relations, social class, and ethnicity, stating that "the beginnings of modernization ... have produced stratification along class lines, with one group – the Amhara – dominating and controlling mass communication, education, religion, ideology, and the political process. Other groups have either been assimilated or have been forced into distinct roles and subordinate statuses."[92] Brietzke focused on land reform as pivotal in structural changes that might promote rural development in Ethiopia, but he linked these with what he called "social integration," which spoke to "the question of the nationalities." With the benefit of hindsight, most scholars of Ethiopian history point to the issues of land and the nationalities question as the two politically unresolved issues of Haile Selassie's reign. His inability to resolve these matters led to the revolution that toppled him.

Others would say there was a distinction between who was affected by these twin political questions: "The Amharas were oppressed by land. The non-Amharas were oppressed by language and religion."[93] In fact, all Ethiopian peasants were oppressed by land alienation and denied citizenship, but only non-Amharas bore the *additional* burdens of language and religious oppressions. Women's concerns were entirely ignored. And this created the conditions for the contested citizenship in contemporary Ethiopia.

Revolutionary and Contested Citizenship

Significant rifts were already in evidence by the early 1960s. In 1974, the monarchy was toppled and the emperor murdered, not by either the church or the nobles as predicted by foreign observers, but by members of the Ethiopian military. At least initially, the military represented the collective force of students and intellectuals who championed a class-based struggle on behalf of Ethiopia's peasants. There followed a seventeen-year rule by a socialist military dictatorship, consolidated under the fiery leadership of General Mengistu Haile Mariam, and popularly called the Derg

92 Brietzke 1975, 45.
93 Interview #64.

(committee). Although a brutal dictatorship, the regime spearheaded profound social and economic transformations, particularly by abolishing feudal structures and centralizing state control of business and development. Critically, the Derg undertook the first legal grant in the country's history of full citizenship to all Ethiopians. Nevertheless, political and social life stagnated under the Derg, and fundamental questions of equality for all ethnic groups remained unresolved.[94]

The 1974 Revolution was first and foremost a class-based revolution, with its slogan being "Land to the Tiller." The Provisional Military Administrative Council was established in the summer of 1974, and by December it had declared the country a one-party state. Focus was put initially on important economic policy proclamations, including public ownership of most economic sectors and the use of collective agriculture. Recognizing the importance of the ethnic and regional component of its political support, the Derg introduced the most radical land reform in the southern regions to address the land expropriations that had occurred under Menilek's and Haile Selassie's reigns. Turmoil occurred in some places as peasants in the south "spontaneously revolted and chased Amhara landlords from their holdings."[95] Land redistribution was begun; abolition of land tenancy and restrictions made wage labor legal only on state farms. This also meant, however, substantial and somewhat sustained social conflict at the local level in which thousands were killed.[96]

Under the policy of Ethiopia Tikdem (Ethiopia First), which included a version of Ethiopian socialism called *hebretesebawinnet*, the Derg expressed its intention to pursue "equality; self-reliance; the dignity of labor; the supremacy of the common good; and the indivisibility of Ethiopian unity."[97] The Derg also laid out a plan of decentralized government founded on rural peasant associations (PA) and urban dwellers associations, called *kebelles*. Proclamation No. 31 nationalized all rural land, abolished tenancy, and established PAs to govern all land matters in rural areas.[98] Proclamation No. 27 nationalized urban land, providing that all businesses and residences not occupied by the owners were

[94] Teshale 1995, 168.

[95] Keller 1995, 195.

[96] It should be noted that as much as land reform was a pivotal and generally popular outcome of the Derg's early policies, there was an ethnic and regional component. Amhara landlords and tenants generally did not benefit as much as Oromos and southern tenants (see Ottaway and Ottaway 1978, 84).

[97] Quoted in Ottaway and Ottaway 1978, 63.

[98] Ottaway and Ottaway 1978, 67; Marcus 1994, 192.

nationalized by the state. But all this belied an intense centralization of power under the Derg, and *kebelles* often became the site of ideological battles between the Derg and their opponents, including the All-Ethiopian Socialist Movement (MEISON) and the Ethiopian People's Revolutionary Party (EPRP).[99] Particularly via the Development through Cooperation Campaign, also called the *zemeccha*, the Derg attempted to educate and politicize the masses of Ethiopia's rural peasants. High school and university students were sent into the countryside to establish PAs and push forward collectivization and leadership changes at the village level.[100]

In April 1976, the Derg launched the Program of the National Democratic Revolution (NDRP), which laid out its political agenda and attempted to bridge ideological and strategic divides. The NDRP officially declared the Derg's commitment to "scientific socialism" and established a "people's democratic republic" through a vanguard political party of the working class. Economic reforms would redress the inequality that had led to ethnic domination, and therefore ethnic associations and political claims were regarded as invalid. While the nationalities were to be accorded autonomy, the unity of Ethiopia was paramount. In line with its ideological orientation, the Derg saw ethnic conflict as merely one aspect of class struggle.

The question of the nationalities, as the Leninist-inspired language suggested, was central to the type of political and social change sought by the Derg. Because the question of land was intimately connected with ethnicity, even policies that on the surface seemed to have no ethnic component, such as radical rural land reform, had tremendous ethnic implications. In particular, its own policies added significant fuel to the fire of ethnic nationalism that had begun brewing during the later years of the Haile Selassie regime, not only in Eritrea, but also in Oromo and Somali regions.[101] Secessionist and irredentist wars were fought by these groups,

---

[99] Briefly, the EPRP was opposed to military rule at any point in the socialist transformation, while MEISON accepted the idea of a period of military rule at the beginning of the revolution. The debate between these groups centered on the type of democracy the leadership of each envisioned and fueled a more radical agenda by the military elements within the Derg. The result was EPRP's break with the Derg and the campaign of urban terror called the "White Terror," to which the Derg reacted with a brutal campaign called the "Red Terror." Keller reports that over an eighteen- to twenty-month period between 1977 and 1978, some 5,000 young people were killed. See Keller 1988; Ottaway and Ottaway 1978; Marcus 1994. For more on the position of these two groups vis-à-vis ethnicity, see Harbeson 1988, 150–151.

[100] Marcus 1994, 192; Ottaway and Ottaway 1978, 70–78.

[101] Ottaway and Ottaway 1978.

and armed ethnic movements fought against the regime throughout its entire reign.

The Derg's solution to this rise in ethnic nationalisms early on was adoption of the principle of equality of all ethnic groups, including the right to self-determination, but within the context of Ethiopian unity. The attention to ethnicity was not just a reaction to militant ethnic nationalisms, however. The earlier Ethiopian Student Movement and other radical groups that had facilitated the political conditions for the revolution considered the question of the nationalities of great significance, trumped only by the question of land. The Derg leadership understood the centrality of ethnicity to the peasants and intellectuals alike, but its commitment to the absolute unity of Ethiopia and its authoritarian nature undermined any policy changes with regard to the question of the nationalities.

The Derg's initial actions, both symbolic and substantive, were focused on the critical principle of equality, which meant the radical introduction of citizenship for all Ethiopians.[102] Despite the eventual discontinuities between its message of equality and its increasingly violent and authoritarian political tools, the Derg evidenced in the earliest years some capacity to tolerate participation and citizen creation. In this, radical reforms were made to equalize ethnic communities. Muslim holidays were for the very first time officially recognized, Radio Ethiopia began broadcasting in all languages, and the Oromo newspaper *Barissa* was officially promoted. The Ministry of Education began considering the feasibility of introducing local languages as a medium of instruction. The 1976 Program of the National Democratic Revolution outlined nine broad aims and activities, including particular attention to the nationalities question:

The right to self-determination of all nationalities will be recognized and fully respected. No nationality will dominate another one since the history, culture, language and religion of each nationality will have equal recognition in accordance with the spirit of socialism. The unity of Ethiopia's nationalities will be based on their common struggle against feudalism, imperialism, bureaucratic capitalism and all reactionary forces. This united struggle is based on the desire to construct a new life and a new society based on equality, brotherhood and mutual respect. Nationalities on border areas and those scattered over various regions have been subjected to special subjugation for a long time. Special attention will be made to raise the political, economic and cultural life of these nationalities.... The problem of nationalities can be resolved if each nationality is accorded the full right to self-government. This means that each nationality will have regional

---

[102] Teshale 1995; Markakis and Asmelash 1967; Keller 1988; Ottaway and Ottaway 1978.

autonomy to decide on matters concerning its internal affairs. Within its environs, it has the right to determine the contents of its political, economic and social life, use its own language and elect its own leaders and administrators to head its internal organs.[103]

Yet even as its edicts claimed that the "right to self-determination of all nationalities will be recognized and fully respected,"[104] the Derg never convinced members of the various nationality groups that its commitments were genuine, particularly because the dogmatic commitment to the territorial unity of Ethiopia undermined any possible attempts at compromise. Some ethnically based liberation movements intensified their antiregime campaigns, and the Derg fought civil wars on several borders, including with the Eritreans (EPLF), the Tigrayans (TPLF), the Somalis (WSLF), and the Oromos (OLF). Despite receiving military and technical support from the Soviet Union, North Korea, Cuba, and Yemen, there were only limited military successes, and the Derg spent most of the country's finances and energy on fighting wars rather than development.[105]

After a period of political consolidation (1974–1978) and a stepped-up war of unification against the Eritrean liberation force and the Somali irredentists, the Derg attempted to respond to growing regional dissatisfaction through the formation of the Worker's Party of Ethiopia (WPE) in 1984. Just prior to this, the Derg founded the Institute for the Study of Ethiopian Nationalities. This organization's mandate was to analyze the sociopolitical conditions of the nationalities and draw up plans for administrative reforms. It conducted a survey of the entire country and drafted a constitution. The 1987 Constitution was approved by a referendum and established the People's Democratic Republic of Ethiopia (PDRE). An 835-member national assembly (Shengo) was formed, but substantial powers were retained by the president, General Mengistu. The assembly immediately took up administrative reorganization of the country, which included the creation of twenty-four administrative regions. The only provision aimed at alleviating ethnic tensions was the designation of Eritrea, Tigray, Dire Dawa, Asseb, and the Ogaden as autonomous regions with varying powers to issue legislation and carry

---

[103] NDRP, quoted in Ottaway and Ottaway 1978, 214.

[104] Ethiopia, ISEN 1986.

[105] Much has rightfully been made of the role of the civil war in facilitating the famine of 1984 and the regime's practice of diverting resources for military purposes instead of famine relief. See Keller 1992; Marcus 1994; Sorenson 1993.

out self-administration. Significantly, Amharic was still designated as the national language.

Owing to the ever-decreasing legitimacy of the regime, "none of the insurgency movements were tempted to accept the new arrangement," but rather intensified their armed struggles against the PDRE.[106] The political leadership of the Derg was composed primarily of Amharas and Tigrayans (two-thirds of all central committees), which did little to alter the perception of continued political domination by former ethnic hegemons.[107] This is interesting in light of the popular perception that the regime also meant to undermine the cultural foundations of the highland state's legacy. In addition to rejecting the legitimacy of the PDRE, these ethnic liberation movements – particularly the EPLF and the TPLF – began to cooperate militarily, which greatly improved their ability to win military victories over the Ethiopian army. The TPLF began in the late 1980s to build a coalition of anti-Derg forces under the name of the Ethiopian People's Revolutionary Democratic Front (EPRDF).[108]

The leadership of the Derg took somewhat contradictory positions on the question of ethnicity. Through Mengistu's political rhetoric and evident in the extensive military campaigns, it was clear that Ethiopian unity was a paramount political objective. Groups that sought increased ethnic autonomy or secession were labeled as "tribalists."[109] Important and truly revolutionary steps were taken under the Derg, however, which facilitated the political organization of ethnic groups within the country. There was a public recognition that ethnicity was a central political identity for many Ethiopians and that inequality based on ethnicity was a primary force behind the revolution. For instance, a WPE document from 1984 stated that "the nationality question was a major democracy question in pre-Revolutionary Ethiopia."[110] Central to the Derg's effort at tackling this issue was the work of the Institute for the Study

---

[106] Teferra 1997, 282.

[107] Keller 1988, 238; Clapham 1988 has a fascinating discussion of the intricacies of Ethiopian naming customs and ethnic identity as related to the leadership of the Derg.

[108] Harbeson considers the relationships of the various liberation fronts to one another, pointing out that cooperation between groups such as the OLF and WSLF and the OLF and the Eritrean and Tigrayan liberation fronts were limited by suspicions of each group's interests; in particular, the OLF was not "entirely convinced that the northern liberation movements [would] fully disavow colonization of the south" (Harbeson 1988, 163).

[109] Marcus 1994, 214.

[110] Ethiopia, Institute for the Study of Ethiopian Nationalities. October 1984, 30.

of Ethiopian Nationalities (ISEN). The institute was formed in 1983 and tasked to conduct a study of the history of Ethiopia's nationalities. Scholars attached to the institute came from a variety of academic disciplines, and they conducted ethnographic and historical studies to determine the territorial boundaries and population distributions of ethnic groups in Ethiopia.

There were five departments of the ISEN: History, Language and Culture, Economics, Law, and the Constitution. In particular, the Language and Culture Department undertook the task of identifying and cataloging the ethnic groups in the country, primarily based on language, and prepared the *Brief Almanac of Ethiopian Nationalities*.[111] But the task of determining borders to both land and ethnic group proved to be impossible as land borders were unclear, and historic processes of assimilation and migration prevented a clear demarcation between the land of one ethnic group and that of another. According to one source, Mengistu was willing to have a type of federal arrangement with eleven regional states, but there was opposition within the party, and they agreed at the end to have five autonomous regions and to divide the country into smaller units called *woredas*. At this time, there were 584 *woredas*, which were defined as territories composed of people who speak a particular language, regardless of ethnicity. Language became the marker of ethnicity and also a central political concept at this time, since all Ethiopians have a mother land and a mother tongue.[112]

The work of the ISEN, in addition to laying the groundwork for the 1987 Constitution that introduced new regional divisions in the country, also prepared the way for the multilingual adult literacy program called the National Literacy Campaign. The series of educational campaigns, conducted in the 1980s, focused primarily on literacy and were popularly known in the countryside as the *meserete timhirt* (foundational education). In official campaign literature, the Derg noted that in previous historical periods "the situation was heavily biased against those for whom Amharic was either not spoken in the home, or was only a second language." The policies of the revolution, however, required that "respect should be given and conditions created for the preservation and development of the different nationalities." Therefore, nationality languages would be used in conducting the literacy campaign. Eventually

---

[111] Ethiopia, ISEN 1986.
[112] Interview #64.

the campaign taught in fifteen different languages, and it was believed to have covered 93 percent of Ethiopia's population.[113]

The *meserete timhirt*, or literacy campaign, was frequently cited by citizens in rural parts of Ethiopia, particularly in the Southern region, during interviews in 2003. It is critical to note here that despite some changes in language policy under the Derg, Amharic knowledge remained an essential prerequisite of any political or economic participation. Critically, the literacy campaign only involved nonformal education and adult basic literacy. Under the Derg, primary schools throughout the country continued to teach in Amharic regardless of mother tongue or ethnic group. The 1987 Constitution clearly made Amharic the official language of the state.

Nonetheless, the *meserete timhirt* and the development of written literacy materials in languages other than Amharic had powerful symbolic and practical effect. In the list of fifteen languages one can see direct correspondence to the important languages of the contemporary language policy. It was an indication of a massive change in the political landscape of language and ethnicity in Ethiopia, and it laid the groundwork for the development of languages other than Amharic, as well as the expectation that literacy in these languages was a meaningful and attainable political right. It also led to the important national census of 1984, which included more detail on ethnicity and mother tongue language than had ever been studied in Ethiopia. Markakis notes the unwillingness of the imperial regime to even discuss categories of citizens such as ethnic or linguistic groups.[114] In light of this, perhaps the Derg's most valuable contribution was the empirical study of language groups and ethnicity, as it provided tools for aggrieved groups to assert citizenship demands in future decades.

Despite the incomplete nature of the changes made in the material and social condition of various ethnolinguistic groups, for the first time in Ethiopian history there was a public, if limited, discussion of citizenship and ethnicity. This may explain the dramatic rise in liberation and armed resistance movements, the majority of whom and most effective of which were ethnically based, such as the Tigrayan People's Liberation Front, the Eritrean People's Liberation Front, as well as the Ethiopian People's Democratic Movement (EPDM), the Oromo Liberation Front, and the

[113] Ethiopia, National Literacy Campaign Coordinating Committee. 1981; Markakis 2003.
[114] Markakis 1974.

Western Somali Liberation Front. Despite some attempts at social and political solutions to the question of the nationalities, the Derg inevitably chose the military solution. Waging battles against liberation movements on multiple fronts, it was unable to address fundamental economic and social issues. In fact, the emphasis on a military resolution "polarized ethnic groups even more and brought the country to the brink of total disintegration."[115] Conditions worsened internally after 1987, and by 1991, a partnership of the TPLF and the EPLF brought the military end to the Derg. General Mengistu fled the country, the army collapsed, and a new regime took the reins of power.

Federalism and Citizenship

The Ethiopian People's Revolutionary Democratic Front entered Addis Ababa on May 28, 1991, and quickly acted to undertake significant reforms of Ethiopia's political, economic, and social structures. The most significant of these was the establishment of what it then called ethnic federalism, which was begun even prior to the ratification of the constitution.[116] The Transitional Government of Ethiopia (TGE) was quickly formed, and included membership by the EPRDF, the OLF, and other smaller coalition partners. A charter was drafted by representatives of thirty-one political movements and a Council of Representatives (COR) was formed. The council was charged with drafting a constitution, which was to be voted on by a constituent assembly. Early on, however, the coalition narrowed considerably, as the EPRDF sought to push other partners to the sidelines. The OLF was forced out of the transitional government when it refused to participate in the 1992 elections, calling instead for dissolution of the council.[117]

With any significant alternate political voices silenced, and with the Eritrean referendum resolving that controversial political question, the EPRDF was able to consolidate power rather quickly.[118] A Constitutional

---

[115] Kidane 1997, 121; see also Merera 2003, 83.

[116] Several scholars have pointed out that the tenets behind ethnic federalism as outlined in the constitution actually emerged through a variety of proclamations in the period from 1992 to 1994.

[117] Keller 1995; Joireman 1997.

[118] I do not mean to suggest that Eritrean secession is an entirely settled political question in Ethiopian domestic politics, as the bloody 1998–2000 border war and the 2005 election platforms of both the ruling party and the opposition groups demonstrate. However, as an internationally recognized sovereign state, there is little reason to think that the independence of Eritrea is in any doubt at this point.

Drafting Commission prepared a draft constitution and presented it to Constituent Assembly for debate and approval. The 1995 Constitution of Ethiopia provides the clearest articulation of what ethnic federalism entails. It includes a fascinating mix of individual and group-based rights unlike any other constitution in contemporary Africa. Important individual rights are guaranteed, particularly the right to life, security, liberty, equality, privacy, freedom of religion, association, movement, assembly, property, development, and environment, among others (Articles 14–44). Special protections are given to women, children, and "nations, nationalities and peoples" (Articles 35–39).[119]

The preamble to the constitution vests power in ethnic groups by opening with the words: "We, the Nations, Nationalities and Peoples of Ethiopia." Power was to be vested in the people *as members of groups*, as indicated by Article 8, which states: "All sovereign power resides in the Nations, Nationalities, and Peoples of Ethiopia." By foregrounding the "Nations, Nationalities and Peoples of Ethiopia," the regime attempted to use a strategy of institutional engineering to prevent ethnic conflict, basing political identification – both in regional states and in national-level political parties – on membership in ethnic groups. This makes ethnic identity in Ethiopia the normative basis for political identification.

While recognizing a variety of individual rights, the Ethiopian Constitution takes the somewhat radical position that political power resides with ethnic and nationality groups. This unique formalization of communal identity as the basis for formal citizenship in Ethiopia has vast political implications. Federalism is a radical departure from the western model that constructs citizenship on a liberal/civic/individual foundation, as discussed in Chapter 1. In this view, federalism is a framework for constructing a constitutional and political role for dual citizenship or communalism found in African sociopolitical contexts. Even as federalism in Ethiopia is perceived as a uniquely African institutional solution to a persistent and vexing source of political conflict and instability, it raises pressing questions about the proper place for "politicized" ethnicity. Critics and hesitant supporters alike have watched the development of federalism in Ethiopia since the mid-1990s with great interest because of this. Although receiving tentative support from western countries such as the United States, there were many skeptics of federalism from the outset. They feared that the departure from commonly accepted political

---

[119] Thorough and thoughtful analysis of the constitution is provided by Tsegaye 2009; see also Assefa 2006.

practice in Africa of nonethnic political institutions was a grave mistake. Because of this, the implications of the success or failure of federalism extend across the entire continent.

The ostensibly ethnic structure of federalism is important to describe. Most of the largest regional states under the federal system are ethnically delineated and primarily monoethnic.[120] A few others have two main ethnic groups, and at least one is multiethnic – the Southern region, with at least forty-five groups. City-states are considered distinct (Addis Ababa and Dire Dawa).[121] The constitution explicitly states that regions should be delineated based on "the settlement patterns, language, identity and consent of the people concerned" (Article 46). As already noted, most have referred to Ethiopia's political arrangement as ethnic federalism. This is in line with general typologies. For example, an ethnofederal state is a federal state in which "at least one constituent territorial governance unit is intentionally associated with a specific ethnic category."[122] We can refer to Ethiopian federalism as ethnic federalism or an ethnofederal system.

There are problems with calling the system *ethnic* federalism, however, since in reality all states are ethnically mixed, and it is unclear how the federal system really guarantees any rights to ethnicity through the "territorial principle."[123] Ethiopian federalism cannot be said to be a pure form of either the territorial or personality principle, as the constitution grants rights based on personality, and in some cases, has upheld rights to members of an ethnic or linguistic group outside of the territory of their ethnolinguistic group. However, this has been done sporadically and inconsistently, and there is arguably a greater protection of constitutional rights to ethnicity and language in the territory of one's ethnic group. But the constitution, as we will see, is clear in intentionally associating the governance unit, the *kilil*, or region, with specific ethnicities in most cases.

The 1995 Constitution also established a federal state. This led to the creation of nine regional states and two special administrative units,

---

[120] I refer to the states in the federation as "regions" or "regional states" since this is the most common translation for the Amharic word *kilil* used in the constitution and in everyday discourse.

[121] Primarily monoethnic states include Somali, Amhara, Tigray, Oromiya, and Afar. Explicitly multiethnic states include Harar, Benishangul-Gumuz, Gambella, and Southern Nations, Nationalities, and Peoples.

[122] Hale 2004, 167.

[123] See the contributors to Kymlicka and Patten, 2003, especially May and Réaume.

Addis Ababa and Dire Dawa.[124] The constitution provides for substantial powers to be held by the regional states, including establishment of their own legislative, executive, and judicial organs (Article 50), as well as State Councils. This also includes the power to write their own constitutions, decide their own regional languages, develop administrative systems – including regional police forces – and to collect certain kinds of taxes. The powers of the two levels of government, the regional states and the federal government, are recognized as separate, distinct, and inviolable (Article 50). Each level has enumerated powers (Articles 51 and 52), and those powers not designated are left to the states (Article 52).[125]

In addition, the constitution established a parliamentary system with a bicameral legislature at the federal government level. The House of People's Representatives (HPR) is the lower house; its members serve terms of five years and are elected by plurality voting. The total number of members is 547, and of these, 20 seats are reserved for "minority Nationalities and Peoples" (Articles 54 and 55). The majority party in the HPR forms the government and selects the prime minister. From the first election to the HPR in 1994 to today, the EPRDF has dominated it. The upper house is the House of Federation, which is composed of representatives of Ethiopia's ethnic groups. Each nation or nationality has at least one member, and one additional representative for each 1 million of its population. Members are elected by State Councils and have the power to interpret the constitution, primarily by organizing a Council of Constitutional Inquiry to study any constitutional issues and voting on the council's recommendation (Articles 61 and 62). A critical aspect of its mandate is to "promote the equality of the Peoples of Ethiopia enshrined in the Constitution and promote and consolidate their unity based on their mutual consent," including deciding on matters of ethnic self-determination and secession (Article 62).

The unconditional right of ethnic groups to "self-determination, including the right to secession," as laid out in Article 39 is by far the

---

[124] The legal and constitutional status of these two regions is distinct. Addis Ababa/Finfinee was considered the locus of the federal government, although the special interest to Oromiya regional state was recognized in the constitution (Article 49). Its location as the capital of Oromiya regional state has also been controversial and, at times, subject to the vicissitudes of national-level politics. Dire Dawa's status is considerably more ambiguous. Its special status seems to have resulted as a political compromise after clashes broke out among rival ethnic groups laying claim to the region, including Harari, Oromo, and Somalis living in and around the city and because of its extreme ethnic heterogeneity (Interview #13).

[125] See Tsegaye 2002, 2009.

most controversial of the entire constitution. Its contested legitimacy remains a substantial barrier to democratization in Ethiopia. Article 39 actually contains five specific provisions. The first guarantees the right to self-determination, including secession. The second guarantees the right of every nationality to "speak, to write and to develop its own language; to express, to develop and to promote its culture; and to preserve its history." The third provision includes the right to "a full measure of self-government which includes the right to establish institutions of government in the territory that it inhabits and to equitable representation in state and Federal governments." The fourth provision outlines the steps to be taken before granting the right of secession, which includes a two-thirds majority in the State Council, a referendum organized by the federal government that ends in a majority in favor of secession, and the transfer of powers and division of assets. Finally, the last provision of Article 39 delineates the criteria for designating a specific ethnic group or national group, which are "people who have or share a large measure of a common culture or similar customs, mutual intelligibility of language, belief in a common or related identities, a common psychological make-up, and who inhabit an identifiable, predominately contiguous territory."

Interestingly, and considerably less contentious, is the fact that Article 47 outlines a similar criteria and political process for a nation or nationality to achieve separate statehood as that for achieving secession, although in this case the State Council would oversee the referendum in its territory and ensure the division of powers between the newly created state and the old one. Disputes between states are to be decided by the House of Federation when they cannot be resolved by the states concerned (Article 48). What makes this of note is that Article 39 is the section of the constitution most cited by opponents of federalism because of the radical inclusion of the provisions on secession from the Ethiopian state. However, this article has not once been invoked in the decade since the constitution came into effect and no serious attempt has even been made in this direction. In contrast, while no new states have been formed, the provisions of Article 47 have been invoked and successfully implemented, resulting in the separation of Siltie zone from Gurage zone in 2001. In light of the hybrid creation of the Southern regional state out of the distinct states of earlier Proclamation No. 7/1992, this can be seen as the political equivalent of statehood for the Siltie nationality. The full context of the Siltie referendum is considered in Chapter 4 of this book.

Article 39 symbolizes the heart of citizenship debates in Ethiopia today. For nationalists, it represents a substantive challenge to historic notions of Ethiopian national identity that are grounded in specific historical and cultural themes– including unity of Ethiopia, territorial integrity, and a specific national identity. It is generally opposed quite strongly by members of formerly dominant ethnic groups, those who can say, "I am Ethiopian" with a confidence that others do not share. In contrast, for ethnonationalists and members of minority and formerly oppressed or marginalized ethnic groups, the inclusion of Article 39 in the constitution can be argued to have been an essential provision guaranteeing a true change in citizenship status. It was a crucial signal to members of these groups that the new regime was interested in making good on promises made decades before for ethnic autonomy, and power sharing. Article 39 is not only about secession, but its proponents and opponents alike focus on the secession language because of the intense symbolic power of the provision. In fact, the most radical part of Article 39 is an articulation of meaningful citizenship, at least for ethnic group members

Writing when the constitution was first ratified, one legal scholar noted that although secession is the most extreme form of self-determination, "the new Ethiopian constitution proposes too few of these self-determination remedies, since nothing is specified as lying in the gaps between secession, quite a narrow form of self-government and a limited cultural autonomy. Remedies could be offered in smaller, incremental steps."[126] While it is difficult to separate the secession provision from the self-determination provisions of Article 39 as currently constructed, it may be worthwhile to consider compromise positions. As the evidence from a study of language policy and ethnic suggests, most Ethiopian citizens, including those who express strong support for the language policy and other elements of the self-determination provisions of the constitution, do not articulate a desire to separate from Ethiopia. This includes many Oromo citizens and political elites, the ethnic group that is most likely to seek such a political dispensation. Parents in all regions of the study consistently articulated a belief that a policy of using indigenous or so-called nationality languages could not harm the national unity of Ethiopia. In fact, despite the dire predictions of the constitution's opponents, secession is not a political option sought after by the mainstream citizenry or political leadership of the vast majority of ethnic groups in the country. The right to self-determination not limited to cultural policy is of vital interest to them, however. Political threats to dismantle the constitution or specifically amend it in order to remove Article 39 entirely fail to account for the centrality of self-determination rights to

---

[126] Brietzke 1975, 35.

the majority of oppressed and minority ethnic groups in the country, and are a recipe for political conflict.[127]

Generally, assessments of federalism in Ethiopia based on various indicators of democracy have focused on four types of flaws in the federal arrangement: ruling-party dominance,[128] resource and human capacity shortages,[129] the persistence of authoritarian traditions,[130] and the politicization of ethnicity.[131] Each of these has some role in terms of explaining the incomplete democratic transition in the country. Most scholars cite a mixture of these variables in their assessments of Ethiopian democracy today. Almost all of them take a national approach in analyzing the impacts of federalism, whereas this study focuses on a specific and local ethnic conflict and the way in which the institutional and procedural parameters provided by the 1995 Constitution addressed it.

This data presented in this book takes up the specific issues of federalism, self-determination, and women's rights. Clearly, the EPRDF has launched a radical reorganization of political life in Ethiopia, drawing from the work of the Derg and the ISEN in particular, to articulate and implement a federal system based on ethnic identity. In fact, ruling-party dominance and resource capacity shortages have seriously undermined the extent of actual power sharing and federalism.[132] Outside the specifics of policy reforms, however, it is clear that the current regime is attempting to shape political identity and the foundations of political life in unprecedented ways. And how does the prioritization of ethnic concerns, as rooted as they are in historical inequalities, over other inequalities such as those based on gender, impact the larger project of citizen creation?

A Women's History of Ethiopia

A surprising absence of women's political history is in evidence in most of the main tomes of Ethiopian historiography. Teshale may be the only

---

[127] This is increasingly important in light of the success of the main opposition party, the Coalition for Unity and Democracy (CUD), in the May 2005 elections. A central pillar of the CUD platform is privatization of land and repeal or amendment of the constitution, particularly Article 39, both of which strike deep into the political psyches of minority and oppressed ethnic communities in the country.

[128] Aalen 2002; Samatar 2004; Medhane and J. Young 2003.

[129] Keller and L. Smith 2005; J. Young 1999.

[130] Merera 2003.

[131] Poluha 1998; Mesfin 2003.

[132] Aalen and Tronvoll 2009; Medhane and J. Young 2003; Aalen 2002; Keller and Smith 2005; Samatar 2004.

historian to at least acknowledge this, including in his introduction this statement: "Due to the hegemonic weight of the Aksumite and Orientalist Semiticist paradigms in Ethiopian studies, the history of peoples defined as outlandish to the Ge'ez civilization has been referred to in passing footnotes. (The most conspicuous silence is on the history of women.)"[133] One wonders why Teshale chose to make that a parenthetical reference rather than an exclamatory one. Even the very elite histories rarely document women's participation and identities. As Heran notes, "Elite women are particularly invisible" in this record, despite the centrality of marriage alliances in cementing diplomatic and political power in imperial Ethiopia.[134]

The near total erasure of women from Ethiopian history, with the exception of the occasional influential royal woman, is surprising in light of the complexity of women's experiences with political and economic power across various ethnic communities in modern Ethiopia and over time. Tsehai Berhane-Selassie contends that there was a certain convergence between the monarchy and successive revolutionary governments in Ethiopia in that "none have truly empowered women,"[135] and her study of rural women under the Derg provides a nuanced view of cultural change and local perceptions of development interventions that should be a model to researchers and policy makers alike. Similarly, Judith Olmstead's study of a female *balabbat* in Gamo, Southern region, should at least make us wonder if there were no other female leaders able to insert themselves creatively and effectively into otherwise male-dominated political structures throughout Ethiopian history.[136] Finally, Pankhurst concludes that Ethiopian peasant women not surprisingly "have found means of expression and rebellion," and she focuses on the somewhat unique and flexible approach to divorce in highland Amhara regions.[137]

All of this leaves us, then, with strikingly little history of women in Ethiopia, and I cannot purport to rectify that here. As historians seem to assume the irrelevance of women to historical processes, contemporary social scientists take for granted the patriarchal nature of Ethiopian society, and one rarely finds discussion of women in Ethiopian politics except as "victims" of poverty or an oppressive political regime. But to offer an analysis of gendered citizenship in Ethiopia is to suggest that the fully

[133] Teshale 1995, xxiii.
[134] Heran 2005, 55.
[135] Tsehai 1997, 184.
[136] Olmstead 1997.
[137] H. Pankhurst 1992, 179.

inclusive and meaningful citizenship of women is distinct from and yet also at an intersection with other types of citizenship, whether national, ethnic, religious, regional, and so on.

Put another way, when one emancipatory or liberatory project such as ethnic equality and meaningful citizenship is pursued, other citizen-creation and citizenship-expansion projects may be sidelined or delayed. Because meaningful citizenship is about how people realize rights already conferred legally or procedurally, women's equal and meaningful citizenship is particularly important in Ethiopia, a country where gendered inequality is rather stark but also where the constitutional and legal reforms have been quite thoroughgoing and bold, but outcomes seem to lag far behind. In addition, because of rather bold affirmative provisions for ethnic and religious communities in the country, it is a crucial case for evaluating the intersecting citizenship-expansion projects of ethnic community groupings and women as a group. This is especially so because women in Ethiopia would be expected, like women globally, to use the tools of their culture to evaluate, resist, and reform cultural and social traditions that might impinge on their exercise of meaningful citizenship.

Battles over the Shape and Meaning of Citizenship

Despite a stated intention to identify the patterns of unity that supported his thesis of a "Greater Ethiopia" cultural area, Levine noted in his 1965 study that "one can scarcely speak of the diverse peoples of Greater Ethiopia as composing a single national society. They remain organized in relatively discrete, autonomous, local social systems, under the umbrella of what is still aptly called the Imperial Ethiopian Government."[138] In fact, different ethnic groups in the country have historically had distinct and competing "societal scripts" for interpreting notions of identity and belonging in the state. As citizenship in the modernizing state, particularly under Haile Selassie, required assimilation to the dominant model, it is little wonder that the Oromo, Siltie, Somali, Anywaa, or Berta increasingly came to identify with their ethnolinguistic group in their resistance to the set of practices embodied by Amharization. Imperial policy facilitated the identification of Ethiopians with their ethnic group through the denial of full citizenship and a structurally unequal partial citizenship model.

---

[138] Levine 2000, 68.

The fact that members of dominant groups frequently identify more readily with the nation as such is instructive to this point. National symbols in Ethiopia are very much implicated in the Amharization process described earlier in this chapter. Therefore, members of dominant ethnic groups in the country will inevitably be less conflicted in their identification with the nation, since the nation and the ethnic group are one and the same. It is members of oppressed and minority ethnic groups who have historically been required to discard or hide the markers of their ethnicity, including their language, religion, and other cultural traits, in order to assimilate to dominant national culture. It is little wonder that it is the members of these groups who find identifying with Ethiopia as such offensive or impossible.

If modern Ethiopian history is, among other things, seen as the steady and contentious pursuit of citizenship claims, achieved through combinations of decrees from above, social relations fought out and negotiated on the ground, and evolving in response to rapid changes in the sociopolitical and economic environment, a whole new perspective on contemporary politics is provided. Rather than merely a series of ethnic conflicts or the balkanization of the state, group claims to self-determination and ethnic autonomy are the result of a historical process of political identification and citizenship creation. They are also funds for democratic participation that, when tapped, have facilitated and deepened democratic processes in the country. Writing during the socialist period, anthropologist Donald Donham made the pointed observation that "Abyssinianization, while successful in holding together a weakly integrated empire in the past, is manifestly maladapted to the later twentieth century.... New notions of citizenship are required, new forms of national identity that are not simply extensions of the old, new notions of the worth of different cultures."[139]

Those new forms of citizenship were somewhat radically introduced during the regime of the Derg, but were limited in impact, and remained fluid and contested. It is not entirely clear that Ethiopians have agreed-on definitions of citizenship that include all within the boundaries of the modern state, nor are the *terms* of this inclusion part of a national consensus. Federalism has created limited forums for social discourse on citizenship claims. It seems to have provided some institutional recourse for some ethnic communities. It has also opened up new social conflicts. And it has had a limited impact on the deep-rooted inequalities for Ethiopian women and girls, as we shall see. To the extent that other factors, such as

[139] Donham 2002, 47.

ruling-party dominance, have undermined the institutions of federalism, they have been unable to create the conditions for democratic debate essential to equal citizenship.

I turn in the following chapters to consideration of several of these themes, providing evidence to illustrate three central claims: first, that the formal institutions of federalism have led to mixed outcomes, in some cases arbitrating interethnic conflict and in other cases contributing to conflict; second, that competing citizenship visions continue to challenge the successful implementation of any institutional reforms or democratization projects; and third, that the major citizenship-expansion project left unfulfilled is that for Ethiopian women. All of this suggests the limited role of formal political institutions and the need for informal and alternative supports to democratization in multiethnic states such as Ethiopia. But first I turn specifically to language policy in Ethiopia, because as noted above, the dominance of Amharic language was perhaps the central tool of Amharization/Abyssinianization, and its rejection has come to symbolize a new iteration of citizenship expansion in contemporary Ethiopia.

THE RESPONSE: THE STATE AND ITS CITIZENS

3

Popular Responses to Unequal Citizenship

In November 1999, the normally quiet trading town of Soddo in the Wolaitta region of southern Ethiopia erupted in violence. During what should have been a peaceful demonstration, police fired on unarmed protestors, and up to ten people were killed, hundreds injured, and as many as 1,000 arrested. In the wake of the protests, many teachers and other civil servants lost their jobs and many more were shuffled off to teach in other regions. The cause of the violence was the decision to combine four previously distinct languages of the region, Wolaitta, Gamo, Gofa, and Dawro, into one Esperanto-style language called Wagagoda. Suggested as early as 1992, the move by the regional authorities to force teachers and students to implement the hybrid language in their classrooms, and the refusal of the regional or central government authorities to formally address these requests, led to the demonstrations. Although the violence was short-lived, as was the effort to use Wagagoda in the classroom, the incident illustrates the potency of language identity to Ethiopians and requires explanation because it seemingly defies a strategic characterization of ethnolinguistic identity.[1]

The challenge for scholars of citizenship and democracy in a place like Ethiopia is that language choice should be a relatively straightforward

---

[1] U.S. Department of State, 2000, 9. See the reports of the Ethiopian Human Rights Council (EHRCO) in *Compiled Reports of EHRCO* (2003), especially the 27th Special Report, dated December 13, 1999; Vaughan's discussion of the Wagagoda incident and the resultant division of North Omo zone into three separate zones and two special *woredas* highlights the critical role of the ruling party and local elites and the challenge of distinguishing administrative preferences from cultural ones (Vaughan 2003; Daniel Aberra n.d.).

policy matter. Ethiopia is home to some seventy-five to eighty distinct language communities.[2] It is also an incredibly poor country. It ranks 174 out of 187 countries in the world on the United Nations Human Development Index. The dominance of one language, Amharic, for most of the last century and up to the present time might also lead one to expect citizens' language choices to reflect a desire to speak the language that guarantees the greatest access to political and economic opportunity. The tremendous financial and labor costs of developing multiple nationality languages in Ethiopia would not suggest the energetic opposition to what are arguably more economically and politically expedient linguistic options, such as the combination of resources into one language.

Even more intriguing is that during interviews conducted in the region, respondents pointed to the importance of Wolaitta *identity* as the object of preservation, more than perceptions of economic, political, or even educational benefits. Typical was the response: "We cannot lose the term Wolaitta,"[3] which would presumably happen if the language were blended with the languages of neighboring ethnolinguistic groups. It is not that respondents did not ever cite economic or pedagogical factors relating to the use of their nationality language. Administrators in the Zone Education Office in Wolaitta increasingly cited the human labor and financial costs associated with a policy of multilingual education in primary schools. Teachers noted the educational benefits associated with instruction in mother tongues, although they too cited the lack of textbooks and teaching resources as hampering their work. Parents were concerned about the prospects for employment and mobility for their children. But the question of Wolaitta identity, as represented by or expressed as language identity, remains pivotal to the political conflict surrounding Wagagoda and the implementation of nationality languages as the medium of instruction throughout Ethiopia.

In this chapter I will contextualize contemporary Ethiopian language policy within the historical and political objectives of citizen formation. In particular, I am interested in the ways that a specific policy intervention such as language policy in educational settings can be seen as an operationalization of meaningful citizenship. The ability to communicate with

---

[2] Hudson 2004. Rather surprisingly, the most recent census in 2007 enumerates ninety-one distinct Ethiopian languages, and Ethnologue gives a number of ninety languages, of which "85 are living languages and 5 have no known speakers."

[3] Interview #48, June 2003.

the state but also within a community of identity and region (a language community) forms a crucial element of how citizenship is expanded. Therefore, I begin by considering the politics of language choice, drawing from the literature in political theory that addresses the role of language in the identity politics of multiethnic and multilingual societies. I present empirical evidence gathered in distinct regions of Ethiopia that points to the relationship between language identities and citizenship formation in the country. Does the revised language policy do more to create a sense of belonging, a meaningful citizenship for Wolaitta speakers or Anywaa speakers within Ethiopia than previous language regimes? What impact has this wide-ranging reform of everyday policy and educational life had on citizenship creation and expansion?

Language is political in Ethiopia precisely because it represents the nation-building project, and because, in the context of limited resources, any language policy change will require a drastic realignment of resources that is politically unpopular with the dominant group(s). The historical distribution of the political goods of communication, recognition, and autonomy has been highly skewed, benefiting native Amharic speakers disproportionately. Because Ethiopian-ness at the national level has become synonymous with Amharic-speaking ability, any local-level reinterpretation of Ethiopian citizenship represents a radical political stance and a threat to the privilege of these dominant language speakers.

Parents, teachers, and school administrators often cited the politics and pedagogy of language during interviews in the different regions of Ethiopia in 2001 and 2003. The reasons for this are tied up with the historical development of meaningful citizenship and the explicit role that language dominance played in state- and nation-building practices of successive political regimes. I outline here briefly the historical processes related to nation-building, specifically as these were influenced by an evolving language policy under successive Ethiopian regimes. Greater attention is given to developments under the Ethiopian People's Revolutionary Democratic Front (EPRDF) and the 1994 National Education and Training Policy (NETP), as related to language policy. I also present the basic changes in language policy and the results of focus group surveys conducted on the topic. But first I consider the relationship between the political goods that language policy can be expected to deliver, and the process of nation-building in modern Ethiopia.

Political Goods

In highly diverse societies, language conflicts are inevitable. Modernizing states are thought to require a united, cohesive, and compliant population. At the very least, this is believed to include mutual intelligibility of language, as well as a certain sense of shared identities, goals, and methods for achieving these. The relationship of language to national identity in the modern period has been thoroughly explored by prominent theorists of nationalism.[4] There has certainly been a normative preference for the notion of "one state, one nation, one language." Historically, modernizing states have pursued policies of suppressing ethnolinguistic claims by minority groups, as well as homogenizing and unifying language systems. International norms have shifted, however, and as indigenous, minority, and formerly oppressed groups throughout the world assert a broad set of political rights – including language rights – states have been compelled to adopt somewhat more flexible and diversified language policies.[5]

As language forms a core rights claim for many ethnocultural groups, language policy has distinctly political implications. It is the politics of language that I seek to explore here, leaving the linguistic, educational, and aesthetic aspects of language to other scholars. It is national states that select the national language(s), and it is states that dictate and control the content of school curricula, as well as the conduct of courtrooms, legislative bodies, and other public spaces where language identity matters a great deal in daily life. It is one area where private business, civil society groups, and even individual families – no matter how powerful some of these may be – have little or no impact. One of the most basic and central aspects of our daily life is choreographed by the state, regardless of whether an official language policy is formally articulated or left implied.

It is not surprising then that language issues emerge as vital and contested in the context of national or subnational appeals for meaningful citizenship. Language is an immediately visible indicator of exclusion.

---

[4] Benedict Anderson's now classic study of nationalism as "imagined communities" is particularly instructive for the study of Ethiopian nationalism, as its modern history is aptly understood as a self-conscious inventing of a nation where one did not exist before, and the "spread of particular vernaculars as instruments of administrative centralization by certain absolutist monarchs" was critical in the creation of nation-ness in Ethiopia (Anderson 1991, 6, 40).

[5] Bilingualism in Quebec Province of Canada is one example, as is the use of Maori in New Zealand. See also Fishman 1989, 1999; Tollefson and Tsui 2004; Skutnabb-Kangas 1995; Skutnabb-Kangas and Phillipson 2000; May 2001, 2003.

Philosophers and political theorists may have the philosophical and personal distance to see language as constructed and in some sense engineered. States, too, may regard language as a relatively inexpensive and highly effective site of intervention in facilitating the political objective of a cohesive national identity. But for citizens, language is most often *experienced* as natural and innate. Because our language is received and mastered well before we become aware of a world that is at all constructed or shaped by forces outside the home, it is one of the most natural aspects of a person's individual identity. Denial of the right to speak one's mother tongue, the language of home, family, clan, ethnic or religious group, is often experienced as perhaps the most undemocratic and autocratic of all policy measures passed by the state.

Language is much more than just speech. It is also a carrier of culture – of individual, community, and even national identity. Some have pointed out that language is much more than an instrumental good, allowing us to communicate with one another, but that it "has an intrinsically valuable dimension..... It is itself a human creation or accomplishment, participation in which is an end in itself."[6] This in part explains the tremendous emotive appeal of language rights to speakers of minority or oppressed language groups. And the language of the state carries with it powerful implicit messages about citizenship. It is a signal of who is included in the political community and on what terms. Language policy can build identification with, loyalty to, and membership in a particular national political community, or it can significantly undermine any efforts in this direction.[7]

These points can be better understood by thinking about the types of political goods any particular language policy delivers to its citizens. Although there are a number of different formulations, it seems that there are at least three primary political goods any language policy will need to deliver to the citizenry:

1. Communication/information: Access to the full range of information that enables the participation of citizens is determined and structured by language policy. As Patten puts it, "A person is better able to exercise his rights if he receives communications from government officials or public utilities in a language he can understand."[8] Those who cannot do so are more vulnerable to having

---

[6] Réaume 2003, 283.
[7] Kymlicka and Patten 2003, 11.
[8] Patten 2001, 696.

their rights and interests overlooked. A democratic language policy, whatever we decide that is, should provide all citizens equal access to the information, education, and opportunities of all others, following the principle of equality.

2. Autonomy: A number of multiculturalist theorists have identified autonomy as a prerequisite for democratic participation. This means that citizens must have not only the freedom to make their own choices, but also what scholars generally refer to as a sufficiently wide range of meaningful options and opportunities from which to choose. This being so, language policy can either promote or hinder individual autonomy by eliminating or providing barriers to participation. This also relates to the cultural component of language identity, since language forms the way we engage and interact with the wider social and political world. It includes the ability to access and express one's cultural identity, which is most typically accessed through the language of that group.[9]

3. Recognition: This includes the individual psychosocial benefit to citizens when the language in which they express themselves most comfortably is recognized publicly and permitted privately; it is also referred to as symbolic affirmation of citizens' identities. In particular, because language identity is so closely related to ethnic identity, recognition of linguistic diversity is an important symbol of the state's position on the various nationalities that compose the state. Citizens who feel that their language is not valued by the state may resist efforts to assimilate or integrate them in other aspects.

An effective and ethical language policy must somehow provide for these political goods. How any state does this will also be subject to various constraints, including history; the total number, relative size, and geographic spread of languages; and the economic and human resources available. We know that many states continue to focus on the first political good of communication only to the neglect of the other two. States that ignore the political goods of autonomy and recognition often face strong opposition, since these are far-reaching and pervasive ideals and often understood as central to the realization of meaningful citizenship. As May notes, "It is not the cultural, linguistic and political expression or mobilization of [minority] ethnicities and nationalisms which are the

---

[9] Réaume 2003, 290–291.

cause of so much contemporary mayhem in the modern world, but their *disavowal.*"[10] This has been the case in the historical development of language policy in modern Ethiopia, as we shall see.

The Politics of Language in Ethiopia

As already noted, Ethiopia is a highly diverse society with a varied and contested history relating to issues of ethnicity and language. The roots of Amhara/Amharic ethnolinguistic dominance, primarily the complex processes of Amharization, have been discussed already. Ethiopia does not have the dominance of a European colonial language more typical in the rest of sub-Saharan Africa. Nevertheless, because of the presence of some seventy-three distinct languages and the type of nation-building project already discussed, language policy in Ethiopia is a highly contentious matter, both historically and under the present political arrangement.[11] Haile Selassie's understanding of the imperatives of the state-building project and the tool kit that he used to accomplish this were strikingly similar to those used by other African leaders of the same period. Under his rule, the Amharic language became the national language and became akin to other colonial languages. Upward mobility and access to political and economic resources of many kinds were obtained through proficiency in Amharic. At times, coercive measures were taken to ensure that children and adults alike became literate in Amharic.

Although official language policy concerns not only education but also bureaucratic administration, legal and legislative communication, and media access, one of the most critical and contentious arenas for the politics of language has been in the education sector. This is particularly the case in Ethiopia, where citizens commonly understand language policy primarily as an issue of language of instruction in schools. This does not always lead to completely accurate information about what the policy is, but it does mean that the language policy is a critical policy sector for Ethiopians in assessing the impact of any particular institutional arrangement, such as federalism.

[10] May 2001, 308, emphasis in the original

[11] Hudson lists seventy-three living languages, "by the criterion of mutual intelligibility of dialects," as well as two extinct Ethiopian Semitic languages – Ge'ez and Gafat (Hudson 2004, 162). The 2007 national census lists ninety-one distinct Ethiopian "mother tongues," with another 119,000 speakers of "other Ethiopian languages" as well as English. It does not include Ge'ez or Gafat, but does include two languages with no speakers, Shetagna and Mejengerigna. Rather strangely, there is no Siltie language (see Chapter 5).

TABLE 3.1 *Language Families in Ethiopia*

Language Family	Number of Speakers for Language Family	Largest Language in that Language Family	Number of Speakers in each of largest Languages (2007)
Cushitic	26,469,394	Oromo	24,930,424
Nilo-Saharan	482,212	Gumuz	179,348
Omotic	3,989,694	Wolayta	1,627,955
Semitic	22,511,505	Amharic	21,634,396

Note: One of the decisions to be made in writing about language policy in Ethiopia is on the choice of transliteration for the names of Ethiopian languages. Although languages have their own rules for indicating a language name, there are conventions that dominate. For instance, the Amharic form of languages is to add the suffix –*nga* to all languages (Amharigna, Oromigna), whereas in the language of the Oromo, all start with the term Afaan (lit. mouth, therefore, Afaan Oromo, Afaan Amhara). For the purposes of standardization and clarity, I have used Hudson's (2004) English transliterations as much as possible, with two exceptions. First, when quoting respondents directly, I used their exact term (Wolaittigna, Afaan Oromo, etc.), and second, when quoting authors and written reports (such as the censuses), I also use their transliterated forms. There are a few places where I have used newer standards of English spelling where I was aware of them (based on interviews and fieldwork), such as Siltie (to refer to the ethnic group, not the language, which will be Silti) and Wolaitta (for the language and ethnic group). I apologize to the reader in advance for the complexity of this, but the politics of a simplified procedure prevented me from choosing one completely standard form throughout.*Source:* Hudson, 2003, 94; 2007 Census.

Historical Development of Ethiopian Languages

Although Amharic is the language of the Amhara ethnic group (not even a numerical majority, and only enjoying official state recognition for barely 100 years of modern history), it is unquestionably the dominant language in the country today. The languages in Ethiopia represent four language families: Semitic, Cushitic, Omotic, and Nilo-Saharan. The total numbers of mother tongue speakers for languages of the four language groups, as well as totals for the most populous language are reported in Table 3.1.

A few points are important to note from this list. Ethiopia has tremendous diversity in language communities, not only in the sheer number of languages spoken but because they come from distinct language families. Learning languages from another language family is a tremendous intellectual and educational undertaking. As the census demonstrates and Hudson notes, "Amharic and Oromo are unquestionably the only truly national languages of Ethiopia."[12] What is clear is that both

---

[12] Hudson's analysis followed from the 1994 census. A constitutionally mandated census was due to be conducted again in 2004 but was delayed to 2007 with results released in 2009.

languages dominate the country, and there are sizable numbers who speak Amharic, probably in towns and cities, although they are not ethnically Amhara.[13]

The use of Amharic stretches back at least several centuries, although it was not spoken outside of the Amhara homeland until recently. Amharic began to be used instead of Ge'ez as the secular language of the country by the early nineteenth century, and particularly through the impetus of Emperor Tewodros, "Amharic became the official written as well as spoken language of the Ethiopian state."[14] However, written Amharic was mainly the language of elites throughout the reign of the first three emperors of modern Ethiopia: Tewodros, Yohannes, and Menilek. It was not standardized in any meaningful way and literacy was not widespread. Reportedly, illiteracy nationwide was as high as 90 percent in the early twentieth century, and only half of Menilek's Council of Ministers could read and write with ease.[15]

It was Haile Selassie's drive for political centralization in the early twentieth century that necessitated the standardization and full-scale implementation of written Amharic. In his discussion of the translation of Ras Kassa's court registers, historian James McCann argues that these registers "represent probably the earliest examples of a systematic, secular use of literacy for public administration in Ethiopia," dating from October 1918 to November 1935.[16] He argues that "Kassa's assertion of written codes of obligations, duties and procedures were part of a transition to a new order of political culture," which primarily involved the centralization of the state.[17] It was no accident that Haile Selassie became the great champion of a national language. Building a centralized and modern state required taking radical political steps to reduce the power of regional nobility, and this was a primary accomplishment of his reign. It was not only his state-building vision, but also his vision of a *nation* of Ethiopians that propelled Haile Selassie toward Amharic. It was the package of policies systematically applied under the rubric of Amharization, and prominently including Amharic-language acquisition,

---

[13] The census counts "mother tongue" speakers, which is the "language used by the respondent for communication with his/her family members or guardians during his/her childhood." See 2007 Census, chapter III.

[14] Girma-Selassie, Appleyard, with Ullendorff, E. 1979; H. Pankhurst 1992, 317; Bahru 1991, 34.

[15] R. Pankhurst 1969, 9.

[16] Leul Ras Kassa Haylu was a close associate of Emperor Haile Selassie and an absentee governor of several areas of the northern highlands (McCann 1991, 1).

[17] McCann 1991, 6.

that explain the tremendous historical significance of language identities, and language policy, in Ethiopia today.

It was especially in 1941, after the end of the Italian occupation, that the language policy assumed a formalized role in the state- and nation-building projects of Haile Selassie.[18] By this time Amharic had become the medium of instruction (MOI) in the first two grades, and by the 1950s it was the MOI in all levels of primary school. Because both Amharic and English were obligatory in certification examinations and entry into the only university in the country, Haile Selassie I University, this gave a distinct advantage to native Amharic speakers. Other languages were suppressed, and it was not legal to teach, publish, or use any other indigenous language for public business.[19]

Making Amharic a national language was critical for consolidating central power and promoting the bureaucratic efficiency Haile Selassie desired. This was not as difficult in the northern highlands, where Amharic and Tigrinya (also a Semitic language), were mother tongue languages of the inhabitants.[20] Not inconsequentially, the Abyssinian highlands were also those areas where the Ethiopian Orthodox Church (EOC) had its base. In the newly incorporated regions of southern, eastern, and western Ethiopia, most subjects were non-Semitic speakers and either Muslim or practicing traditional religions. Haile Selassie used foreign missionary workers to accomplish the dual tasks of language homogenization and religious conversion. These early foreign missions were often forbidden to enter the strongholds of the EOC but were encouraged to concentrate in the newly conquered areas of the south and west of Ethiopia. Although European missionaries had been working in Ethiopia since at least the sixteenth century, they had had very limited impact, owing to the strength of the Ethiopian Orthodox Church in particular.[21] But beginning in the

---

[18] Space constraints do not allow full consideration of the impact of the Italian occupation, but it is worth noting that Italian policy on the matter (issued in 1936) was for teaching in main local languages of the six administrative units: Tigrinya in Eritrea; Amharic in Amhara; Amharic and Oromo in Addis Ababa; Harari and Oromo in Harar; Oromo and Kafficho in Galla-Sidamo; and Somali in Somalia. Arabic was also to be used in Muslim areas (R. Pankhurst 1969, 33; Mekuria, 1997).

[19] Boothe and Walker, 1997, 2; Keller, 1988, 160; Mekuria, 1997.

[20] It should be noted, however, that Tigrinya speakers, both in Eritrea and in Tigray region, resented the increasing dominance of Amharic over Tigrinya. Tigray regional state leadership was a strong supporter of the multilingual policy after 1991 (Harbeson 1988, 69).

[21] R. Pankhurst 1969, 11.

1940s, these missionaries were also required to teach in Amharic. Of course, most of the missions had a policy and practice of promoting local language use, particularly for Bible translation. Generally, Protestant missions promoted Bible translation as a matter of theological principle – new converts should access the Bible in their own language. This often required consolidation of regional languages or selection of critical language groups, since missionaries had a finite set of resources. The missions brought in experts to assist with developing orthographies and dictionaries for languages with no written forms, and most especially, for translating the Bible.[22]

The post-occupation period saw a standardizing of language provisions with respect to missionary activity. Imperial Decree 3 of 1944 mandated that missionaries would have to teach Amharic "as a general language of instruction," as well as learn it themselves.[23] They were allowed to teach in indigenous languages other than Amharic, but only orally and only in the early stages of missionary work until they and their pupils had learned Amharic. As one linguist of the time noted, "Missionaries are customarily permitted to work only in those areas in which the Ethiopian Orthodox Church is not well established. Since these areas are largely inhabited by people whose first language is not Amharic, the missionaries bring Amharic to people who might otherwise not have an opportunity to learn it."[24]

The missionaries became the workhorses of Haile Selassie's national integration project, although some continued to conduct other language development activities, particularly Bible translation projects. The success of these latter projects sometimes brought the missionaries, and their converts, into direct conflict with the imperial government. The successful and prolific Oromo scholar and evangelical Onesimos Nasib, for instance, translated the Bible and other religious literature into Afaan Oromo and compiled an Oromo dictionary and translated some secular works. As they became popular cultural and educational tools, they threatened the hegemonic project of Amharization, and in 1906 he was banned from preaching and teaching.[25]

---

[22] The relationship between Amharic-language instruction in these schools and national integration was explicitly made by Pankhurst when he stated: "Schools were thus accepted as contributing to the nation-building process. It was for this reason that Amharic, as will have been noted, was the sole language to be employed in government schools" (R. Pankhurst 1969, 30).

[23] Markakis 2003; Boothe and Walker 1997, 3; McNabb, 1990.

[24] Cooper 1976, 189.

[25] Mekuria 1997, 2002; Bahru 2002.

Language assimilation and suppression of other nationality languages became a primary source of resentment by non-Amharic speaking eth-nolinguistic groups. Some complained that it contributed to the "dehu-manization and subsequent alienation of groups speaking nonofficial languages."[26] Similarly, others connect the suppression of Oromo with the general degradation of Oromo culture, including the destruction of Oromo shrines and forced religious conversion.[27] Mekuria highlights the absurdity of judges, litigants, teachers, and students conducting legal pro-ceedings or educational programming in Amharic, through translators, when most or all parties were fluent speakers of Oromo. Education in particular was a site for humiliation and alienation, contributing to high attrition rates and low levels of literacy among non-Amhara peoples.[28] Muslim residents of border regions, for instance, sent their children to neighboring countries such as Sudan because of their strong association of language instruction in primary schools with religious conversion.[29] These same regions have seen a rapid growth in school enrollment under the more recent policy of nationality language instruction, highlighting the association of Amharic-instruction with hegemonic political forces.

There is little doubt that Amharic-language hegemony was a critical pillar on which the Amharization policy stood. Although there was a small opening in the late 1960s when four ethnic languages – Tigrinya, Tigre, Somali, and Afar – began to be broadcast by government-owned radio stations, these were not genuine attempts to reinvent or redefine the content and nature of belonging in the Ethiopian state. Significantly, the continuing ban on the use of Oromo, by far the largest group of any language speakers in the country, provides compelling evidence that this practice was not intended to allow a flourishing of cultural or linguistic identities. Interestingly, despite several decades of official language domi-nance, Amharic never achieved complete nationwide status. For instance, studies in the early 1970s showed that there was no lingua franca for trade in Ethiopia, based on a comparative study of market transactions in eight major urban market towns.[30] This was particularly striking in light of several decades of concerted language policy directed at elevating Amharic to just that status.

---

[26] Arity, quoted in McNabb 1989, 59.
[27] Keller 1988, 160.
[28] Mekuria 1997.
[29] Interview #71, October 2003.
[30] Bender et al. 1976, 253.

In general, the language policy under Haile Selassie fostered a strong sense of pride in Amharic among mother tongue speakers who had privileged access to employment, unrestricted mobility, and the resources of the state in both corpus planning and status planning of Amharic. The attachment to Amharic among fluent Amharic speakers today is closely linked with their sense of Ethiopian citizenship and identity. However, language identity among non-Amharic mother tongue speakers is similarly deeply felt and represents their unequal inclusion into the Ethiopian state. The close association of language with religious, ethnic, and regional identities made the preservation of local languages a critical component of the political and social movements that eventually toppled the imperial regime.

Language Policy under the Derg

Under the socialist dictatorship of the Derg, there was some movement away from full linguistic domination. Overall, however, the centralist bent of the regime and the ethnolinguistic composition of the Derg itself contributed to a perpetuation of Amharic-language dominance at all levels and certainly the continued local perception of Amharic dominance. At the outset, there was a flourishing of ethnic identity heralded by the Derg's early social and economic reforms and a sense that the question of the nationalities was to receive redress under the new leadership.[31] The 1976 Program of the National Democratic Revolution of Ethiopia (NDRP) explicitly guaranteed the right to "regional autonomy ... [including] the right to use its own language."[32] However, as the Derg centralized its control over the various movements that had initially supported its platform, and as power came to rest increasingly with General Mengistu, there was a change in rhetoric and practice. Ethnolinguistically based groups were labeled as counterrevolutionary and "narrow nationalists." Many have pointed out that despite the rhetoric, Mengistu merely merged his socialist ideology with the imperialist ideology of his predecessors and "continued with their politics of centralization and homogenization of the multi-national and multi-cultural empire."[33]

---

[31] For instance, the Oromo quickly organized literacy and translation projects in Oromo in the early years, including the launch of a weekly newspaper, *Bariisaa* (Dawn) and the holding of a cultural show in 1977 (Mekuria 1997).

[32] Reprinted in Ottaway and Ottaway 1978, 214.

[33] Mekuria 1997, 346.

The literacy campaign was one of the early and most dramatic social interventions of the Derg regime. The first *zemeccha,* or Development through Cooperation Campaign, as it was officially called, was held from late 1974 through mid-1975 and set the pattern for later literacy campaigns. It involved the use of high school and university students, primarily to explain and implement the new land reform program and to establish the Peasant Associations (PA). This campaign was met with limited success in programmatic terms, although it did much to educate and sensitize these young leaders to conditions of the peasantry. The literacy component was conducted in Amharic, Tigrinya, Oromo, Somali, and Afar languages. Materials were produced in these languages in the Ethiopic/Amharic alphabet.

Later service campaigns in the 1980s were to focus exclusively on literacy and were popularly known in the countryside as the *meserete timhirt.* In the official description of the campaign, it was asserted that in previous periods, "the situation was heavily biased against those for whom Amharic was either not spoken in the home, or was only a second language." Therefore, nationality languages would be used in conducting the literacy campaign. Eventually the campaign was taught in fifteen different languages and it was believed that they covered 93 percent of Ethiopia's population.[34]

Some have argued that the preparation and delivery of the literacy campaigns were both cursory and ineffective, particularly as they did not involve experts or representatives from non-Amharic groups and because the selection of languages was somewhat arbitrary. At least it can be said that it did not involve popular or widespread discussion among Ethiopian citizens about which languages would be used or what would be covered. Overall, despite receiving significant international attention, the success of the literacy campaign was quite limited. Because curricular materials were poorly written and there were very few additional resources for deepening literacy through supplemental materials, it did not have much long-term effect on literacy levels.[35] Some asserted that the people were reluctant to abandon Amharic because they realized they still needed it for economic reasons, particularly access to employment.

In addition, at this time the nationality languages were written in the Ethiopic script. The Ethiopic, or Amharic, script refers to the system of

---

[34] NLCCC 1981; Markakis 2003.
[35] For information on the implementation of the *meserete timhirt* see Markakis 2003; Hoben 1994; and Cohen 2000.

letters of the alphabet in Amharic, called *fidel* in Amharic.[36] It has been argued that whereas the Ethiopic script is appropriate for Semitic languages such as Amharic and Tigrinya, it is not well suited linguistically to languages from other language families, such as Oromo.[37] The selection of orthography for each of the nationality languages in Ethiopia has been fraught with controversy because the political and symbolic attachment to the *fidel* is so great, and rejection of its use since 1991 for most non-Semitic languages in the country is seen by Ethiopian nationalists as a further symbol of their linguistic and cultural defiance. Despite important substantive changes in language policy under the Derg, Amharic knowledge remained a prerequisite of political or economic participation. Critically, the literacy campaign only involved nonformal education. Primary schools throughout the country continued to teach in Amharic regardless of mother tongue or ethnic group. The 1987 Constitution clearly made Amharic the official language of the state. Scholars writing during this time pointed out that "a relentless imposition of a national language is the likely outcome of national language policy."[38]

Nonetheless, the *meserete timhirt* and the development of written literacy materials in languages other than Amharic had powerful symbolic and practical effect. Even if it did not create full literacy for adult peasants, stories of the literacy campaign reverberated through our focus group discussions across multiple subregions of the country in 2003. People had participated, at least for a time, and been energized by the prospects of literacy and, especially, the translation and promotion of their nationality/ethnic languages. In the list of fifteen languages, one sees direct correspondence to the focal languages of the contemporary language policy. It was a very dramatic indication of a massive change in the political landscape of language in Ethiopia, and it laid the groundwork for the development of languages other than Amharic, as well as the expectation that literacy in these languages was a political right that could facilitate meaningful citizenship.

---

[36] There are 231 letters in the Amharic alphabet (Bender et al. 1976, 121).

[37] This is in part because Cushitic languages have a greater number of long vowel sounds that cannot be adequately represented in Ethiopic script, and there is also a gemination (doubling) of consonant sounds (see Cohen 2000, 92). Others argue that the Ethiopic alphabet is better suited to Oromo than Latin. There is considerable debate about the "scientific" basis for choice of script. I am not a linguist and not qualified to contribute to this debate. I merely cite here some of the common reasons given by those for and against the use of Ethiopic script for non-Semitic languages in Ethiopia.

[38] Bender 1985, 277; see also McNabb 1990.

Language Policy under the Federal System

When the Transitional Government of Ethiopia (TGE) replaced the Derg in 1991, it confronted declining enrollment rates in all levels of education. Because of the complex relationship of Amharic dominance, together with ethnolinguistic demands for autonomy and self-government, the TGE quickly attempted to demonstrate the extent of self-determination provisions for ethnic groups. The language policy was perhaps the earliest and most striking manifestation of how the new government intended to demonstrate its commitment to these principles. In 1991, the Ministry of Education (MOE) drafted a policy statement on language that provided for the use of nationality languages, specifically identifying Amharic, Oromo, Tigray, Wolaitta, and Sidama, beginning in the 1991–1992 school year. Studies were to be done on the introduction of other languages as a medium of instruction as soon as feasible, and a national referendum was to be held on the question of a language of national communication.[39] This also included a policy switch emphasizing the Latin script for Cushitic languages in particular and decentralization of language choice. Tigray region was already teaching in Tigrinya and would not have tolerated a return to Amharic only. The Oromo Liberation Front was also conducting literacy campaigns in Oromo. Other regions were interested in following suit.

As early as spring of 1993, the MOE moved forward with a large-scale translation of textbooks. In addition to instruction in Tigrinya in the Tigray region, other languages of instruction in 1992 were Oromo, Sidamo, and Wolaitta languages, and plans were in place for Kambatta, Hadiya, Gedeo, and Somali languages by 1993.[40] The National Education and Training Policy (NETP) of Ethiopia, published in April 1994, laid out the policy objectives for education under the new government. It clearly stated that one of the objectives of the policy was "to recognize the rights of nations/nationalities to learn in their own language, while at the same time providing one language for national and another one for international communication." It goes on to say that "primary education will be given in nationality languages," and "nations and nationalities can either

---

[39] This referendum was never held. By the time of the 1994 policy statement, the referendum was dropped entirely, and Amharic was specifically designated as the "language of countrywide communication" (Ethiopia, Transitional Government of Ethiopia, 1994, 24). Boothe and Walker 1997, 5

[40] S. Hoben 1994, 190.

learn in their own language or can choose from among those selected on the basis of national and country-wide distribution."[41] Nationality languages or Amharic are the languages of instruction in primary school. English is given as a subject beginning in grade one, and it is the language of instruction in secondary schools and institutions of higher education, usually beginning in either grade seven or grade nine. In regions where a nationality language (NL) other than Amharic is taught, Amharic is given as an additional subject from grade one or grade five, depending on the region. This is presumably because of the special constitutional status of Amharic as the national "working language."

This rather specific set of policies on language took shape under the TGE but was formalized in the 1995 Constitution. Article 5 of the constitution guarantees that "all Ethiopian languages shall enjoy equal state recognition. Amharic shall be the working language of the Federal government. Members of the Federation may by law determine their respective working languages." In Article 39 it provides that "every nation, nationality and people in Ethiopia has the right to speak, to write and to develop its own languages; to express, to develop and to promote its culture; and to preserve its history." Language policy has been without a doubt a pivotal dimension of federalism in Ethiopia and intended as a signal of the EPRDF's dramatic commitment to self-determination for all nations and nationalities in the country. The regime has made language policy a pillar of its citizenship-expansion project.

In addition to the use of nationality languages as a tool for improving educational effectiveness, regional states were supposed to have authority to devise methods and materials suited to the unique needs and goals of their student population. Access issues were to be addressed through widespread construction of new schools as well as repairs and additions to existing schools. The massive need for teacher training was identified as a high priority. Programs were proposed for teacher certification, distance learning, and the use of other teaching aids and materials to foster improved teaching. Boarding schools, hostels, and pilot nomadic (mobile) schools were to be constructed or organized in regions – including Afar, Somali, Benishangul-Gumuz, and Southern Nations, Nationalities and People's Region – where nomadic children's education has been hindered by lack of access.[42]

---

[41] Ethiopia, Transitional Government of Ethiopia 1994.
[42] Ministry of Education 1999a, 7.

Implementation of Language Policy in Education

In addition to the presence of significant disparities in human and financial capacity among regions, conflicts over language use and curriculum content, particularly in multiethnic states, represent an example of how the federalism arrangement in Ethiopia remains contentious. Conflicts over language policy in schools and regional administrations have occurred mainly within the regions and between the regional governments and the federal government. At the national level and in urban areas in particular, there is a general dissatisfaction with the current language policy. In rural communities, far from towns and cities, rapidly rising enrollment rates in primary school suggest satisfaction with the language policy and a general support for educational goals.

The economic cost of the multilingual policy in education is substantial and has contributed to the overall growth in regional disparities, without necessarily lessening the political conflict over ethnicity. Some smaller ethnic groups in the Southern region have opted to continue the policy of Amharic instruction. They contend that the use of nationality languages is a policy of the ethnic group in power to marginalize minority ethnolinguistic groups, especially in light of the fact that Amharic is the official language of the state and widely used in multiethnic cities such as Addis Ababa.

In the case of those that have chosen to use nationality languages, especially in multiethnic states, a tremendous burden is put on their Regional and Zonal Education Office to translate educational materials provided by the Regional Education Bureau from Amharic to these languages. For instance, there are at least eleven nationality languages being taught in Southern region, and at least two more are in the process of being added, as outlined in Table 3.2.

In Amhara regional state, and the other large and ethnically homogenous regions such as Tigray, Somali, and Oromiya, the Regional Council has approved the use of the respective NLs as the MOI in different grade levels of primary school. Even in the case of considerably larger ethnic groups located in primarily homogenous regional states such as Tigray and Oromiya, the costs of standardizing the use of the nationality language, training teachers, and producing supplementary reading materials in that language continue to be significant. Yet the question of linguistic minorities is a source of conflict even within the more homogeneous states. Oromiya regional state in particular has attempted to address the presence of significant populations of non-Oromo speakers, especially

TABLE 3.2 *Languages of Instruction in the Southern Nations, Nationalities, and People's Region (SNNPR)*

Language	Grade level
Sidama	1–6
Gedeofa	1–6
Koreta	1–6
Wolaitta	1–6
Gamo	1–6
Kambata	1–6
Hadiya	1–6
Kefa	1–4
Silti	1–6
Dawro	As a subject only
Kabena	1–4
Konta	Being prepared; grade level not decided
Gofa	Being prepared; grade level not decided

Note: List current as of June 2005, but likely to change over time.

in regional urban centers, by adopting a mixed policy. The state requires that schools with a significant proportion of other language communities must offer instruction in Amharic, either by designating one primary school as Amharic or certain classrooms within a school as Amharic mother tongue classrooms.

In the so-called emerging regions, including the South, Benishangul-Gumuz, Gambella, and Afar, there are strikingly different policies. Afar has an official policy of the use of the Afar, but it is widely understood that both the lack of trained Afar teachers and the lack of materials and resources mean that Amharic remains the language of instruction. In Benishangul-Gumuz, where there are five indigenous nationality languages, there is a plan to introduce all five of these as an MOI within the next five years, although they are still teaching in Amharic in most cases. Somali region, despite its low socioeconomic capacity, has benefited from the standardization of Somali in neighboring states.

Many of these languages have never been written before, requiring local experts to select orthographies, develop standardized grammars, and oversee translation. It is unclear who these "experts" are and whether those zones using nationality languages receive additional budgetary supplements to support the translation of Amharic materials into nationality languages. Teachers who have always taught in Amharic must now be instructed in these languages. Authorities report that site visits often find teachers using Amharic, or Amharic interspersed with the nationality language, throughout their teaching, despite the written policy.[43] In other cases, teachers who are not familiar with the nationality languages must be reassigned and qualified teachers hired.[44] All these factors affect educational quality, as well as the perceived success of the decentralization arrangement.

The Southern Nations, Nationalities, and People's Region has the greatest ethnolinguistic diversity of all of Ethiopia's regions, with approximately forty-five ethnic groups in all. Of that, there are 23 languages with more than 50,000 speakers.[45] Therefore, the Southern region has the tremendous task of meeting the needs and wishes of many sizable nationality groups. To address MOI and language policy priorities, some zones are using Amharic and some are using their respective NL. For instance, all *woredas* of Gurage zone except one use Amharic as the MOI, while in one *woreda* the NL of Kabena is being taught as a subject. In Wolaitta and Siltie zones, the NL is the MOI, but only in grades one through six, when there is switch to English. There is a desire in at least Wolaitta zone to switch to English instruction in grade four. There is a remarkable gap between the demands for NL by even small groups in the Southern region and the capacity of the Regional Education Bureau in Awassa to meet those demands. At the time of this research, there was only one designated staff member in the entire region working on nationality languages, and his own linguistic and technical abilities were obviously limited.[46]

Presently, Ethiopia is pursuing a hybrid of several policy models with respect to language. There is some weight given to supporting and developing even minority languages, which looks much like the "language maintenance" model.[47] In this, the mobility of Ethiopian citizens has been affected, as regional states are allowed certain political rights to require

[43] Interview #17, February 2003; Interview #46, June 2003.
[44] The question of teacher reassignment is an emotive topic, particularly for opponents of the present language policy (Teshome 1999). Although it is true that teachers not fluent in nationality languages have been reassigned in a number of cases, particularly at the start of the policy, every school has at least one Amharic teacher, as Amharic is always taught as a subject. In most of the schools we visited this individual was actually Amhara, not the ethnic nationality of the region. This fact alone contradicts the charge that teachers are dismissed based on ethnicity, not language ability. In at least one other school, a teacher who was Amhara but fluent in Oromo was teaching other subjects and spoke in favor of the language policy. Of course, under the Amharic language policies of the past many competent nationality language speaking teachers were unable to obtain jobs because of the preference for fluent Amharic speakers.
[45] Hudson 2003, 101.
[46] Interview #46, June 2003.
[47] Patten 2001.

knowledge of a local language as a prerequisite for employment and elected office, and to require all children to learn the language in school. Still, under the federal arrangement this is a matter for the territorial entities known as the regions, and therefore the national policy is more of the official multilingualism model in that it allows but does not guarantee the maintenance of all Ethiopian languages.

The language policy in Ethiopia is illustrative of the trials of implementing public policy to ameliorate or prevent political conflict, particularly in the presence of a highly diverse population. Repeatedly, language choice, both the EPRDF policy and the policies of the various states, is cited by Ethiopian citizens as emblematic of the federal arrangement, both good and bad. It has resulted in the proliferation of administrative units and has consumed a large proportion of regional education budgets, particularly in historically disadvantaged regions already suffering from a wide variety of obstacles to efficient regional budget management. Although some connect increasing enrollments in primary school to the new language policy, it is unclear whether this policy is contributing to political empowerment, and certainly it consumes significant proportions of regional budgets. There can be little doubt, however, that the language policy has been a crucial tool of citizenship expansion, providing previously excluded groups access to the halls of learning, justice, and government administration in strikingly more equal ways.

Further complicating our efforts at categorizing Ethiopia, however, is the de facto "linguistic rationalization" that one finds, particularly in the capital and at the federal level, where Amharic continues to dominate. One does not find street signs in Addis Ababa in each of the twenty languages in use in the regions, for instance. In fact, the constitutional provision for Amharic to serve as the "working language of the Federal government" (Article 5) undermines many of the potential equity and recognition-based norms behind the more general language policy.

Despite the rhetoric of a unified language policy, there are two language policies, one explicit and formal and one informal. The dominance of Amharic as the working language is understood by many categories of Ethiopian citizens as a continuation of their marginalization and a threat to their ethnic self-determination rights. Although the language policy gives new voice to some members of ethnolinguistic groups, it is an incomplete project, particularly as unequal citizenship in Ethiopia is only partially about language, but also because of the imperative of some working language for a country as linguistically diverse as Ethiopia.

Popular Responses to the Language Policy

Since the introduction of the language policy in the early 1990s, there have been few studies of the language policy.[48] Writing in the first five years of the new policy, Boothe and Walker noted the problems of resource shortages, rushed translations, and inadequately trained teachers. Nonetheless, they were optimistic about the prospects of the policy to improve educational outcomes. In particular, they noted that

decentralisation, use of the mother tongue, and curricular revision have all helped to bolster community support for primary education.... Across the board, parent, student and teacher attitudes about using the nationality languages were positive. Children were excited that for the first time they could legally use their mother tongue in schools. Parents were pleased that they could talk to school officials in the mother tongue rather than through an interpreter. Teachers were encouraged by the students' willingness to engage in class discussions now that they could express themselves in the language in which they were most confident.[49]

In a more recent study of language policy in Southern region (SNNPR), Cohen determined that "local pride and self-identity are clearly increasing in response to the reform."[50] Cohen's study is the most exhaustive and qualitatively rich, even if limited by the focus on one regional state. He found that although public consultations were limited prior to the introduction of the language policy, there was considerable public debate after the policy was implemented. Parents and teachers noted concerns that the policy would limit their children's opportunities and might divide the country. Importantly, Cohen found variation in popular responses based in part on literacy levels and ethnic diversity. More literate ethnic groups tended to favor the use of nationality languages, as did those living in ethnically homogenous areas.[51] The historical role of labor migration and higher literacy and educational levels points to the relationship between ethnic identity and opportunities for social mobility. Members of ethnic groups who have a history of migrating within the country, such as the Gurage and Wolaitta, tended to favor the use of Amharic. Those who were more rural based, Muslim, or had lower literacy levels tended to favor the use of nationality languages.

---

[48] However, there are many good senior essays and master's theses submitted to Addis Ababa University that provide additional information specific to particular languages and regions.

[49] Boothe and Walker 1997, 11, 13.

[50] Cohen 2000, 122.

[51] Cohen 2000, 146, 171–182.

Many of these findings were echoed by respondents in the focus group sessions I conducted in Southern region, Oromiya region, and Benishangul-Gumuz region. The very first question asked related to local understandings about what the meaning of ethnicity/nationality/*behereseboch* includes. While there were many fascinating and sometimes insightful types of responses, most respondents identified language identity as one of the core markers of ethnicity or nationality in Ethiopia.[52] Nearly all respondents favored the use of nationality languages at some point in primary education, but there were differences based on rural versus urban location, and among members of different ethnic groups. For instance, the Gurage and Wolaitta continued to prefer Amharic in far greater numbers than the other groups surveyed, and the Siltie and Oromo were the strongest supporters of the policy of nationality languages. There was also a general consensus for English as the second language for Ethiopia, although this was considerably stronger among Oromo than members of other ethnic groups. Interestingly, one of the only surveys ever done, published in 1976, found similar patterns of language preference in Ethiopia, reporting that "the language most frequently cited as desired [by factory workers] was English."[53]

I summarize here some of the main findings of the focus groups. I have organized the responses by the types of questions asked and an analysis of the responses. Those quotes selected for inclusion here represent the *types* of different perspectives offered by respondents rather than an exhaustive list. They are meant primarily to illustrate the way that Ethiopians in different regions and from different backgrounds articulate their understandings of ethnic and language identity, and the range of pedagogical and political issues associated with language policy in the country.[54]

Knowledge of Language Policy and Level of Participation

Somewhat surprisingly, the knowledge-based questions were often the most difficult for parents and teachers to answer. Whereas most knew that the present language policy came with the "new government" (meaning with the EPRDF in the early 1990s), few knew who had formulated the

[52] See L. Smith 2005, 2008.
[53] Bender et al. 1976, 271.
[54] The text of the full questionnaires and the list of schools visited in 2003 can be found in L. Smith 2005.

policy or even at what grade levels children were required by the policy to learn in their nationality languages in their region. The most common response was that the policy "came from above down to us" or it "came down through the chain." Parents generally understood that the federal government imposed the policy, although a fair number also indicated that the regional governments had a role to play in its formulation. Almost no parents had attended a meeting about the new language policy at the time, and when they had, they usually described a meeting at which they were told about the policy, certainly not consulted or asked to provide input.

Participation in making policy

Is there supposed to be a meeting on these things? I did not hear of the meeting. (Borana town parent)

The decision came down from above. It came through the government chain. If the higher government does not say something, the school and local government have no authority. (Bale town parent)

It came from above. But I am not sure it did not start from here. We are old and do not know everything. (Bale town parent)

It is not because of participation in a meeting, but it is according to what the constitution states. (Siltie town parent)

It was in this government. I do not remember exactly when it was. But it was after the coming of the EPRDF and after the law that every nation should have the "nationality right." And the Siltie language replaced the Amharic language. (Siltie rural parent)

Political choice

It was asked as a right. When the system started, we became beneficiaries. So it was by the local people. (Siltie town parent)

No one was forced about the language policy. It is based on interest. It was said that Amharic is suitable for our people, and if our society uses Amharic, in the future it will be developed. (Gurage rural parent)

Educational or pedagogical reasons

There are certain people who are famous in education and other professions. These people declare the advantages of learning in Amharic to the society and the society accepts their idea. These people have done this thing, not for political reasons. (Gurage rural teacher)

Opinion of Using Nationality Languages

As stated above, most respondents in the zones and regions of this study supported the use of nationality languages. The few who were most opposed were mother tongue speakers of Amharic.[55] They often indicated that their children were struggling to master a new language, and they as parents were struggling to help their children learn their material in a language they themselves did not speak, read, or write. None of them had the reflexivity to acknowledge that the reverse situation would be true for the majority of the local population if the nationality language were not in place for that region.

Every respondent felt that learning in a nationality language was important for teaching children about their culture and history, for helping students understand their subject matter better, and for motivating them to learn and stay in school. To this, parents frequently added a factor we had not asked them about – the role that learning in a nationality language plays in facilitating parent-child learning. Many stated that because their children were learning in their own language, the parents were better able to help answer children's homework questions, and children were less afraid to ask questions of parents and teachers alike. Other parents said that they were learning from their children, sometimes specifically learning to read and write their mother tongue or learning about their history.

Cultural argument

When we used to learn in Afaan Amharic, no one mentioned the history of the Oromo. The history we learned is the history of the language we are learning. Now our children are learning the culture and history from their father's history to their ancestor's history. (Borana rural parent)

In previous times, no one mentioned Oromo culture and history. Since we have started learning in our language, our culture is spreading all over the world. We are very happy. (Bale rural parent)

When they ask us in our language the questions they have from school, we can give answers about it, such as about the culture. (Bale town parent)

They used to learn in Amharic. During the Derg time a person who spoke Oromo was disliked. Now they are even learning in Oromo. (Bale rural parent)

I have a daughter at home. One time she came to me with twelve questions. I myself did not know my own language. She was asking me who was the participant of this war and that war. I answered to her, "I do not know." I could not

---

[55] Approximately 10% of all respondents were not of the dominant ethnic group in the region, even in town schools. For instance, in Mega town, Borana zone, one father was an Orthodox priest assigned to the region by the EOC. In Yabello town, one mother was half Oromo, half Amhara, but she and her children spoke Amharic as a first language. There were no Amharic-speaking respondents in any rural schools, and parents and teachers usually indicated that all children in those schools were nationality language speakers.

answer her twelve questions. I felt so happy that she knew all this. I thought I was born again. I thought my language was born again through her. (Siltie rural parent)

Practical/communicative argument

I guess it is important. If the person goes to an office, he does not need an interpreter. Therefore, I am happy, since we do not know Amharic. We can tell our problems in our language, so we are happy. (Siltie town parent)

For example, if we teach them Guragigna, and if they do not learn things like the national language and they go far from this place, they may face difficulties. In the class, when they do not understand things in Amharic we explain it in Guragigna and they understand it quickly. But as Amharic is the national language it is better if they learn it. (Gurage rural teacher)

In the past, what we were learning was like spreading the education in the air. In the past with this language, everything was taught in Amharic and the courts were in Amharic. Now things are changed. It is the other way around and the schools and court system are in our language. That makes me wonder how things can change. (Bale rural parent)

They are happy that they are learning in the language of their nationality. They see it as another victory. After that, the number of students [enrolled in the school] has increased.... Even the lessons are better when they learn in their language. Before, in the text there was something they did not know. It was about Bahir Dar, Gojjam, or Blue Nile. Now, it is based on their area. Therefore, their understanding is better. (Siltie town school director)

Even if, according to the diversity of Ethiopian ethnic groups, it is beneficial to learn in one's own language, in my opinion, when students go to higher levels they may encounter difficulties. This is because the national language is different than their first language. So their perception becomes poor and they will be not benefiting. They can express their culture but they will be poor in language, writing, and reading skills. Due to this, I can say that they will lose more than they gain. (Gurage rural teacher)

Impact of Language Policy on the National Unity of Ethiopia

In response to a question about the impact of the use of nationality languages on the national unity of Ethiopia, participants expressed a consensus that it would not harm the national unity of the country. They were, however, generally divided on the specifics, with roughly half citing the concerns of regional mobility and the need for a language of national communication as a way to foster Ethiopian unity. The other half felt that unity was not implicated at all in the use of nationality languages, particularly as all nationalities were using their own language and all were learning Amharic and English. Respondents often indicated a nuanced understanding of national unity and ethnicity, wondering why learning a particular language could hurt a country as large, diverse, and secure as Ethiopia.

We do not create unity. It is not our job to create unity. (Borana rural parent)

Everybody in Ethiopia is learning in their own languages. So I do not think this will create a problem for the unity of Ethiopia. (Bale rural parent)

We must love Ethiopia. It is our motherland and our country.... If I have my own language, if I learn by my own language, if I develop my culture – that is not to be separate from Ethiopia, or to have another way to go out of Ethiopia. Culture is something which makes Ethiopia more beautiful.... When you go to the garden, and you find the garden has only one flower, one type of flower, I think it is not a good thing. So we all develop our language, respect together, work together, believe others, trust others, we can build a smart and beautiful Ethiopia. (Berta political leader in Assosa town, Benishangul-Gumuz)

What is the problem with learning? If somebody learns, how can it harm something? I do not think it [the language policy] will create a problem. Ethiopia is Ethiopia. If anyone learns in their language, in their *fidel* [alphabet], it does not bring a problem. (Bale rural parent)

It might bring conflicts for students as they move up levels [grade levels]. (Borana rural parent)

I do not think it is a harm.... It is good for the country because people get educated in what they understand. That helps the country. (Bale town parent)

In my opinion, it helps. Because any nation and nationalities of their own language like the Amhara nation, the Amhara they have their own language and also Oromo and Gurage the same way. As anyone's language has a certain contribution to the people and the country, and the Siltie people's language as the other languages if the people can use them, I think it will help the country's unity. (Siltie rural parent)

In my opinion it may affect individuals, but it may not affect the country. They may not be competent to get jobs nationally. If a person is affected it implies the country is also affected. But the effect is mainly on the individual so I do not see the effect on the country. (Gurage rural teacher)

Conclusion

Language policy in schools is a critical tool of citizen creation and citizenship expansion, as is language policy more generally (courts, government facilities, public resources, and educational and health-care venues). The various respondents to focus group surveys in southern and western Ethiopia might justifiably find any modern state that did not provide for basic education and access to government services in the most inclusive and respectful way to be an obstacle to the making of citizens. In fact, the contemporary Ethiopian state has undergirded efforts at citizenship on a bedrock of linguistic inclusion, despite the opposition from some and the steep resource requirements.

There is little doubt that language policy has been and will continue to be foundational in creating the conditions for meaningful citizenship in Ethiopia, particularly as long as illiteracy and poverty persist and especially as these are structurally related to ethnicity and regional state. Communities were near unanimous that the use of local nationality languages contributed to their sense that the government was concerned about including them in some types of decision making. They had reasonable worries about mobility and employment for their children, and about how communication and national identity in a multilingual political entity such as Ethiopia could be cultivated. But it can also be said that Ethiopian citizens have a sophisticated and nuanced understanding of the conditions of national unity. In a context where all ethnolinguistic groups have the right to use and develop their language, they do not worry that such a policy will undermine the solid foundations of Ethiopian unity. Their perception of the strength of the Ethiopian polity is perhaps reflected in this assessment, but it is nonetheless not for lack of an appreciation for how language contributes to political unity.

Evaluating language policy is not only about measuring the practical implications of the policy, such as efficiency, financial costs, labor needs, constraints or impetuses for social mobility, and so on. This research documents not only the varied opinions of Ethiopian citizens about the language policy but also varied outcomes, some of which highlight the practical problems posed by a multilingual policy. But there are also significant ethical dimensions – recognition, autonomy, and democratic participation – to language identity, which cannot be overlooked. The state cannot choose to be silent on language policy, but restricting language choice may be costly to the citizenship-expansion project, as the history of Ethiopia shows us. Language is both the vehicle and the subject itself of vital political goods for citizens, and it will always have a political nature. Even as there are a variety of models for addressing language in a multilingual society, none seems immediately ideal, particularly as soon as we move to real-world contexts such as those in Ethiopia today. Not only are there administrative and political costs to implementing a truly egalitarian language policy in multilingual states such as Ethiopia, but there are significant democratic costs to ignoring language diversity or pursuing a policy of linguistic domination.

Language policy has proved central to the citizen-creation and citizenship-expansion process in Ethiopia because of the symbolic meaning and practical consequences of language choice. The language policy has been a tool of expanding recognition and participation for members of ethno-linguistic communities in the country, and it has undoubtedly contributed to important gains in educational enrollment as well as popular participation in some levels. But it has been an uneven good of citizenship, one that relatively larger and better-resourced groups such as the Oromo have been able to put to more direct political use than members of other language groups, whose incentives for English, if not for Amharic, are considerably greater. The Anywaa woman of the Shola market may prefer to have her children learn her language for the purposes of cultural education and ethnic uplift, but she may recognize that their economic prospects would be better served by knowledge of Amharic, or perhaps of English.

4

A Referendum on Ethnic Identity and the Claims of Citizenship

The Anywaa woman of the Shola market is not the only citizen of Ethiopia imperfectly and incompletely incorporated into modern Ethiopian citizenship regimes. Other individuals and groups, some numerically small, and some rather large in size, have contested the terms of their inclusion in recent decades, testing not only the present regime's federal system, but a century and a half of a narrative of expanding citizenship. One prominent case came to fruition in early 2001, when voters in a poor region of southern Ethiopia were presented with a unique referendum on ethnicity. The Siltie, previously considered a subclan of the Gurage ethnic group, were asked quite simply, "Are the Siltie Gurage or not?" Their answer was overwhelmingly that the Siltie were *not* Gurage. This unique exercise in voting for an ethnic identity is one of the most dramatic modern experiments in injecting direct political competition into what has traditionally been regarded as a social or cultural matter. It followed years of campaigning, both for and against Siltie separation, by members of both the ruling political party and opposition parties, and prompted debate and eventually arbitration at the highest political authority on questions of nationality in Ethiopia: the House of Federation, which had ordered the referendum.

The complex and contested meanings underlying Siltie and Gurage identities provide a critical window into the citizen-creation and citizenship-expansion processes in Ethiopia and the potential of public policy with respect to ethnic identities in the context of conflict. Vesting a decision regarding the boundaries and content of ethnicity in the hands of ordinary citizens is a somewhat unusual political maneuver. Some would call it inherently democratic, as democratic procedures were followed and the results were accepted by all major parties. This is the argument, for instance, of Laitin and Reich's "liberal democratic approach" to language policy.[1] Others would decry it as the inappropriate politicization of ethnicity resulting from the flawed and politically divisive institutional structures of federalism, and sure to lead down a slippery slope to further ethnic conflict. Even the success of the referendum itself can be contested: Was it successful because it was peaceful – no riots or clashes broke out at the time, or have done so up to the present?

The Siltie referendum is a critical test of the citizenship-expansion project that is central to the country's present federal system. The focus of analysis in this chapter is the use of sociopolitical institutions for the purpose of creating a common sense of national citizenship among Ethiopia's disparate ethnic populations, and for creating the conditions of dialogue and participation central to democracy. Conflicts over the most appropriate political institutions in a multiethnic state frequently indicate competing visions of citizenship, not just competing political interests. Different ethnolinguistic groups in Ethiopia have strikingly different visions of what citizenship should entail, and at least some of these conflicting visions represent distinct and competing institutional arrangements. It would seem that there are institutional procedures that can accommodate the fluid, situational, and constructed nature of ethnic identities while simultaneously taking the value of those identity groups seriously. But the Siltie case also suggests that citizenship expansion may entail other trade-offs among ethnic communities.

The granting of constitutional rights to "Nations, Nationalities and Peoples," rather than to individuals, inherently makes the boundary-drawing exercises between ethnic groups highly politicized. The most controversial section of the Ethiopian Constitution, Article 39, which grants to all of the country's constituent "Nations, Nationalities and Peoples" the right to self-determination, "including the right to secession," is arguably more about rights to ethnic self-determination than rights to secession, although the symbolism of the secession provision is profound. In the April 2001 referendum, members of the Siltie ethnic group voted overwhelmingly in favor of declaring themselves a distinct "nationality" or ethnic group. In addition to being an administrative and political move to separate the Siltie from the Gurage group of which they were previously a part, the referendum is a fascinating test of the role of institutions in managing conflict, promoting democratization, and

---

[1] Laitin and Reich 2003.

arbitrating between disparate identity groups. Other ethnic groups have tried to do the same, but not all attempts have resulted in the hoped-for grant of self-determination rights. Some of these are discussed in later chapters of the book.

Ethnic Self-Determination for the Siltie

Located in the Southern Nations, Nationalities, and People's regional state (SNNPR), the Siltie are predominantly Muslim and are economically poorer and less likely to migrate than the Sebat Bet Gurage, who live to the west.[2] Few studies of the Siltie people have been completed, although political and administrative changes in recent years are likely to lead to more focused research on them.[3] In the modern period, the Siltie were considered a subclan of the Gurage ethnic group.[4] Although the Gurage were understood as a loose collection of related clans, the term "Gurage" came to be operative at the national level, and subsumed the identities of ethnic groups that were distinct in certain ways, and some of which had little interaction with others.

The commonalities among Gurage groups include high levels of political fragmentation, the cultivation of *ensete*, or false banana, and cultural factors such as housing patterns. The so-called subclan distinctions mark off different languages, dialects, and religions, in addition to other social and cultural characteristics. Historian Bahru Zewde notes that the three categories of the Gurage were formed largely on the basis of linguistic studies, and that "in spite of the strong tradition of their common identity, these are mutually unintelligible categories."[5] Similarly, linguist Grover Hudson points out in his study of the 1994 Ethiopian census that "Gurage is not a single language but at least five languages."[6]

One of the most important early studies of the Gurage was an ethnographic study of one group, now referred to as the Sebat Bet (seven houses) or seven clans of western Gurage, comprising the Chaha, Ezha,

---

[2] The Gurage are known in modern Ethiopian history as successful businesspersons who are highly mobile. Even in remote parts of Ethiopia, shop owners and businesspeople tend to be Gurage. This is far less true for the Siltie (see Bahru 2003; Markakis 1998; Worku Nida 2000).

[3] Important studies of the Sebat Bet Gurage include Shack 1966 and Gebreyesus 1991; of the Soddo/Kestane Gurage by Fekadu 1972; and of the Azernet Berbere Siltie by Abraham and Habtamu 1991, which is discussed below. See also Sherif Leri 1985.

[4] Shack 1966.

[5] Bahru 2003, 20–21.

[6] Hudson 2003, 95.

Geyto, Muher, Ennemor, Akilil, and Walani-Woriro. Under the imperial administration, the Gurage formed their own *awraja* (sub-province), within which there were three politico-administrative divisions: Chaha, Walani, and Selti.[7] Since then, several scholars have contradicted or clarified some of the assumptions and assertions made in this early work. For instance, Fekadu Gadamu's dissertation on the Soddo Gurage and the Alemgana-Walamo Road Construction Association provided a critical counterargument to the developing ethnographic and historiographic representation of a pan-Gurage identity.[8] Fekadu's argument was that the Gurage do not form one cohesive society, and that many of the "generalizations and conclusions [of Shack] do not apply to the Soddos."

In addition to ethnographic and political counterclaims to the notion of a pan-Gurage ethnic identity, linguists have also reassessed the relationships between the languages and dialects of the so-called Gurage languages. Early scholarship designated as Gurage some "fourteen 'tribal' divisions in the Gurage cluster ... each comprising a number of politically independent clan chiefdoms, [and] further distinguishable on the basis of the language or dialect spoken by each tribal unit."[9] Recent scholarship, rather than ignoring significant linguistic and politico-territorial differences, has corrected the historical tendency to cluster the Gurage linguistically. Hudson notes twelve to fifteen recognized varieties, "within which six or seven languages and/or dialect clusters may be distinguished, in three distinct groups," the northern (Soddo), western (Chaha), and eastern. He also notes that the "eastern Gurage languages are more divergent from western and northern Gurage languages than, for example, Amharic is from Tigrinya."[10]

The history of linguistic and ethnographic contributions to the construction of a pan-Gurage identity is only part of the story. More recently, John Markakis has developed these insights in his argument for the "contextual, multidimensional and fluid" nature of ethnic identity through a brief study of Gurage ethnic-identity formation. He argues that the clan (*bet*) provides the primary source of identity for the western

---

[7] Shack 1966, 67.
[8] Fekadu 1972, 3.
[9] Shack 1974, 94.
[10] Hudson 1994, 692; Shack (1974) reviews the classifications of Gurage speakers given by various scholars of the time. Significantly for our point, all agree on the separation of an eastern (prominently including Siltie) and a western cluster distinction, although strangely, these languages have not been distinctly counted in subsequent censuses (1994 or 2007).

Sebat Bet Gurage, territoriality (*ager*) for the Soddo or Kistani Gurage, and religion for the Siltie speakers of the east. In fact, Markakis concludes that historically there was no group who self-identified as Gurage, and that the Siltie speakers would traditionally have identified themselves as "Muslims," something consistently confirmed in focus groups throughout Siltie in 2003.[11] What is significant for our purposes is Markakis's conclusion that, while the notion of a cohesive and united entity known as Gurage did not come from within those groups who were classified as such, it suited the Gurage to develop this "pan-Gurage universe." This was useful both to expand social networks in urban areas and to provide the Gurage with political and economic currency when dealing with Ethiopian imperial authorities.[12]

It is surprising that the Transitional Government of Ethiopia (TGE) and later, the Ethiopian People's Revolutionary Democratic Front (EPRDF), unproblematically built federalism on ethnographic work of the Derg regime. This is a little-known fact, buried in the 1994 census, nowhere mentioned in early TGE proclamations, the 1995 Constitution, or other related government policy statements such as the National Education and Training Policy (NETP), and never discussed by supporters or opponents of the federal arrangement. In fact, the EPRDF, despite a stated interest in the self-determination of all nations and nationalities in the country, has done little to contribute to either scholarly or public discussion on the content and nature of ethnic group identities. In the case of the Siltie, by using ethnic categories from previous regimes, the EPRDF itself laid the groundwork for the contentious issue of Siltie self-determination. In this, the work of the Derg's Institute for the Study of Ethiopian Nationalities (ISEN) represents the most systematic and thoughtful attempt to conceptualize and standardize the terms and categories of ethnicity and language in Ethiopia. This is recognized in the 1994 census, which explicitly attributes the ethnic and linguistic categories it uses to those that were created by the ISEN.[13]

The Politics of Self-Determination for the Siltie

Scholarly research, state- and nation-building imperatives, and a historic lack of precision with regard to defining ethnic or linguistic groups, all colluded to create a murky and ambiguous terrain for federalism

---

[11] Markakis 1998, 130
[12] Markakis 1998, 134.
[13] For more on the ISEN, see Chapter 2 and L. Smith 2005, 2007.

in Ethiopia. It is of little surprise that earlier regimes, particularly that of Haile Selassie, had intentionally subverted the clear development of indicators of ethnolinguistic identity and categorization. The nationalist vision of modern Ethiopia has always been of one dominant culture, unified not only territorially but culturally. On the other hand, despite the contribution of the ISEN's work, especially the preparation of the *Almanac* of ethnic groups on which the present-day institutions of federalism rest, there had yet to emerge clear criteria for determining ethnic group boundaries, nor was there a procedure for arbitrating disputes or contested claims. The Siltie pursuit of recognition as a distinct "nationality" under federalism has resolved procedurally, if not politically, essential political and constitutional questions.

Despite some precedence for a political designation that was pan-Gurage in content, the Siltie mobilized early in the transitional period to receive status as a separate nationality. This is attributable to several factors worth considering here, including change and continuity in administrative and political categories of ethnic groups and evolving social relations among Gurage groups as well as nationwide. The position of Siltie ethnic group members with regard to their earlier designation as Gurage is unclear. Some indicate that the experience of subjugation and exploitation under Emperor Menilek united the Siltie with their Gurage neighbors. "They saw themselves as the same because of this mistreatment."[14] The Siltie experienced military conquest and processes of labor displacement caused by their unequal incorporation into the Ethiopian empire similar to that of the Gurage, although they tended to remain more rural and considerably poorer than the Gurage. There are also historic patterns of interaction between the groups, particularly in border towns and regions. Yet in these same areas where Siltie came into contact with Gurage and Hadiya, they were also more likely to become aware of their difference, as they were often referred to as *not* Gurage or Hadiya by members of those ethnic groups.[15]

Even prior to the referendum and the separation, the Siltie pushed for the use of their own nationality language in their own administrative districts (*woredas*). At a symposium on the question of language policy, the Siltie decided in about 1992/1993 to use their own language, and informed the Gurage zone administration.[16] This was facilitated in part

---

[14] Interview #85.
[15] Interview #85.
[16] Interview #67.

because the Siltie language was one of the languages of the Derg's literacy campaign, and therefore more educational materials were available in the language.[17]

Today, most agree that unequal development was a primary impetus for Siltie separation. It was argued that the location of Welkite, the Gurage zonal capital town, was too far away, and the isolation meant that the Gurage zone government was not adequately addressing the development needs of the Siltie.[18] When the economic development gains did not materialize, resentment built against Gurage leadership, and a sense of distinct Siltie suffering emerged. A political organization called the Siltie Gogot Democratic Party was formed in the early 1990s, calling for separate Siltie representation and self-administration based on the claim that the Siltie were a distinct nationality. Later, there was a split and a new party, the Siltie Peoples Democratic Unity Party (SPDUP), was formed. Shortly thereafter, anti-separation Siltie formed the Siltie Gurage People's Democratic Movement, apparently funded by a wealthy Siltie merchant.[19] Finally, the Gurage themselves mobilized to oppose the separation. The Gurage People's Revolutionary Democratic Movement (GPRDM), which controlled the Gurage zonal government, used its power and influence to work against the separation.[20]

The political wrangling was played out in the early years over questions of ethnography and identity. The distinctions among the Gurage groups, including particularly the Soddo Gurage and the Siltie, were important from the very beginning of the federal arrangement. During the initial stages of designing and building federalism, only two Sebat Bet Gurage representatives attended critical early meetings of the TGE, and intragroup representation concerns led to the development of procedures for determining which of the three main Gurage sections (east, west, north) would represent the Gurage on the two seats they were allotted on the Council of Representatives. Particularly after the establishment of the EPRDF affiliate, the GPRDM, the splits between these groups became political, with the first important conflicts between Soddo Gurage in the north and their Oromo neighbors, known as the Soddo Jida. This involved the call for the Oromo of the region, known as the Soddo Jida, to be included as part of the new Oromiya regional state government,

---

[17] Interview #54.
[18] Markakis 1998; interview #67.
[19] Markakis 1998, 142.
[20] GPRDM is the Gurage arm of the EPRDF umbrella.

rather than part of Gurage zone in SNNPR, despite the close connection between Oromo and Soddo Gurage in this area. Somewhat later, but still early in the transitional period, the Siltie began to agitate for separate status, based primarily on their Muslim identity, distinct language, and relative underdevelopment.[21]

The early period of Siltie mobilization was characterized by attention to developing local ethnographies and a unified discourse of Siltie identity, followed by what could be called a civil-society building phase. In particular, Siltie from the Azernet Berbere area, who were contributors to the important Gurage Road Development Association but had not reaped the expected development benefits from the association's work, formed their own association. This association sponsored a report that was to be written by two university professors. There were some who wanted the report to focus on the Siltie people as a whole, while others pushed for the study of the Azernet Berbere people only. This is in part because of the distinct identity development of the Azernet Berbere Siltie, who are the most rural and remote of the Siltie. Azernet Berbere was administered as part of Hadiya region under Haile Selassie and the Derg. This is where Siltie identity developed most distinctly, as the Azernet Berbere Siltie were the most removed from the Gurage. This development involved the creation of associations and eventually, political parties that could advance Siltie interests in the political realm. A short time later, these Siltie political parties began to pursue legal and constitutional recognition of the Siltie ethnic group, an unprecedented move in Ethiopian political history. The constitutional provisions of federalism concern themselves directly with questions of self-determination of ethnic groups, requiring the establishment of procedures for groups to be delineated as such, thereby qualifying them for self-determination.

Because the constitutional and institutional framework attached primary political importance to ethnic groups, determining ethnic group boundaries emerged as a pivotal political exercise, and the Siltie case became the test for claims to autonomy and distinct identities. Until this point, it is unclear how groups were or were not designated as separate

---

[21] Markakis (1998, 143) also summarizes the claims to separation from the Kabena of northwestern Gurageland, and the Wollene of northern Gurageland. At least one Siltie respondent noted the conflict over the Wollene in interviews in 2003, although it appears that the Wollene are for the time being considered part of the Siltie. The Kabena are still administered by Gurage zone, although they are the only *woreda* of the zone to be teaching in their nationality language, while the rest of Gurage zone uses Amharic as the medium of instruction (interview #58).

ethnic groups. The ambiguous legal nature of ethnic group specifications, however, could not continue, as the distinctions between groups involved tremendous political and economic resources, not to mention social status. As one EPRDF document itself states, "Without resolving such nationality issues the building of a stable democratic society and progress in the political and economic life of the people cannot materialise." Interestingly, the position of the party was that "in most cases there was no ambiguity in the ethnic identity of the people of Ethiopia ... [but] that there has occurred one case which has special attention" – the case of the Siltie people.[22]

At this point, those in favor of separation for the Siltie made a petition to the House of Federation. The House of Federation's decision initially was that this matter must be handled at the regional level, if at all possible.[23] Thereafter, a meeting was organized in the town of Butajira in 1997, with representatives from various parts of the Siltie community. Butajira is a town in what is now Gurage zone but on the road to Worabe, bordering the new Siltie zone. It is considerably closer to the Siltie region than Welkite, the capital of Gurage zone, which is on another main road. The importance of proximity should not be underestimated, as access to decent roads between towns can make all the difference in the perception and realization of development objectives. Rival political parties were present, as were regional and zonal officials of the dominant party, the EPRDF/GPRDM. A resolution at the end of the meeting opposed separation, and the matter was considered closed by the ruling party. But there is strong evidence that the ruling party's position against the separation inhibited free discussion and nullified the decision of the group assembled. As one respondent noted, "The people did not feel free because the EPRDF was campaigning strongly that the separation was wrong."[24] The EPRDF's own report on the issue concluded that "the fact that EPRDF took a position on the matter threw doubt on the sincerity

---

[22] EPRDF n.d.b, 1.

[23] Because the constitution is clear that nations and nationalities, through their regional state governments, have the right to self-administration, there were questions of authority, particularly whether the House of Federation is the first-instance court in such cases. It was determined that the right of self-administration (self-government) made this question one on which the Regional Council should make a decision, as provided for by the constitution. The House of Federation would only become involved if the regional government could not make a decision in two years, or if the plaintiffs were unsatisfied with the regional government decision (interview #23).

[24] Interview #85.

of the ballot to many observers.... This made the Butajira conference and its outcome undemocratic."[25]

The initial position of the EPRDF was that the Siltie were indeed part of the Gurage ethnic group. According to one respondent close to the process, the feeling of the EPRDF was that they were the same people, only speaking different languages, and that they would "evolve as Gurage.... [Whereas] the population [of Siltie] as a whole is more inclined to see themselves as different."[26] But even the ruling party acknowledged that the Siltie people had a distinct language, and since language was a primary designator of ethnic group identity under the ISEN studies that were foundational to the boundaries of federalism, it could not resolve this anomaly. The EPRDF report [27] cites three reasons for the "growing nationalism" of the Siltie people: a distinct language, a clearly defined territorial boundary, and the "absence of a strong local economy." Therefore, the party admitted that they "mishandled" the matter from the start. The EPRDF report on the matter states that the party "failed to appreciate the rise of nationalism and misconstrued this trend, fearing it might lead to the break-up of the Guraghe people.... At the start of the campaign the EPRDF took a defensive position. It felt it had to take a stand on the identity of the Siltie and therefore supported the unity of the Guraghe people as one body. EPRDF has always struggled for the unity of people but in this instance this support was misplaced."[28]

This "recognition" by the EPRDF appears to have allowed or at least facilitated the legal process undertaken by separatist opposition political parties, particularly the SPDUP. Once the matter was brought before the House of Federation the second time, it was sent to the Council of Constitutional Inquiry, which is tasked by the constitution to consider in depth any issues relating to the nations and nationalities and make a recommendation to the House of Federation for a vote.[29] Their recommendation in 1999 demonstrates that the council saw the constitutional issues at hand to be twofold: (1) "According to the FDRE Constitution, who has the power to decide about the identity of a given group of people?"

---

[25] EPRDF n.d.b, 2.
[26] Interview #85.
[27] EPRDF n.d.b, 2.
[28] EPRDF n.d.b, 2.
[29] Articles 61–68 of the constitution specify the role of the House of Federation, particularly its mandate to "interpret the Constitution" through the organization of the Council of Constitutional Inquiry for all "issues relating to the rights of Nations, Nationalities and Peoples to self-determination, including the right to secession." Ethiopia 1995.

and 2) "What procedure should be followed to do that?"[30] Within the council's decision is therefore to be found the most explicit procedural answer to the political question of determining ethnic identity under the new federal arrangement.

Because the Council understood the Siltie case as an issue of self-determination, particular provisions of the constitution were considered for their relevance. Articles 39(4), 47(3), 52(2), and 62(3) were considered to be most relevant to the "question of identity" (*mannennet teyyaqe*). The recommendation of the Council was that "a demand for the determination of identity must be entertained by the Council of the State where the issue is raised" because of the requirements of Article 52(2). But "if there is a procedural irregularity or complaint that the issue was not resolved in accordance with the constitution; or if there are similar reasons, or if the group and the state council do not agree, the case will be submitted to the House of Federation for a final decision." However, Article 39(5) was seen to have some bearing with respect to determining the procedures for the group to make their wishes known. In particular, the "State Council to which the case is submitted is expected to conduct research that is cognizant of the conditions under Article 39 (5) and then present the case for referendum. For the referendum to be democratic and fair, the members of the group which has raised the demand must participate directly, and the process should be free and held by a secret ballot." The use of a referendum as the procedural answer was argued to be provided for by Articles 39(4), and 47(3) of the constitution, which relate to secession and statehood, respectively.

As provided by the constitution, this recommendation went for a vote by the House of Federation, which supported the Council's recommendation. Thus, the historic decision of the House of Federation was that the Siltie had made a sufficient case for their status as a distinct nationality to at least have the right to a referendum on the matter. The question on the ballot was simply: "Are the Siltie Gurage or not?" A referendum held on April 1, 2001, in the Siltie area and other places where the Siltie lived resulted in a vote of more than 99 percent for the separation of the Siltie from the Gurage. Siltie residents in Addis Ababa were reported to have taken to the streets to "express their happiness on the results of the referendum."[31]

---

[30] EPRDF "Constitutional Right: The Question of Identity", n.d.b. I use an unofficial copy of the Siltie case, and a translation done by a senior law student at Addis Ababa University.

[31] *Addis Tribune* April 13, 2001.

The economic, political and administrative results have proved significant for the Siltie people. Moving from the status of several *woredas* within Gurage zone, the Siltie now have their own zone, with the attendant resources and direct access to higher levels of administration. Officials at zone administrative offices, some of whom had previously performed their duties for the Siltie area from the Gurage zone offices in Welkite, reported that the location in Worabe, which is inside the Siltie area, and the greater financial resources, were both tangible signs that the referendum had given the Siltie a greater share of the political and economic power they needed and deserved. By late 2003, a number of new government and private buildings were under construction along the main road. Several self-help organizations with links to urban entrepreneurs were advertising their work in schools, as well as other poverty-alleviation and development projects. A large mosque was under construction just as one entered Worabe from the north.

Echoing the words of the EPRDF report, although presaging them, the council concluded that the important constitutional principle "is that the group itself is the decision-maker. Thus, the House of Federation and the State Council's role should be seen in light of that."[32] This historic decision of the House of Federation and the outcome of the Siltie referendum mean that future decisions about who is an ethnic group and who is not will be decided procedurally according to processes somewhat similar to those for secession and statehood, notably a referendum of the people concerned.[33]

It is instructive to note that the position of the EPRDF was initially focused on the "unity of Ethiopian peoples," and therefore the party leadership considered the Siltie to be part of the Gurage. One respondent close to the issue said that, while "unity could not be forced," the party has long been of the view that "the people do not want disintegration and they do not want their own mini-states. They have common interests and the same problems."[34] This is quite a different view from that claimed by the EPRDF's opponents, who cast the regime as interested either in eternal divisions as part of its divide-and-rule strategy, or in breaking up the country completely. By grounding its initial opposition to the Siltie separation in the complex question of unity versus separation, but still being willing to acquiesce when it was clear that popular opinion was not with them,

[32] EPRDF n.d.b.
[33] Baylis 2004.
[34] Interview #85.

it could be argued that the EPRDF advanced a certain type of citizenship expansion in this process. In the early days of the federal arrangement, the EPRDF struggled with the contradiction between upholding constitutionally protected rights to self-determination and maintaining the unity of the country at the most basic level. Sometimes it has come down in favor of unity – particularly, it would seem, when unity as a political principle coincided with retaining a firm hold on central power.[35]

Popular Responses to the Referendum in Siltie

Relatively little has been understood about the perceptions of Siltie and Gurage citizens themselves regarding the goals and outcomes of the Siltie referendum. While the electoral response to the referendum was a resounding affirmation of Siltie identity, we have little data by which to track the change over time in Siltie attitudes toward self-determination. Even earlier studies, such as John Markakis's article from the late 1990s, do not give much attention to the popular sentiment at the time. What were the motives of the Siltie, and what do they perceive to have gained (or not gained) from the separation?

In 2003, in addition to asking the standard set of questions about language policy in the region, we asked Siltie and Gurage parents a series of additional questions specifically focused on the 2001 referendum.[36] Siltie parents and teachers in the zone reported almost unanimously that they had participated in the referendum, that they had voted to separate from the Gurage, and that they were happy with the decision to separate.[37] Typical reasons given for the desire for separation were the distinct language, culture, and religion of the Siltie. A member of the government said that issues of language had always loomed large in Ethiopian politics because "if you dismiss language, you dismiss people."[38]

The Siltie Response
The Siltie, like other ethnic groups in Ethiopia, have nuanced understandings of how their ethnic identity is constructed and how their separate

---

[35] The Wagagoda language incident and the subsequent breakup of North Omo zone is another example of this. See Chapter 3 of this text and Vaughan 2006.

[36] See Appendix IV for those questions asked in Siltie and Gurage zones related to the Siltie referendum.

[37] Only one Siltie parent, an elderly illiterate peasant woman, did not vote, although she had heard about the referendum. A few Siltie teachers also did not vote because they were out of the area for a training workshop.

[38] Interview #85.

identity contributes to the unity of Ethiopia. They are generally in agreement that separate ethnic identities, and language development in the zone, will not harm the unity of Ethiopia. At the same time, they described feelings of shame and loss of identity associated with being included in a Gurage grouping. There was a distinct link between attributes of ethnicity for the Siltie, particularly language and religion, and the sense that their inclusion under a pan-Gurage umbrella of identity had robbed them of the fullest expression of that identity.

Interestingly, whereas intellectuals and even Siltie political leaders cited the economic marginalization that preceded the referendum, and that for many explains the political impetus for the separation, none of the parent or teacher respondents noted Siltie-wide underdevelopment as the reason for the referendum. A couple of respondents cited specific individual costs, including a preference for Gurage over Siltie in hiring. But many more cited the constitutionally protected right to "be a nationality," by which we can infer that they meant the right to self-determination guaranteed in Article 39, as well as the language and culture-promotion provisions of the constitution. There was enough political education along the way for many respondents to use the language of rights and democratic rights in their explanations. For others it was a question of representation, implying the link between designation as a distinct nationality under the federal arrangement and having ethnic representation and political influence. Many were cognizant of the perceived threats to Ethiopian unity raised by the separation vote and were interested to dispel those ideas, signaling their "patriotism" as Ethiopians first, Siltie second.

Who told you to vote? How did you learn about the referendum?

It came from the high officials. (Siltie town parent)

The *kebelles* ordered us to vote. (Siltie town parent)

As it was heard from the mass media, it means it was by the central government. According to the chain, it came up to the *kebelles*. So it was told on the mass media that there would be a vote. (Siltie rural parent)

It came from above. (Siltie town teacher)

Why did you vote in the referendum?

It is to confirm that we are Siltie. (Siltie town parent)

Since Siltie, like other nationalities, has a language and a culture, therefore a chance has been given to other nationalities, and I wanted the chance to be given to Siltie too. Therefore, I voted. (Siltie town teacher)

Why we wanted to vote is because of influence.... There were also people who died. Now we are past all that. I want to thank Allah for achieving this. I cannot finish telling the influences we were in [*sic*]. There were many who died and who were imprisoned. There were many who were forced also to pay a tax for three years. The story is much. I cannot finish now saying all that. We got to be Siltie by struggle. We reached to this, after struggling and finishing all that we have for eight years. There was a time that our children were banned not to pass by the gate side. It is better if you do not remind us of that. (Siltie rural parent)

Why we asked to be Siltie and why we voted was [because] EPRDF made the law that every language should be respected. Siltie is Siltie, not Gurage. Siltie must be separated from Gurage. We are two different people. We have no relation in culture, custom, and many things. We have no common relation. That is why we voted, to get our right. (Siltie rural parent)

It is good to tell the truth. We are Siltie. We go to the office and can speak in our language. We will not be afraid and ashamed when we speak in Siltigna. That is why we wanted to speak in our language. We know we are Siltie from our mother, father, and ancestors. That is why we wanted to vote for Siltie. (Siltie town parent)

Are you happy with the decision of the Siltie people to separate from the Gurage? Why or why not?

When people say, "You are Siltie, you are our relative," I am happy. When my people win, of course I am happy. (Siltie rural parent)[39]

Before, the possibility to get work when we were in Gurage, the margin was narrow ... there was influence by the Gurage, especially to get a job. They would ask if we are Gurage or Siltie. (Siltie rural teacher)

We want Ethiopia to be one and united. Of course we do not want division into nations and nationalities. This division came from the government. We do not want the division into nations and nationalities. Even we Siltie people and Gurage people want to live together. (Siltie rural parent)

We have not brought this idea. This is a proclamation from the government. This follows the right that was given to the other nations and nationalities. There is no reason that Siltie is not led by Siltie. The case is based on this. The question of Siltie people is not about the separation of Siltie people and Gurage people. (Siltie rural parent)

The Gurage Response

Fieldwork in neighboring Gurage zone revealed a marked difference in perception in that area about the referendum. The Gurage respondents from two *woredas* of the zone were also almost all aware of the purpose and outcome of the referendum in Siltie but expressed the view that the Gurage include the Siltie. The Gurage, at least the Sebat Bet Gurage,

---

[39] Interestingly, this is the one Siltie parent (and the one woman respondent in this area) who did not vote in the referendum. She is also the respondent who said she never attended school meetings.

seem to have a view of Gurage heterogeneity that incorporates linguistic and religious differences within the category of Gurage. The pan-Gurage conception of citizenship that scholars such as Markakis has described does seem to resonate with the average Gurage peasant.[40]

Significantly, the non-Siltie Gurage, which includes the Sebat Bet and Soddo and Kestane Gurage, were not involved at all in the political process regarding the Siltie decision. They did not submit a written position or participate in the pre–House of Federation decision meetings, nor were they given the opportunity to vote on the same question: "Are the Siltie Gurage or not?" Perhaps some would assert that they should not have had a vote. It can also be argued that the larger Gurage grouping has political and administrative incentives to oppose a separation of the Siltie, or any other subclans, since clearly Gurage as a numerical and political category decreased in size with the results of the referendum.

The EPRDF recognized the Gurage resistance to the referendum implicitly in its report on the matter. It was concluded that "the rest of the Guraghe people needed to be reassured that by raising the question of identity, the Siltie people were not negating their historical and cultural ties fostered over many centuries. The Siltie people were asserting their constitutional right to recognition of their nationality. The exercise of this constitutional right shows the maturity and strength of our democracy. This fact should be celebrated by both the Guraghe as well as the Siltie."[41] The House of Federation's ruling, while affirming the right of a nationality to self-determination, did not address the role of the larger community of nations and nationalities who are surely also parties to at least some self-determination disputes.[42]

When conducting fieldwork in the area it was clear that the Gurage do not generally celebrate this result at all. Most were not happy with the results of the referendum. All felt that the Siltie *are* part of the Gurage and that the Siltie vote was a reflection of manipulation by political elites interested in advancing their own political positions. They were unsympathetic to the factors that may have led the Siltie to support separation. Especially along border areas with Siltie (such as Chenchen), there is tremendous pressure caused, in part, by the language policy differences. At Chenchen Primary School, teachers and the school director acknowledged that most of the students are mother tongue speakers of

[40] Markakis 1998.
[41] EPRDF n.d.b, 3.
[42] Baylis 2004, 567.

Silti, but the school, because it is in Gurage zone, teaches in Amharic. The nearby high school is Silti- speaking. The primary school uses Amharic, purportedly at the request of the parents.[43] Gurage is an interesting zone for study not only because of the Siltie referendum but also because it is one of the few nationalities in the country that has chosen to continue the use of Amharic in education and zonal government, and this despite having even more resources for nationality language development than other poorer ethnic groups do.

What is your opinion about the results of the Siltie referendum and the separation?[44]

The separation brings no benefit. It is better to remain together developing the country in cooperation. (Gurage rural parent)

Some people are trying to spread hatred through the societies. These people agitate the illiterate society on the basis of the society's language and culture. I am sad to see such types of political activities which are trying to reverse the respectful approach of the two societies. They are thinking not to develop the country. It is rather for their own benefit to get political power. (Gurage rural teacher)

I believe that unity is strength. Working together leads to the required result and more development. I do not think unity retards the country. Separation brings failure with no other result. As they said, few people are trying to get political power but it is not for the sake of the people. (Gurage rural teacher)

This is a political question. As I know in history, Siltie is Gurage. But now after EPRDF controlled the country, due to the right in the constitution, they said that they have to separate from the Gurage. According to their right, their separation has no problem but when they say they are not Gurage, it touches our feelings deeply. (Gurage rural parent)

We are very sorry for their separation because we are neighbors. The coordination, harmony, and unity will lead us to development. They said that they are not Gurage, but instead if they say for us that we are Siltie, we happily live with them together. (Gurage rural parent)

Conclusion

The Siltie referendum is an interesting test of some critical assumptions of procedural and institutional models of linguistic and ethnic justice.

---

[43] This was the claim of the school director in our interview. He said that the parents signed a petition saying they wanted their children to learn in Amharic, not Silti.

[44] Prior to this question, I had asked respondents if they had heard about the referendum. All respondents knew of the referendum and the result.

The question of ethnic identity was central and was subjected to political contestation through a process of meetings, petitions to government entities, constitutional interpretation, and, eventually, a referendum. Critically, it was a peaceful process, remarkable in light of the tensions surrounding ethnicity and language in the country.

The Siltie case may be the only significant example in two decades of the peaceful use of formal political institutions to resolve competing ethnic group claims in Ethiopia. Consideration of the failures – ethnic conflicts that might qualify for institutional resolution but either have not been pursued or have not been successful in resolving the conflict – provide an even more complex picture of how formal institutions are an incomplete solution to the conflicts of identity between ethnic groups.[45] Asnake also considers the issues along the Somali-Oromiya borders in this context.[46] And in other work, I provide specific examples, such as the Sidama conflicts in 2002, the ongoing Oromiya-Somali border disputes, and the violence in Gambella in late 2003.[47]

For each of these three examples, there are myriad others. Rather than being just a few discrete conflicts based on ethnic identity, there are in fact quite a number of dissimilar and low-intensity conflicts across the country. Although I have suggested that there are considerable implications of not including the Gurage in the referendum process, the relatively successful resolution of the Siltie case to date reflects an exception to the rule rather than the standard by which federalism can be judged. In part it is the rarity of such peaceful and institutionalized responses to ethnic disputes, no matter how great the level of political violence that precedes them, that makes the Siltie case important. Nevertheless, the peaceful resolution does suggest the potential for institutional and legal processes to resolve disputes rather than deepening and strengthening conflict. In Ethiopia, the House of Federation and the Council of Constitutional Inquiry are powerful democratic institutions yet to be fully utilized for democratic processes or outcomes.

The institutions of federalism have in some cases peacefully arbitrated and managed conflicts, particularly ethnic conflicts. At times,

[45] Baylis (2004, 570) has an interesting discussion of Oromo claims for self-determination as a counterexample to the Siltie case. I agree with her that the Siltie and Oromo cases are different in both the character of the disputes and the identity of groups involved, but I think there are better examples than the Oromo question, which one might expect to have found institutional resolution, but which in fact have not.

[46] Asnake Kefale Adegehe 2009.

[47] L. Smith 2005.

the institutions have demonstrated a surprising flexibility in resolving ethnic conflicts, as the Siltie case illustrated. Rather than hardening ethnic claims, the House of Federation and the Council of Constitutional Inquiry in particular have been pivotal tools of citizenship expansion. Yet, in a number of other cases, these institutions have not been utilized at all, and in other cases they have not been so successful. For instance, there have been no national tests of the unequal citizenship of members of ethnic communities from the emerging regions like our Anywaa woman of the Shola market. Such a case might theoretically have emerged in Addis Ababa or in Gambella, where multiple, violent, and unresolved ethnic and regional clashes have led to an appalling loss of life and property for members of different communities. As we shall see, there have been no such legal or constitutional tests of her citizenship as a woman either, although we might have expected such. As I discuss in the next chapter, the single most important citizenship test of future decades in Ethiopia, the question of Oromo terms of citizenship, has also not been addressed through the institutions of federalism. In part, these failures result because the institutions have not been merged with the process of social discourse about the nature and terms of meaningful citizenship in the contemporary Ethiopian state.

5

No Going Back on Self-Determination
for the Oromo

Perhaps no other ethnolinguistic group's experience better illustrates the complex and contested realities of ethnic politics in the modern Ethiopian state than that of the Oromo people. Although the largest ethnic group in terms of population size, they have been understudied historically and their people subjected to intense political and social pressures for assimilation and acculturation. Recent scholarship on the Oromo people has enabled a fuller discussion on their place in regional history. This includes study of the internal social and political dynamics that led to the formation of an "Oromo people," the various subclan groupings that constitute the Oromo, and, particularly, their historical relationship to both the historic highland empire and the modern Ethiopian state. Considerably less, however, has been written about the implications of contemporary political processes on Oromo identity and, especially, about the accomplishments and limitations of citizenship expansion for members of the Oromo ethnic community.

In particular, the study of the Oromo question in Ethiopia today demonstrates that on matters of identity politics and citizenship, there can be no turning back on strides made in citizen creation and meaningful citizenship for members of ethnocultural communities. Although there are vocal challenges made by those opposed to federalism, these are often veiled attempts to return to an assimilationist or structurally Amhara-dominant political system; it is nearly impossible to imagine such an outcome. This is in large part because of the tremendous impetus to regional self-determination provided by the Oromos' embrace and successful implementation of reforms in this direction. I will describe the extent of this with regard specifically to language policy and self-determination claims, arguing that any and all future political configurations will have to incorporate meaningful autonomy on matters such as language but including at the very least other cultural and identity matters.

The significance of this is the realization that citizen formation and citizenship expansion is a forward-moving process, even if it harks "back" in language and imagery. The nationalist nostalgia is found in icons of identity, such as the pictures of the stately Emperor Haile Selassie in his military attire that grace the walls of many Amhara homes and businesses around Ethiopia and around the globe. As well, the battles over national symbols such as monuments and tourist destinations within Ethiopia represent deeply contested notions of what is Ethiopia, past and present. For instance, some in Ethiopia campaigned extensively to have a replica of Emperor Tewodros's cannon erected in a prominent square on Churchill Road in downtown Addis Ababa. But for many ethnic groups, these symbols of the empire are insulting as they represent the conquest of their people. As one Oromo intellectual phrased it, we need a "day of national day of mourning ... not more statues of Tewodros' cannon in the squares of our towns."[1]

In addition to the majority groups' fear of what citizenship expansion means for them within Ethiopia, there is an insistence, more likely to come from those members of formerly oppressed ethnolinguistic groups, that what we are seeing is in fact not a genuine and meaningful flourishing of ethnic self-identification. Rather, they point to the political dominance of ethnic elites in the ruling party and the majority of important political positions as evidence that cultural and political hegemony by the highlander minority continues even under the federal arrangement.

In a strange sort of way, both these points of view share a common negative view of federalism. The first, the Great Tradition nationalists discussed earlier, see the political events since the early 1990s as a dangerous dismantling of the foundations of unity that hold Ethiopia together. Their political assessments are full of notes of impending political doom, as if Ethiopia were about to split into two, three, or four separate countries at any moment. Whereas these dire predictions might have held some sway in the early years, particularly after the Eritrean referendum, they seem strangely misplaced today. At the same time, the ethnonationalists base their criticism on an opposite argument, asserting that the federal arrangement has done little to meaningfully empower ethnic nations within Ethiopia and that the political veneer of federalism has in fact

---

[1] Interview #61; see also Alemseged 2004, 611.

obscured central political control and ongoing domination by particular ethnic coalitions.

In this chapter I consider the citizen-creation and citizenship-expansion project for the Oromo people and their place within modern Ethiopia. I do this by looking at the present situation of Oromo citizens in Ethiopia, with a focus on educational decentralization and language policy, as well as Oromo elite perspectives on self-determination and secession under the present constitutional order. Oromo autonomy and self-determination symbolize the nationalist fear over the secession provision of Article 39 and is at the heart of debates over inclusion and integration and over what it means to be an Ethiopian. Because of their size and political and ethnic power, the Oromo represent perhaps the only significant threat to the political hegemony of northerners in the central government, in part because their withdrawal would delegitimatize any attempt at national government.[2] One observer warns that "an independent Oromia would almost certainly result in the disintegration of Ethiopia."[3]

At the same time, the Oromo have benefited from the provisions of federalism, in part because of their size and relative resource endowments. They have been able to meaningfully initiate ethnic renewal projects, particularly with regard to promotion of their nationality language, with far fewer of the resource constraints than most of the small- to medium-sized ethnic groups have faced. This means that Oromiya regional state, for instance, has developed a flourishing and generally successful policy of Oromo language instruction in primary schools in all parts of the state. They have the technical expertise and the general homogeneity of regional language to their advantage, and the spread of Oromo has proceeded apace. Although language is surely only one element of political control, if we take the centrality of language claims in earlier political and intellectual literature on the Oromo question as a crucial platform, we can assess one important element of the federal arrangement with regard to demands for full, meaningful, and inclusive citizenship. In this, the Oromo fared better than other ethnic communities

---

[2] Population figures are contentious in Ethiopia, but particularly for the Oromo people. The 2007 census puts their total population at 25,488,344, or 34.5% of the population, up from 32.1% in the 1994 census, and higher than the next largest group, the Amhara at 26.9% of the total population (down from 30.1% in 1994). These figures were controversial in 2007, as they have been for all of Ethiopia's censuses (1974, 1984, 1994, and 2007).

[3] Shinn 2004, 1.

seeking meaningful citizenship in part because of their size and relative educational backgrounds.

Critically, I do not look in this chapter at the question of political party control. The use of ethnically affiliated parties within the Ethiopian People's Revolutionary Democratic Front (EPRDF) umbrella and the centralized control and co-optation of those parties is a vital political concern to the Oromo people, but it is outside the scope of this work. The increasing use of local administrative structures to violate the most fundamental human and political rights of the Oromo and suppress genuine political representation is an alarming development that speaks to the tenuous position of Oromo self-determination and self-government.[4] I am concerned here with citizenship formation and with the centrality of language and ethnic identity to Oromo demands for self-determination and some meaningful measure of ethnic autonomy, as evidence of the relationship between institutional changes and the citizenship-expansion projects within the larger context of Ethiopia.

Oromo Nationhood: Foundations and Development

Unlike some ethnic groups whose political incorporation into the Ethiopian state was relatively recent, the Oromo people have a centuries-old history of political interaction with their Abyssinian neighbors to the north. Still, as the esteemed historian Mohammed Hassen has argued in his study of the Oromo of Gibe region, those earlier Oromo were the makers of their own history, and they lived "beyond the military control and political influence of the medieval Christian kingdom of Abyssinia" up to the early 1880s.[5] The historical relationship of the Oromo peoples to the evolving, sometimes expanding and sometimes contracting Abyssinian state is a fascinating one for which a full accounting is only beginning. Generally, the Oromo place in the recounting of this history has been peripheral. Scholarship on the important Oromo migrations of the sixteenth century, for instance, is often exaggerated tales of barbarity and violence. Oromo culture, religion, and political institutions were not taken seriously and were not treated independently. In the development of the modern state, the Oromo people formed a pivotal role as justifying the

---

[4] See Merera 2003; Mekuria 2002; Interviews #35 and 88; Medhane and J. Young 2003; Human Rights Watch 2005a; Ethiopian Human Rights Council 2003c; State Department Human Rights Reports, Pausewang 2005.

[5] Mohammed 1990, 1.

"civilizing missions" of colonial powers, in which Shoan Amhara rulers were complicit with European colonialists in their shared vision of a regional economy and subregional political hegemony.[6]

Scholarship on the historical origins of the Oromo indicates the existence of a common ancestor of the Borana and Barentu peoples, part of what are now called the Oromo peoples. It is also now generally agreed that while some Oromo were pastoral nomads, others were practicing settled agriculture and living in what is now the region of Shoa prior to the fourteenth century.[7] The Oromo ancestral homeland seems to have been the highlands of Bale. Although not a single tribe, the Oromo were groups fused together through the interaction of the tribes, through important religious and cultural institutions such as the Qallu and the *gadaa* political system, and through their steady movements, migrations, conquests, assimilations, and interactions with other groups.[8]

Much has been written about the *gadaa* in recent years, not only as a corrective to previous scholarly neglect but also as a crucial example of indigenous democratic political institutions and because of its pivotal role as a source of identity and continuity among the Oromo. The *gadaa* is a concept with multiple meanings and connotations in Oromo society, and I use Asmarom Legesse's basic definition: "a system of classes (*luba*) that succeed each other every eight years in assuming military, economic, political and ritual responsibilities."[9] Crummey notes the role that the *gadaa* played in fueling the great Oromo migrations up from Bale, into the northern and eastern regions now decimated by the bloody wars of Ahmed Gragn. He contends that "for the bulk of the sixteenth century much of the dynamic of Oromo expansion came from the need and desire of each succeeding *gadaa* to distinguish itself and enrich society" through war.[10]

The Oromo migrations of the sixteenth century were a pivotal period in Oromo history. Historian Mohammed has noted that those Oromo communities practicing settled agriculture, such as those in historical Dawaro, Ifat, Waj, and other parts of what is now southern Ethiopia, were not part of this important population migration that put the Oromo into direct conflict with the highlands tribes of the north. These migratory groups came to compose the five Oromo Gibe states that settled in

---

[6] Mohammed 1990; Holcomb and Sisai 1990; Keller 1995; Mekuria 2002.
[7] Mohammed 1990, xii; Crummey 2000, 54.
[8] Mohammed 1990, 4–17.
[9] Asmarom 1973, 8; Mohammed 1990.
[10] Crummey 2000, 54.

what is now southwestern Ethiopia around the 1570s and lived there until the late nineteenth century, at which time they were annexed by Emperor Menilek.[11] For respected scholars such as Mohammed Hassen and Donald Crummey, the Oromo population migrations of this time were less the result of the power of the invading Oromo forces as they were the consequence of many years of tremendously destructive wars between the northern Christian kingdoms and the Muslim jihadists. These wars of mutual destruction uprooted those in the zones of conflict, leaving an open swatch of territory and battered peoples, making Oromo settlement and integration with these peoples remarkably easy. Although the historical record is still limited, it is understood that this was most likely the result of a constellation of demographic and environmental pressures, the role of the *gadaa* imperative, and opportunities provided by Amhara and Tigrayan political weakness.[12]

This was the apogee of Oromo politics: when the Oromo groups dispersed geographically and developed distinctive Oromo tribal groupings, and when these groups acquired new lands and integrated with new groups of people. Some formed states (such as Jimma), and in many places sedentary or mixed agriculture assumed new prominence, even if it was not an entirely new activity for these Oromo. It was a time marked by "rapid religious, social, culture, political, industrial and commercial progress unsurpassed in any of the other Oromo areas in what is today Ethiopia."[13] In particular, the assimilation of members of other ethnic groups into Oromo identity has been emphasized by a number of scholars, as well as the learning and adaptation that occurred through increased Oromo interaction with other ethnic groups.[14]

Despite this historic independent and interactive relationship with the rulers of Christian Abyssinia, the end of the Zamana Mesafint and the consolidation of Abyssinian hegemony considerably altered the political relationship between the Oromo peoples and other groups in Ethiopia and, critically, Oromo self-identity. Most see the Oromo weakness at this time as the result of rivalry and power struggles within the Oromo leadership that prevented them from responding to the growing threat posed by neighboring rulers, as well as the superior weaponry of the Amhara to the north in particular.[15] The experience of conquest and subjugation

[11] Mohammed 1990, xiv.
[12] Mohammed 1990, 20, 27, 46; Crummey 2000, 54–60; Marcus 1994, 37.
[13] Mohammed 1990, 93.
[14] Mohammed 1990, Asafa 1993; Marcus 1994.
[15] Mohammed 1990, 197.

suffered at the hands of northern governors, administrators, and settlers in Oromo lands, particularly during the reign of Menilek and Haile Selassie, contributed most powerfully to a sense of pan-Oromo identity where one had only loosely existed previously.[16] Like other conquered peoples, the Oromo were viewed as merely subjects, not citizens of the expanding Ethiopian state, and Oromo lands were given as crown lands to the Amhara invaders and settlers. Peasants and pastoralists found that the heavy cash tax burden forced them into relations of production with Amhara landowners that were exploitative and oppressive in ways described in greater depth in Chapter 3.[17]

Although there was some resistance against the imposition of external rule, after the initial subjugation of the Oromo peoples by Menilek, there was no sustained nationalist ethnic movement among the Oromo until the early 1960s.[18] This began the period of Oromo ethnogenesis. Two pivotal moments in Oromo history, the Bale rebellion (1963–1970) and the founding of the Macha-Tulama Association, represent the development and articulation of an organized Oromo political identity in the modern era.[19] The Macha-Tulama Association was initially founded as a self-help and mutual aid organization, but it quickly became a platform for ethnic identity formation and articulation of a desire for full citizenship rights by the Oromo peoples and an important force in developing a sense of pan-Oromo identity.[20] In addition to consolidating Oromo identity and articulating cultural and political demands, the Macha-Tulama was a mass movement calling for "accommodation of differences, recognition of identity and equality of citizenship."[21] Although Haile Selassie's government

---

[16] Crummey 2000; Mohammed is one of the scholars of Oromo history who points to the developing consciousness of a unity of Oromo identity in earlier periods, particularly during the reign of Abba Bagibo, who sought to unify the Gibe region through diplomacy and political marriage (Mohammed 1990, 196); Keller 1995, 626.

[17] Keller 1995; Mohammed 1990; Gebru 1991, 129.

[18] Ezekiel (2002a) considers instances of Oromo resistance, notably the creation of the Western Oromo Confederation of 1936 under Italian rule, as evidence of long-standing Oromo opposition to Amhara/highlander rule.

[19] Gebru Tareke documents the social and economic contradictions in Bale that contributed to the rebellion, as well as its implication for Ethiopian politics (Gebru 1991; see also Bahru 1991, 215).

[20] There is a long tradition of self-help and mutual aid associations in Ethiopia. Some examples include the *iddir* (funeral associations), *iqqub* (credit associations), and *mahaber* (neighborhood associations); see A. Pankhurst and Damen (2000) and their list of sources on the topic. While serving invaluable social and development functions, they have often become important instruments of ethnic group identification, facilitating contact and mobilization and serving as springboards into more direct political action.

[21] Mekuria 1996, 59.

tried to crush the organization by banning it and later condemning its leader, Tadesse Biru, to death in 1966, the foundations of identity and citizenship had been laid. Part of the work of the Macha-Tulama Association included the "revival and preservation of the Oromo language," and they built schools and promoted literacy as part of this.[22]

In 1973, the Oromo Liberation Front (OLF) was formed by members associated with the Macha-Tulama Association. It was opposed to the Derg, and its mandate was to ensure the "total liberation of the entire Oromo nation from Ethiopian colonialism."[23] It launched a military offensive in Hararge in 1974, and later it conducted military campaigns, particularly in Wallaga in the western Oromo lands, which it launched from bases in Sudan. At times, the OLF was a significant military force and even established some kind of coordination with other ethnically affiliated military fronts such as the Tigray People's Liberation Front (TPLF) and the Eritrean People's Liberation Front. Although the OLF was given twelve seats on the eighty-seven-seat Council of Representatives of the Transitional Government of Ethiopia (TGE), its leadership quickly came to believe that the EPRDF was not a genuine democratic partner. After the EPRDF began to create political organizations to represent ethnic groups outside of its base, particularly by establishing the Oromo People's Democratic Organization (OPDO), the OLF withdrew from the electoral process and was then forced out of the coalition government.[24] Since that time it has been operating from outside the country, first in Sudan, then Somalia, and finally in Eritrea. It has continued to conduct low-intensity warfare against the EPRDF government, although there have also been several attempts at negotiations between the ruling regime and the OLF in particular.

In general, the OPDO lacks grassroots support from among the Oromo people. In some areas of Oromiya, the OLF continues to have popular local support, although it is very difficult to gauge this owing to the use of harassment and intimidation of its supporters. As Shinn notes, participants at a 2004 OLF conference in Europe "talked confidently about

---

[22] Mekuria 1997, 343.

[23] Platform of the OLF, quoted in Keller 1995, 628.

[24] Keller 1995, 630. Other opposition parties also withdrew from the electoral contests of 1994 and 1995, including the All-Amhara People's Organization, the Southern Ethiopia People's Democratic Coalition, and other smaller parties (Joireman 1997). Some of these parties rejoined the political process as opposition parties and participated in subsequent elections. The OLF is barred from standing as a registered political party because of its refusal to renounce violence as a legitimate means of political opposition.

overwhelming support but realized they have no empirical proof of that assertion.... They acknowledged that there is a certain mythology about the OLF among Oromo peasants."[25] While the OLF's grassroots support may be greater than can be substantiated, the OPDO has effectively used local government structures to control the Oromo population politically, socially, and economically. One powerful tool is to label any political opponent as belonging to or supporting the OLF, which leads to political reprisals.[26]

In other areas of Oromiya where legal opposition parties have formed, supporters and local residents alike have experienced tremendous political persecution. For instance, the politicization of invaluable development assistance such as fertilizer is often mentioned as a tool of OPDO control.[27] In 2005, Human Rights Watch issued a scathing report focused primarily on western Oromiya, documenting that the "government systematically stifles and punishes dissent and uses its coercive power to prevent genuine opposition parties from emerging."[28] In particular, this report cited the use of quasi-governmental structures in local areas to control and restrict the labor and political activities of Oromo citizens. The EPRDF has long used the Derg-era local government structures, particularly the *kebelles*, to control local populations.[29] There is little doubt that political control of the Oromo people is evidence of the limitations of the citizenship-expansion project occurring under federalism today. Earlier attempts at a negotiated settlement facilitated by international observers will undoubtedly be adversely affected by the recent evidence of increased EPRDF control over the Oromo population.[30]

Language Policy and Identity in Oromiya

Language is a matter of paramount concern to the Oromo. For decades the Oromo people resisted the imposition of Amharic language. In fact,

---

[25] Shinn 2004, 10.

[26] Human Rights Watch 2005a; Shinn 2004; Interviews #35, 27, and 28; multiple U.S. State Department Human Rights Reports.

[27] Interview #35; Human Rights Watch 2005a.

[28] See Human Rights Watch 2005a; Ethiopian Human Rights Council 2003c, 2004.

[29] Pausewang et al. 2002.

[30] Shinn provides evidence of some of these attempts, and also the stalemate created by the EPRDF's unwillingness to show good faith through, for instance, release of Oromo political prisoners (Shinn 2004, 7). Human Rights Watch reports that there are at least 25,000 Oromo political prisoners, including many Oromo teenagers, and probably many more than that number (HRW 2005).

the Oromo language, hereafter referred to as Afaan Oromo, has survived, and more recently, seen a renaissance of sorts. Nearly every book or article on the status of the Oromo focuses on the suppression and persecution of Oromo and the desire of the Oromo people to use and develop their language. Therefore, the regional government of Oromiya has invested considerable resources into the task of language development and promotion, far more than most other regional governments have been able to do.[31] The present language policy in Oromiya is highly successful in terms of standardization and pedagogy. The Oromo have benefited from the relative homogeneity of language within the regional state. There are regional variations in dialect, but most respondents indicated that the language is generally mutually intelligible across all of Oromiya. The nonprofit organization Ethnologue lists three distinct Oromo languages, but others disagree.[32] To address variations in vocabulary, the Oromiya Regional Education Bureau publishes dual vocabularies, when needed, in dictionaries and textbooks.[33] At the same time, the question of Amharic's role as the national language and its ongoing dominance in the federal government demonstrate the challenges of even "successful" language policy in regional governments under the federal arrangement.

Afaan Oromo (lit. mouth of the Oromo), often called Oromigna by Amharic speakers and outsiders, or also Oromiffa, has a long history as a spoken language.[34] Interestingly, Bender and his co-authors, in their otherwise exhaustive and meticulous study of Ethiopian languages, give no linguistic history for Oromo. One of the challenges is that Afaan Oromo was not a written language until relatively recently, unlike Amharic and its forerunner, Ge'ez. In this, it is similar to most other African languages with long-standing oral traditions and the difficult task of developing written forms in rather short order. Afaan Oromo began to be written

---

[31] Clearly, Amhara regional state has the benefit of decades of state-sponsored Amharic language development, making the policy of mother tongue instruction in that state relatively unproblematic. At the same time, the only other state that has been able to use its mother tongue extensively is Tigray regional state, but again, the benefits of long-written language development in Tigrinya, proximity to Eritrea, and access to central government resources by virtue of the power of the TPLF/EPRDF explain this.

[32] Hudson 2004.

[33] Interviews #50, 51, 52.

[34] Some readers may be familiar with the term "Galla" (the people) and Galligna (the language) are pejorative terms, widely used during the regimes of Menilek, Haile Selassie, and the Derg, but publicly discredited today (see Baxter in Markakis 1998, 55). The use of the term "Galla" in recent years has sparked incidents of violence in places such as Addis Ababa University.

during the eighteenth century by Muslim Oromo scholars producing religious literature. By the beginning of the nineteenth century "*Oromoo* was the language of correspondence for all Oromo kings and it was also the language of education, law, high culture, business and government administration."[35]

The true renaissance period for Afaan Oromo, however, was in the late nineteenth century under the leadership of Oromo Protestant evangelists, particularly Onesimos Nasib and Aster Ganno. Captured in Oromo lands as children and sold as slaves, these two were later freed and educated at a Swedish mission in Massawa, Eritrea.[36] Both demonstrated an early gift for language and interest in translation and language development. Onesimos's main linguistic contribution, with Aster's aid, was the translation of the Bible, as well as translation of many volumes of other religious literature. He also compiled an Afaan Oromo dictionary and translated secular literature, in addition to an active proselytizing and social service campaign in Neqemte, Wallaga.

Aster, in addition to serving as a valuable partner to Onesimos in his Bible translation project, engaged in her own literary and translation projects. She collected some 500 Oromo riddles, fables, ballads, proverbs, cradlesongs, love songs, and stories that she transcribed from memory, and she coauthored an Oromo literacy text, *The Spelling Book*. Like Onesimos, Aster was a prominent evangelist, and she was a powerful advocate for female education. She was instrumental in making Wallaga the first region in Ethiopia to open a school for girls, to employ female teachers, and later to ordain female priests. All of these language and literary materials, in addition to advancing Protestant missionary work among the Oromo, had a significant role in fostering Oromo literacy and elevating the status of the language and the Oromo people. Their work was supported by Oromo intellectuals and elites, particularly in the Wallaga area, despite persecution by the imperial government, in part because these written materials were such poignant cultural symbols.[37]

Because the development of Oromo language and literature coincided with the conquests of Oromo lands by the rulers of the expanding Abyssinian empire, the language itself became a critical target of the agents of the state. Regional elites and settlers, as well as the leaders

---

[35] Mohammed, quoted in Mekuria 1997, 328.
[36] For more on Onesimos, see Mekuria 2002; Bahru 2003. For more on Aster, see Mekuria 2002.
[37] Mekuria 2002, 131; Mekuria 1997, 329.

of the Ethiopian Orthodox Church, banded together to discourage the development of Oromo for disparate reasons – the former, political, and the latter, religious. But both being agents of the state, they used their influence to stem the spread of Afaan Oromo. Despite these early setbacks, Onesimos and his colleagues, with the support of the foreign missions, were able to expand their work in western Oromiya, particularly after the death of Menilek. As well, the period of Italian occupation saw the further flourishing of Oromo literature and education, and "by the end of the Italian occupation of Ethiopia in 1941, literacy in the Oromo language had made some significant progress."[38]

As discussed thoroughly in previous chapters, however, Haile Selassie's return to Ethiopia in 1941 marked a new political era. It was a time of intense centralization and consolidation of the empire. The use of Afaan Oromo was declared illegal. Literature in the language was destroyed. All formal education, including religious and missionary education, was to be conducted in Amharic, as were proceedings in all public institutions, including courts and government administrative functions. The mere possession of the Oromo Bible or other literature was illegal. Even when Haile Selassie's government initiated minute changes on the edges of the language policy, including the provision of some radio programming in Tigrinya, Tigre, Somali, and Afar in the late 1960s, Oromo was not included. This is not surprising in light of the perceived political need to prevent linguistic competition between Oromo and Amharic.[39] But it was also this same policy of Amharization that provoked and strengthened the development of ethnic consciousness among the Oromo people.[40]

In addition to the structural obstacles that the Amharic-only language policy created for Oromo education and literacy, it had a political cost. Although some may see a national language policy as important national integration, when it is accompanied by deep-rooted prejudice and discrimination, it fosters unequal integration that militates against the nation-building project. The development of modern education across Ethiopia was interwoven with patterns of discrimination and domination. Amharic was the only language sanctioned for educational use. Therefore, nearly all teachers at all levels were Amhara, because they were native speakers of Amharic and because as a group they received disproportionate access to employment and educational benefits of modernization

[38] Mekuria 1997, 331.
[39] Mekuria 1997, 341.
[40] Mekuria 1997, 335 and 1996; Keller 1995, 632.

under Haile Selassie. As one sociologist notes, "The problem was not that the teachers spoke Amharic, but the fact that children who did not speak Amharic were expected to communicate in it from the very first day of school."[41]

The educational and social inequality fostered by the policy of Amharic only was substantial. Schoolchildren were often ridiculed for their poor Amharic. The language policy meant that children struggled to comprehend their subject materials, making the relevance of their education highly suspect to parents whose daily lives were marked by the quest for survival. Children's labor was needed at home. The lack of educational relevancy and high levels of discrimination also led to very high drop-out rates among the Oromo and higher levels of illiteracy – as high as 80 percent of primary school children.[42] Acquiring some Amharic knowledge but often forced to drop out of school early, they spent their lives in a middle position – fluent but illiterate in their mother tongue, Oromo, and literate but lacking proficiency in the dominant language, Amharic. Because political participation and communication in public requires relatively high proficiency in a language, nonnative Amharic speakers such as the Oromo were denied the ability for "public articulation" of political goals and concepts because of lack of language skills.[43]

Much like the period of the Italian occupation, the Derg regime was a time of mixed benefit to the Oromo people. The land reforms had tremendous impact on the basic conditions of land ownership and economic and labor obligations under which most Oromo lived. There was also some public recognition of the rights to self-determination for members of ethnic and linguistic communities, and although Afaan Oromo was no longer banned, Amharic continued to be the official language of government at all levels. Public administration and, most notably, public schools, continued to be exclusively Amharic-language only domains. The nationwide literacy campaign was conducted in Oromo in those areas where Oromo lived, although it was taught using the Amharic script, and few resources were put into language development or promotion. By and large, however, the benefits to the Oromo were limited, as the Derg's authoritarian and centralist policies and intensified military campaigns took a heavy toll on Oromo life and productivity.[44]

[41] Mekuria 1997, 337.
[42] Mekuria 1997, 336; Balsvik 1985, 7.
[43] Interview #61.
[44] Mekuria 1997, 2002.

In light of this history, the introduction of federalism can surely be seen as a time of tremendous change for the Oromo people, particularly with regard to cultural policy and citizenship expansion. The language policy was one of the very first policy actions taken by the TGE and allowed for the immediate establishment of Oromo as the language of the Oromo people. The OLF had long stated as one of its objectives: "To develop the Oromo language and bring it out of the neglect that colonialism has imposed upon it."[45] As an early member of the TGE, it actively pursued this objective. During the Derg regime, it had promoted the use of the Latin script for the language, developed the alphabet, and even began publishing educational and political materials in Oromo.[46] After the removal of the Derg, the OLF immediately began to administer Oromo lands and began an active literacy program of Oromo using the Latin script. Even after the withdrawal of the OLF from the transitional government, the new administration of Oromiya regional state, including the leadership of the newly established OPDO, continued and expanded the language policy.

Presently, Oromo is the language of the regional state government of Oromiya. In terms of education, it is the language of instruction as well as one subject of study for grades one through eight throughout Oromiya. English is taught as a subject from grade one, and is the medium of instruction beginning in grade nine, as is the national policy. Besides Tigray and Amhara regional states, Oromiya is the only regional state that extends mother tongue instruction through grade eight. For other regions, if they have the resources or the desire to implement mother tongue instruction at all, it is only through grade four or grade six. It was suggested by at least one respondent that the ICDR had tried to insist that all regions begin instruction in English in Grade 5 and Oromiya resisted. The position of the Institute for Curriculum Development and Research (ICDR) and the Ministry of Education (MOE) is that these decisions are left up to the region, but it is likely that the MOE did try to enforce a hegemonic policy that was resisted by powerful regions such as Oromiya. One can speculate that Amhara and Tigray regions would have resisted such a policy imposition as well.[47]

In Oromiya region, Amharic is given as a subject from grade five, as was decided by the Oromiya Regional Council.[48] Because there are

---

[45] OLF Political Programme, quoted in Mekuria 1997, 347.
[46] Mekuria 1997, 348.
[47] Interview #50.
[48] Interview #41.

certain urban areas within Oromiya where there are large groups of linguistic minorities – particularly Amharic speakers – policy was developed to address this. The policy stipulated if the enrollment numbers indicated such, schools would have to accommodate the other nationality language(s) as the language of instruction. In some cases, this has required designating entire schools as Amharic speaking, but in most cases it involves setting aside particular classrooms within a school. There is a similar policy in Amhara regional state, where a zone has been created to address a substantial pocket of Oromo people living there. But there are far greater numbers of Amharic speakers in Oromiya than vice versa, primarily because of the historical settlement of Amharas under the expanding empire. Most of these Amharas are third- and fourth-generation immigrants to the region with few if any ties to the regions of the northern highlands that they left behind. Older generations tend to be bilingual in Oromo, but this was certainly not a requirement under previous governments.[49] For instance, in Bale zone, there are Amharic-language schools in Robe, Goba, and Dodola towns.[50] It is somewhat unclear how the determination of thresholds of language speakers is made and how potential conflicts are resolved on these issues. Even in these Amharic-language schools, the policy requires that students take Oromo as a subject beginning in grade five, just as Oromo speakers begin learning Amharic as a subject in grade five.[51]

In terms of the issues of resource capacity and language development that plague other regions, Oromiya is in a considerably better position. There are two language experts at the Regional Education Bureau who are devoted exclusively to language development, in comparison, for example, to Southern region, with only one devoted staff member to the twelve-plus languages of instruction in the region. Because of a relatively longer history of language and literacy development than most other languages in the country, there are more Oromo dictionaries and educational materials, more fluent speakers with advanced degrees, and a greater number of supplementary reading materials available. All of these are crucial to successful implementation of both language and subject learning. In addition, there is a higher percentage of qualified teachers in Oromiya than other regions, and it is easier to train teachers at

---

[49] Interviews #41 and 87.

[50] Interview #76.

[51] Interview #41. One respondent indicated that the policy had recently changed to require Oromo as a subject from grade one in Amharic-language schools in Oromiya, but I could not verify this (Interview #66).

the regional Teacher Training Institutes and Teacher Training Colleges, as they have only to train all primary school teachers in one language, Oromo.[52]

Yet despite some considerable structural advantages in Oromiya and a clear widespread support for the use of Oromo at all levels, similar issues, including lack of knowledge and participation in decision making, were noted in the region. One study done in 2002 found that most teachers and education experts from the Oromiya region had not been involved at all in the decision and that discussion had not occurred at any level outside of the federal government in Addis Ababa.[53] Still, they were nearly unanimous that mother tongue instruction helped "the nationality facilitate their culture … increased cognitive and pedagogical benefits … [and the] absence of language differences between home and school helps children understand and express concepts."[54] In my focus group discussions in 2003, most Oromo parents were not involved in policy formulation, although they consistently and strongly supported the use of Oromo. A number of these themes were highlighted by the comments made by Oromo parents in Chapter 3 of this book.

The question of script choice for Oromo in particular, but other also non-Semitic languages in Ethiopia, is a highly emotive one. The Oromo have chosen the Latin script as the Qubee Oromo. All of the non-Semitic language speakers have chosen, through their regional state governments and implemented through their regional educational bureaus, to use the Latin script. This decision has generally received harsh criticism from those opposed to the multilingual policy. In fact, the discourse over script represents a set of much deeper-seated feelings about Ethiopian citizenship and opposition to multilingualism. Oromo intellectuals are adamant that the Amharic script is completely inappropriate for transcribing Oromo sounds.[55] But beyond any attempts at "scientific" and linguistic conclusions about script choice, there is a tremendous symbolism to this policy action. It is a rejection not only of the Amharic language, but the very essence of Abyssinian identity, as the *fidel*[56] and the tradition of written

---

[52] Teacher Training Institutes are one-year programs that train first-cycle primary school teachers (grades one through four), while Teacher Training Colleges are two-year programs that train second-cycle primary teachers (grades five through eight). There was a policy shift to make the colleges three-year programs in 2003.

[53] Interview #76.

[54] Interview #76.

[55] Respondent after respondent repeated this same assertion during interviews in 2003. Mekuria also cites several sources on this (1997, 351).

[56] The *fidel* are the Amharic letters, and *qubee* is the Oromo word for the lettering system.

Amharic (and Ge'ez) are foundational to the monarchy, the Ethiopian Orthodox Church, and Abyssinian national myths of identity.

On a more pragmatic level, critics of the Latin script argue that it makes it all the more difficult for Oromo students, educated and literate in Oromo, to master Amharic, which is still the working language of the federal government. They fail to acknowledge, however, that it also makes comprehension and possibly mastery of English, the "international language" of Ethiopia and the language of all formal education from secondary school through higher education, that much easier.[57] This is one of the central tensions of the present national education policy with respect to language. It is undeniable that the policy of nationality languages is a political imperative that is likely to remain the policy into the distant future. The federal government, however, cannot decide which language should be the *second* language. To appease the nationalists, it has made Amharic the national language and in fact, promoted it actively through official government channels. Every aspect of the federal government, from Parliament to the line ministries to the federal judiciary, operates in Amharic. On the other hand, perhaps recognizing the global importance of English and the need for Ethiopia to carve out some kind of economic niche, the official policy designated English as the language of education beyond primary school but with very little active support or promotion. Importantly, it has not chosen English as one of its repertoire of languages to rectify the past hegemony of Amharic, or Amhara ethnic domination, and this inconsistency in its policy makes the domination of Amharic in the government a critical marker of unequal citizenship. But because English proficiency is so central to all formal education beyond primary school, it can be considered the second language, even if it is not explicitly designated as such in the National Education and Training Policy. This is highlighted by the priority given to English-language instruction over Amharic as a subject, for instance.[58]

Illustrative of the inconsistent reasoning applied to the present policy on nationality languages by its opponents is the idea that, because of the de facto dominance of Amharic, non-Amharic speakers are the ones who will suffer the most under the language policy.[59] Defending the justice of a particular policy, or the democratic (or undemocratic) nature of

---

[57] Transitional Government of Ethiopia, 1994.
[58] Consistent requests were made for improving English-language education by regional, zonal, and *woreda* education officials and school directors and teachers, particularly in Southern regional state.
[59] Teshome 1997, 398.

its formulation and implementation, cannot be done by reference to the status quo. This only reinforces the hegemony of particular ethnolinguistic groups in the country. Arguing that the use of nationality languages is unjust to non-Amharic speakers through reference to the unjust and inconsistent policy application of Amharic dominance in the federal government is a tautology. It cannot hold up to democratic scrutiny. Rather, the fundamental question of a democratic language policy involves the question of what the second working or national language of Ethiopia should be. It is an unanswered question.

Amharic continues to dominate at the federal level, contributing to resentment and concerns of alienation and charges of ongoing hegemony by members of formerly oppressed ethnic groups such as the Oromo. Some ask: Would not English be a more appropriate language of national communication, particularly in light of the current language policy? Where is a young person, educated in the regions, expected to acquire high levels of proficiency in Amharic, which is, according to the policy, the *third* language in a line of languages learned? At least one scholar has suggested that the justifications for the designation of Amharic as the federal working language are demonstrably wrong. Law professor Abera Degefa has pointed to three reasons that the policy on the federal working language should be changed: (1) the numerical size of the speakers of a certain language in proportion to the general population of the country should be considered – that is, leaving out major language groups such as the Oromo cannot be justified; (2) the numerical size of related languages should be considered, since the major Cushitic languages constitute a majority of the total population, and these groups speak languages more closely related to each other than to Amharic (a Semitic language); and finally (3) the dominance of English in the global setting requires an elevated role for it.[60]

Opponents of the present language policy often explain their position as a practical one (never symbolic or in the interests of the dominant group): How will children educated in the regions in their mother tongue communicate with others in the capital city, where Amharic dominates? It is a reasonable question when posed in such a way. But many members of minority and formerly oppressed ethnic groups such as the Oromo pose a different question: Why are we not strengthening the teaching of English, making it both the national and international language? Would this not resolve the tensions over the historic role of Amharic while also

---

[60] Abera 2003.

preparing Ethiopians to enter the global world system? It is not that members of minority groups in Ethiopia are oblivious to the challenges of selecting a language of national communication. It seems that they are concerned with the questions of justice and recognition reflected by state policy on language. Reframing the question sheds light on the ethical considerations implicit in language policy.

The Language Policy in Oromiya

The Oromo are a powerful political force in Ethiopia. Their social and political position and the status of their language are, however, ambiguous under the current government. There is little doubt that the regime has gone far, both on paper and in its actions, in granting greater rights of self-determination and cultural autonomy to nationalities such as the Oromo. The language policy in Oromiya can generally be judged a success. It has received the institutional, financial, and labor needs to become a standardized and widely used language at all levels of government and public administration, including the courts, schools, and government offices. Although slow and imperfect, educational materials, supplementary reading materials, audio programming, and other media sources and teacher training have kept pace with general trends for Amharic and Tigrinya and enabled Oromo to compete with these languages more than ever before.

Nevertheless, there are problems at the national level that even a successful language policy cannot solve. As one intellectual has commented, "Without the democratization of politics, the language policy is suspect," leading people to question the government's interest in pursuing the policy.[61] There is some evidence of government suppression of private associations that use Oromo, even in Addis Ababa. The dominance of generally illegitimate political leaders in the courts and the People's Democratic Organizations has a restraining effect on the positive aspects of the language policy.

Consistently, Oromo intellectuals point to the need for English-language ability and the contradictions in the government policy. As one respondent put it, "In Ethiopia we always talk about the past, about the 'good old days.' But the policies should reflect the present and the future."[62] This individual personally favored English as the medium of instruction in all levels of education, with the nationality languages as subjects. Not

[61] Interview #35.
[62] Interview #61.

a single Oromo respondent favored the use of Amharic as a national language, although they differed on the relative weight between English and Oromo for such a purpose. This was not confined to Oromo intellectuals but included Oromo peasants as well. A similar perspective was offered in Southern region, where linguistic diversity is far greater than in Oromiya and where English-language instruction has not been very successful. In all regions, parents and communities are equally concerned with the economic prospects for their children.

As some have noted, the evidence of central government control over regional affairs is demonstrated in the reluctance or inability of the regional states to implement even symbolic reforms reflecting regional or ethnic autonomy.[63] For instance, revised regional state constitutions, most of which were drafted in 2001 in the wake of the EPRDF's internal split and Tehadso (renewal), are largely believed to be the product of central government directives. Even when the new constitutional language contains powerful expressions of ethnic autonomy, the influence of the TPLF/EPRDF leadership has undermined these efforts. The Oromiya Regional State Constitution opens with the statement, "We the Oromo People, cognizant of the fact that we have paid enormous sacrifices, with other nations, nationalities and peoples of the country, to uproot the oppressive system which was imposed upon us and violated our human and democratic right ... and thereby threatened us as second-class citizens."[64] Article 5 clearly states that "Oromo language shall be the working language of the Regional State. It shall be written in the Latin Alphabet." Although Article 2 makes clear that the Oromiya region "is the uninterrupted territory inhabited by the people of the Oromo Nation and Other peoples who made a choice to live in the Region," Article 8 clearly states that "sovereign power in the region resides in the people of the Oromo Nation." Article 113, the last of the constitution, states that the "Oromo language version of this Constitution shall have final legal authority."

At the same time, there are some highly visible symbols of Oromo autonomy. On the road from Bole International Airport in Addis Ababa, visitors and citizens alike pass the Oromiya Regional Parliament (Regional

---

[63] Interview #9.

[64] *Magalata Oromiyaa* Proc. 46/2001 "Revised Constitution of 2001 of the Oromia Region." As mentioned previously, transliteration from Ethiopian languages into English has not been standardized, which is true as well for Oromo. The English version of the Oromiya Constitution spells the regional state name as "Oromia," although the Oromo version (in Latin script) spells the regional name as "Oromiyaa." I have chosen the somewhat conventional spelling "Oromiya" for English throughout this work.

Council) buildings, with the Oromiya regional state flag flying boldly and the large sign, in Oromo, clearly identifying the capital city as Finfinnee.[65] Other symbols of Oromo government are highly visible, particularly the *odaa* (the holy sycamore tree), which has powerful symbolism. In the shade of the *odaa*, elders met, religious duties were fulfilled, and it was the place where the assembly of Oromo gathered in the *chaffee* (meadow) to participate in debate and decision making.[66] The *odaa* tree now appears on the Oromiya flag and other public symbols of Oromo self-administration. *Chaffee* is also the name used for the modern Oromiya Regional Council. In addition, every evening, one-hour news programs in Oromo, Tigrinya, and Amharic are aired on Ethiopian Television.[67] Oromo newspapers, magazines, dictionaries, and other reading materials can be found on street corners and bookshops around town. All of these symbols of Oromo identity are extremely powerful, both for Oromo peoples and non-Oromos. They are irksome to many nationalists. Humorous and trivial tales circulate about town – my personal favorite is that organizations or individuals writing to the Oromiya regional government offices with the address of "Addis Ababa" rather than "Finfinnee" will find their mail returned unopened. This is suggestive of the power of symbols to stimulate new power configurations and threaten old hierarchies.

Besides being irritating to the Great Tradition nationalists, Oromo intellectuals more and more cite these public displays of Oromo cultural identity and political autonomy as evidence of the increasingly vacuous nature of federalism. It is nearly impossible to ascertain how important the symbolic elements of self-determination are to the rural Oromo peasant in comparison to the daily struggles of economic and political survival. It was clear from interviews in the region, however, that Oromo citizens not only support the present language policy but also would be unlikely to acquiesce to any policy reversal in the future.

Oromo Views on Ethiopian Unity

Few national constitutions in the world recognize a right to self-determination and even fewer, a right to secession. There are few

---

[65] The regional capital has officially been moved to Adama (Nazareth) and then back to Finfinee several times. A proposed move from Finfinnee to Adama is controversial among many Oromo elites and intellectuals, who see it as a capitulation of the Oromo people's special claim over Finfinee (which is recognized explicitly in the constitution).

[66] Mohammed 1990, 14.

[67] ETV is the state-owned television station.

incentives for political regimes to promulgate rights that could ultimately lead to the diminution or even dissolution of the state they control. Ethiopia's constitutional reforms of 1995 are a significant departure
from international norms because a robust right to self-determination for
ethnonational communities, including a right of secession, is guaranteed.
This is remarkable not only in the international context but in the domestic one as well, as Ethiopia's modern history has mainly been focused on
an expanding and centralizing state. The tensions between an ethos of
national unity and the demands for self-determination by some groups,
including armed movements, became particularly pronounced after the
Eritrean referendum on independence. Prominent among the Ethiopian
groups with a history of contesting both the "national unity" practice
and rhetoric are the Oromo people's movements, which have been active
since at least the 1960s in advancing the political rights of the Oromo
people. As the Oromo represent a plurality of the Ethiopian population
and occupy some of the most fertile agricultural areas in the country,
there are reasons to expect the Oromo to have organized to activate these
rights. This expectation is compounded in light of their historical as well
as contemporary marginalization and oppression.

Generally, despite a strong push for cultural and political autonomy, it
seems that the Oromo people do not favor full secession from Ethiopia,
despite the fears of Ethiopian nationalists. There have always been divisions among the Oromo leadership about the prospects for statehood
versus the possibility of full and equal citizenship within the Ethiopian
state. But there is good reason to think that the moderate leadership of
the OLF favors full inclusion of the Oromo in a democratic Ethiopian
state. In fact, the OLF is a supporter of some of the foundational principles of federalism, particularly the self-determination principle of Article
39, as well as the language policy. The political platform of the main
opposition parties from 2005 seems inimical to Oromo interests, particularly those who wish to repeal Article 39 entirely. In order to consider
the citizenship-formation processes under institutional reforms such as
federalism and the complex dynamics associated with it, it is useful to
analyze the evolving and diverse conceptions of Oromo political identity
vis-à-vis questions of national unity and self-determination.

There has been an evolution in the Oromo political identity. Some
would argue that Oromo citizens are as committed to a notion of
Ethiopian national unity as other communities within the country,
although one grounded in greater freedoms for the Oromo people, particularly expanded civil and political rights. The main contention is that

Oromo political identity, shaped as it is by elements of what we also refer to as ethnic identity, such as language, region, culture, and so on, is modern, contested, and most of all dynamic. It is not static or unitary. Not only is there a multiplicity of visions of Ethiopian citizenship, there is diversity in the vision of Oromo political identity that represents the richness of human expression, both individual and group based. As I have argued with particular reference to the Siltie referendum, institutional arrangements such as federalism are no more likely to reify ethnic identity groupings in ways that are essentialist or unyielding. While there are many interesting puzzles related to Oromo claims to self-determination and secession, the most interesting one is what Oromo views on national unity are – Oromo unity and Ethiopian national unity – and what that reveals about citizens' views of unity in the context of ethnic diversity, inequality, and institutional reforms such as federalism.

It should be noted that it is virtually impossible to ask ordinary Oromo citizens (or any Ethiopian citizen for that matter) what her views are on self-determination, secession, or the future of the Ethiopian state and Oromo politics. The Oromo people in Ethiopia have faced an increasingly hostile and defensive Ethiopian regime on such questions, and free expression has been seriously circumscribed. Some of the most significant incidents of human rights violations by the current regime have occurred in parts of Oromiya where politically active groups attempted to engage these sorts of questions.[68] During focus groups on the topic in 2003, I did ask Oromo citizens and others what they thought of the state of national unity in Ethiopia with regard to the language policy.

Meaningful Self-Determination

Article 39 symbolizes the heart of citizenship debates in Ethiopia today. It represents a substantive challenge to historic, and distinctly modern, notions of Ethiopian national identity that are grounded in specific cultural ideas – including unity, territorial integrity, and a specific ethnocultural identity. It is bitterly opposed by members of formerly dominant ethnic groups. In contrast, for ethnonationalists and members of minority and formerly oppressed ethnic groups, the inclusion of Article 39 in the constitution can be argued to have been an essential provision guaranteeing a true change in citizenship status. It was a crucial signal to members of these groups that the new regime was interested in making

---

[68] See Human Rights Watch 2005a and Advocates for Human Rights, 2009.

good on promises made decades before for ethnic autonomy, self-rule, and power sharing. Article 39 is not only about secession, but its proponents and opponents alike focus on the secession language because of the intense symbolic power of the provision.

Article 39, as discussed in Chapter 2 of this text, concerns the "Rights of Nations, Nationalities and Peoples." It is worth citing the full text here:

(1) Every Nation, Nationality and People in Ethiopia has an unconditional right to self-determination, including the right to secession.

(2) Every Nation, Nationality and People in Ethiopia has the right to speak, to write and to develop its own language; to express, to develop and to promote its culture; and to preserve its history.

(3) Every Nation, Nationality and People in Ethiopia has the right to a full measure of self-government which includes the right to establish institutions of government in the territory it inhabits and to equitable representation in the state and Federal governments.

(4) The right to self-determination, including secession of every Nation, Nationality and People shall come into effect:

a. When a demand for secession has been approved by a two-thirds majority of the members of the Legislative council of the Nation, Nationality or People concerned;

b. When the Federal Government has organized a referendum which must take place within three years from the time it received the concerned council's decision for secession;

c. When the demand for secession is supported by a majority vote in the referendum;

d. When the Federal Government will have transferred its powers to the Council of the Nation, Nationality or People who has voted to secede; and

e. When the division of assets is effected in a manner prescribed by law.

(5) A "Nation, Nationality and People" for the purpose of this Constitution is a group of people who have or share a large measure of common culture or similar customs, mutual intelligibility of language, belief in a common or related identities, a common psychological makeup and who inhabit an identifiable, predominately contiguous territory.

Interestingly, in an excellent study of the state constitutions (most of which were revised after 2001) by legal scholar Tsegaye Regassa, he notes that many of the constitutions, such as the Oromiya constitution, include language from the country's Transitional Charter regarding the conditions for seeking secession. The charter "says that secession is to be exercised when a group is denied self-rule, democracy is on the wane, and there is a violation of human and democratic rights – and these problems cannot be solved within the Ethiopian union. The Oromiya constitution says that secession is to be exercised if the group is 'convinced that the rights under Art.39–13 have been violated, suspended or encroached upon and when such cannot be remedied under the auspices of a union with other peoples.'"[69] Similar language is in the Tigray, Benishangul-Gumuz, Harari, Amhara, and Afar constitutions. As Tsegaye notes, the state constitutions have actually attached conditions to the right to secession, which is unconditional as per the language of the federal constitution.

Generally, despite a strong push for cultural and political autonomy, it can be argued that the Oromo do not favor full secession from Ethiopia. Parents in all regions under study, for instance, consistently felt that a policy of nationality languages could not hurt the national unity of Ethiopia. In fact, despite the dire predictions of the constitution's opponents, secession is not a political option sought after by the mainstream citizenry or political leadership of the vast majority of ethnic groups in the country. Nevertheless, self-determination including, but not limited to, cultural policy is a vital interest to them. Political threats to dismantle the constitution or specifically to amend it in order to remove Article 39 entirely fail to account for the centrality of self-determination rights to the majority of oppressed and minority ethnic groups in the country, and are a recipe for political conflict. All of this points to a citizen-formation process actively being created, contested, and reshaped.

As Mekuria has noted, the Macha-Tulama was not seeking the secession of the Oromo, but the "demand for cultural rights and recognition of Oromo identity which included the use of the Oromo language ... [and it] dispelled the wrong belief about the 'readiness' of the Oromo to assimilate and Amharize."[70] There have always been divisions among the Oromo leadership about the prospects for statehood versus the possibility of full and equal citizenship within the Ethiopian state.[71] As in earlier periods of Oromo history, the diversity of Oromo experience and opinion

[69] Tsegaye 2008, 16.
[70] Mekuria 1997, 344; see also Alemseged 2004, 605, 608.
[71] Joireman 1997, 391; Keller 1995.

has at times been cited as a weakness for the consolidation of identity rather than a source for political power.[72] Sorenson notes that "there is considerable diversity among Oromos in terms of class, region, urban and rural differences, subsistence activities, religion and politics."[73]

Historian Mohammed Hassen summarizes a common viewpoint well when he states, "Without unity, the future of the peoples of Ethiopia including the Oromo appears to me to be bleak. Of course there are competing nationalisms in Ethiopia ... what is at stake is the question of establishing a genuine federal system based on democracy.... The strength of the federal system is that it combines self-rule (which satisfies the aspirations of the Oromo and others) and shared rule (which takes into consideration the geography, demography, culture, history, and economic interdependence of the peoples of Ethiopia)."[74] In his study of the Macha-Tulama movement, Mohammed takes up the question of why Oromo nationalism did not develop until the 1960s. He points out that the Ethiopian state's exaggeration of regional and religious differences among the Oromo, coupled with underdevelopment and lack of Oromo leadership and the tight control of the government, contributed to this rather late political and organizational development.

Bulcha Demeksa, who until his recent retirement was the head of the Oromo Federalist Democratic Movement, similarly supports the realization of Oromo rights to self-determination within a fully democratized Ethiopia. At recent meetings with the Oromo diaspora in Minnesota, he energetically took on those who favor armed resistance, arguing that violence begets violence. He stated in a 2005 interview that the question of secession is evolving in Oromiya, and that while the OLF argued for secession in the 1990s, it now believes that "the Oromo people are not really interested in secession or being an independent country."[75] According to Bulcha, what they want is the Oromo language to be an official language, to "be the masters of their own destiny, controlling their resources and lands, and to share it with the federal government according to law"; to control their state while playing a major role in the federal government. Although he shares a critique with other Oromo elites

---

[72] This observation about the Oromo is itself instructive to larger questions related to secession, because there is a view that ethnofederal arrangements that guarantee autonomy will necessarily "increase the group's cohesion and *willingness* ... and *capacity* to act" are flawed (Cornell 2002, 252, emphasis in original).

[73] Sorenson 1993, 227.

[74] Mohammed 1998, 185.

[75] Wiren 2005.

of the EPRDF's stranglehold on political parties, he wants to advance issues such as promoting the Oromo language and making a change to a presidential system, as well as supporting communal, not state, control of land (with government regulation). He seems also to be advocating a set of preferential policies such as affirmative action for Oromos to rectify past inequalities, citing the example of African Americans in the United States.

From a political action perspective, the OLF's stance has been more ambiguous. In a resolution at its October 2008 National Council Extraordinary Meeting, it repeatedly discussed the need to "struggle against the EPRDF regime" and to "safeguard the unity of the Oromo people and the cause of national liberation," but it did not clearly state what "national liberation" means. In a recent interview, Chairman Daud Ibsa stated that "enabling the Oromo people to exercise its right to self-determination remains our core objective. The final decision is up to the Oromo people."[76] Daud's comments reflect a common tension – he concludes that "to talk about democracy in Ethiopia is to talk about the Oromo people. Democracy is about majority rule ... and the Oromo people makes up close to 50% of the population. And because of the mobilization that has been going on for the last 14 years, the Oromo have become a force, a real force in Ethiopia and a real force in the region."[77]

There is good reason to think that the moderate leadership of the OLF favors full inclusion of the Oromo in a democratic Ethiopian state; at least it did as recently as 2005. There are factions within the OLF as well, and some do prefer an Eritrean-style solution – a referendum on independence. In general, the OLF's position has been to call for a referendum sponsored by the UN.[78] What evidence from local communities in Bale and Borana regions of Oromiya suggests would support the public pronouncements of Oromo politicians and intellectuals within and outside Ethiopia – that Oromos seek inclusion within Ethiopia but with meaningful citizenship, including unmediated political representatives and far less political repression in their communities. Whether and how this will come to Ethiopia is an open question. There are strong suspicions of Oromo citizens by members of other ethnic communities, and it does not seem that those are based only on the fears of majoritarian dominance. Rather, historic prejudices and biases rear their heads when the subject

---

[76] Delsol 2006.
[77] Delsol 2006.
[78] Markakis (2011, 284) summarizes these development succinctly.

of the Oromo question is raised, a striking unwillingness to even discuss such a topic framed in that way, which of course hints at the intensity of mistrust and misunderstanding among groups in Ethiopia, particularly centered on the Oromo.

Conclusion

Meaningful citizenship probably has no more complex a landscape than the Oromo peoples and their place within the modern state of Ethiopia. It is such an emotive subject that it is rare for anyone but an Oromo nationalist to write on the topic, and nationalists of other stripes talk of it often, but usually only in closed circles. The myths and misperceptions of what goes on in the contemporary regional state of Oromiya are myriad, particularly in the diaspora, but also in cities such as Addis Ababa. Venture to towns and communities inside Oromiya and one finds what might be expected – ethnically mixed towns such as Jimma and Robe, where businesspeople and administrators and teachers fluidly shift back and forth in language between at least Amharic and Afaan Oromo, working and living together. Those in smaller villages outside towns are occupied primarily by Oromo in ethnically homogenous communities, visiting towns for market days or religious events and using interlocutors in Amharic as needed. The point here is that 35 percent of the country is Oromo, and the vast majority live quite peacefully with their neighbors – Oromo and non-Oromo – and while some individuals were forced out in earlier historical epochs (especially 1974 but also a bit after 1991), many non-Oromo live in Oromiya. Despite rumors to the contrary, I found ethnic Amharas, particularly those Afaan Oromo–speaking teachers, businesspeople, and government administrators working in all parts of Bale and Borana during my research.

The language policy in Oromiya has been generally successful when judged by both the historical claims to linguistic identity and self-determination articulated and supported by the Oromo people and by more general measures of language standardization, implementation, and entrenchment. In this, Oromiya is clearly unique in Ethiopia in its ability to implement such a thoroughgoing reform of language policy in the region. This is a tremendous accomplishment for which credit goes to generations of Oromo intellectuals, educators, political activists, and ordinary peasants who never fully assimilated into Amharic-language repertoires. Their successes continue to be an inspiration to other ethnic groups throughout Ethiopia. The excitement that Oromo parents and teachers feel about the use of their own language is testament to that success and an indicator of what meaningful citizenship can look like. The Oromo especially are now able to access education, justice systems, and administrative apparatuses operating through the use of Afaan Oromo and generally with Oromo leadership at the helm of those institutions.

The persistent and at times intense political repression of the Oromo people under the present political regime demonstrates as well the limits of formal institutions in fostering the conditions for meaningful citizenship. The Oromo would be expected to be the ethnic group most likely to benefit from the provisions of the constitution, particularly those relating to self-determination. Because of the political control of the Oromo people, however, they have not yet seen the use of these institutional or constitutional channels as have other smaller, less politically threatening ethnic groups, such as the Siltie. Specifically, federalism has done little to resolve the fundamental question of Oromo citizenship, although it has surely advanced important political and cultural elements of Oromo rights to self-determination. But the treatment of the Oromo peasantry in particular indicates that the terms of Oromo inclusion in the modern state, their citizenship claims to full and inclusive and equal participation, remain as yet largely unfulfilled. This is partly the result of government oppression and state-sponsored violence, but it is also because the institutions themselves have not been utilized to initiate or facilitate a social dialogue between and among different ethnic groups.

The contradiction for the Oromo is summed up well by this statement: "If they start talking about seeking the resolution of the Oromo question within the context of the Ethiopian state, then they are easily accused of entertaining domination due to the size of the Oromo population. If they persist in seeking the restoration of the rights of the Oromo people alone, then they are accused of being separatists."[79] This is well illustrated by any discussion of what the national or working language of the Ethiopian state should be, English versus Amharic in particular, as a corrective to the suppression of Oromo. Talk of resolution based on a plurality in the Ethiopian state is dismissed as majoritarian dominance. At the same time, the use and development of Afaan Oromo are given as evidence of Oromo secessionist aspirations. The fact is that institutional solutions have eluded the Oromo for decades under successive political regimes.

The Oromo case is one of the most important on the African continent today to study with regard to what meaningful citizenship means

---

[79] Leenco 1999, 239.

in actual practice. The fears of granting ethnic self-determination rights notwithstanding, the Oromo case suggests an adamant refusal to consider this option by the regime in power, and the debates about self-determination are often implicitly and silently framed by the fears of other groups regarding the growing activism of Oromo elites and citizens. Meaningful citizenship as the expansion of citizenship rights and responsibilities carries with it anxieties for other groups that may militate against realization of meaningful citizenship at any particular moment in time.

6

Ethiopian Women and Citizenship
Rights Deferred

While ethnic groups have pursued equal citizenship in the contemporary Ethiopian polity, Ethiopian women and their allies have been similarly active in advancing gender equality and meaningful citizenship for women in Ethiopia. The intersectional nature of ethnic and gendered inequalities in Ethiopia and the unique constitutional provisions related to both identity groupings provide critical insights into the ways that expanding citizenship can provide new opportunities and new challenges. As diverse and divided societies confront legacies of inequality and exclusion based on race, ethnicity, and national origin, rights for these communities at times have been resisted based on how they might disproportionately harm female members of the community. How are such competing rights claims to be resolved? Are these rights even "competing" at all? And in, particular, are women uniquely harmed by the protection of the rights of ethnocultural groups within the state?

This is particularly important in places where a history of social inequality is deep-rooted and where this inequality is somewhat equally distributed between women as a group and ethnic and racial communities as a group. It is also important because scholars have argued that African feminisms tend to be "corporate," viewing individuals as members of interdependent human relations, including family and community, rather than individualist, as in the west.[1]

As noted in the Introduction and demonstrated throughout this book, Ethiopia is a unique and critical context in which to examine questions of citizenship and multiculturalism, in part because of its distinct form

[1] Mikell 1997.

of federalism. Because of the affirmative and radical provisions for ethnic communities discussed already, and because of the distinct gendered nature of unequal citizenship, it is also a crucial case for assessing the issues at stake with respect to women and multiculturalism. Few constitutions as innovatively adhere to multiculturalist principles as the 1995 Constitution of Ethiopia. As described in Chapter 2 federalism in Ethiopia grants constitutional rights and protections for Ethiopian citizens as members of ethnic communities. At the same time, the constitution includes exciting protections for women that were subsequently incorporated into a comprehensive revision of existing legal parameters as the Revised Family Code of 2000, which stands apart across much of the world for its thoroughness in the reform of legal codes that impact on women. How do these two documents and the principles they enshrine – rights for ethnic communities and rights for women – reconcile what will surely arise as conflicts? I am particularly concerned here with how these two sets of group rights might actually reinforce and support each other in ways that theorists and policy makers alike have underappreciated.

There are a number of ways to approach the sets of questions that emerge from thinking about gendered citizenship in Ethiopia and its implications for the democratizing potential of citizenship creation and expansion. Is gender inequality in Ethiopia to be addressed through the institutional structures of federalism? Have the strong constitutional and legal provisions for ethnic communities impacted Ethiopian women, as a group, in positive ways? These two questions are rooted in somewhat distinct constellations of empirical data: one related to women in Ethiopia in particular and the other arising from global experiences with gender and multiculturalist concerns. An interesting corollary to the attention to ethnic claims in Ethiopia or even elsewhere in Africa, even if consistently framed as ethnic conflict, is to consider the ways in which being "ethnic" (Oromo, Tigrayan, or Siltie, for instance) presents a challenge to national identity in a way that being "gendered" (a woman) not does. Is a gendered approach to Ethiopian politics also a challenge to the essential foundations of Ethiopian-ness? If not, why? Put another way, does federalism in Ethiopia, with its relatively strong protections for ethnic communities, provide the Anywaa woman of the Shola market with additional resources to challenge and expand the norms and practices that impinge on her full and meaningful citizenship, or are these a further obstacle to such? Is her Anywaa-ness an identity of actual citizenship expansion, or the most direct source of patriarchy and inequality? And how is her identity as a woman also part of the Ethiopian-ness of her political and social life?

In this chapter I explore women's citizenship status in Ethiopia today. In turning to the questions of how federalism and ethnocultural provisions such as those of the 1995 Constitution impact women's citizenship expansion, we see that there are evident tensions between these two general sets of group-based rights. Although the contradictions of cultural rights for ethnic groups and substantive protections for women are myriad, they are not incompatible in the ways that liberal scholars or critics of federalism in Ethiopia have suggested. Rather, there are compelling examples of cultural traditions within ethnic communities that actually do a better job of protecting and supporting the rights of women in Ethiopia than western-inspired liberal principles of individual rights. One interesting example comes from the concept of *wayyuu* among the Arsi-Oromo in Bale, Ethiopia, and the types of practices traditionally associated with it. Constitutional protections for ethnic groups in Ethiopia are a rich resource for gender-equality activists, although they will have to engage with cultural traditions in creative and multifocal ways. Some cultural traditions will undoubtedly be antithetical to the constitutionally protected rights sought by women and their allies. Feminist activists will be more successful at challenging these practices *through* ethnocultural traditions than by trying to banish the latter from the public sphere.

If it is true that gender equality can be achieved through ethnocultural traditions in at least some cases, then women's rights are not at odds with cultural rights but supported by them. What is missing is a theoretically informed and detailed inventory of cultural traditions regulating gender and women's rights in many societies. At the same time, such possibilities for cultural – and gendered rights –promotion require a political climate of open and substantive – as well as respectful –debate, which is unfortunately missing in some of the contexts under consideration. These minimum conditions must be met for both women's rights and ethnocultural rights to be fully realized.

The Historical and Cultural Context for Women's Citizenship

An exhaustive study of women in Ethiopia is impossible here, but it is not inaccurate to say that Ethiopian history is mainly a story of men, and of some very few elite women. In this, modern Ethiopian history shares much with the rest of the modern world. Of course, women were always there, and they were as much political and economic actors as men, in addition to active social and moral agents. But their place within the rigid hierarchies of family and society were mostly understudied and certainly undervalued, and historical analyses are just beginning to account for their contributions. In some cases, elite and royal women played a direct role in state and church politics in Ethiopia. For instance, Donald Crummey focuses on the role of Mentewwab, consort of Emperor Bakaffa (1721–1769) of the Gonder period, arguing that "continuity during this half century was maintained by one of the more remarkable, and most prominent, women in Ethiopian history."[2] Other prominent Ethiopian women in history include Empress Taitu, an influential and powerful actor in the reign of Emperor Menilek, and his daughter, Zawditu, as well as lesser-known women such as Bafena, Menilek's consort. Heran concludes that "both Bafena and Taitu's force of personality and their positions make them obvious studies of exceptional Ethiopian women. Finding women outside institutional positions is more challenging, since they are nearly invisible."[3]

Peasant women and women of other socioeconomic classes were mainly prominent in fulfilling social reproduction and economic functions in particular. Most of the ethnocultural communities of modern Ethiopia tended to limit women's political and economic participation through practices of male-dominated political and religious leadership, as well as economic practices restricting or limiting ownership and control of valuable productive assets such as land and cattle. Bahru Zewde's history of intellectuals in the early twentieth century points out that interest in female education sparked opposition from the religious establishment and led elites at the time, including Haile Selassie, to send their daughters abroad for education. The opening of the first national girls' school in the capital in 1931 heralded a substantial shift in thinking about women's and girls' education, if only for the children of the highest elites of the time.[4]

The modern period of Ethiopian history and citizen creation, elaborated on in Chapter 2, really had very little impact on Ethiopian women. Women do not figure prominently in political life until the Derg. Despite the influential role of particular women in earlier periods, neither

---

[2] Crummey 2000, 94.
[3] Heran 2005, 68, 73; see also Belete Bizuneh's excellent review of the extant literature on women in Ethiopian history as of 2001.
[4] Bahru 2002, 28.

Menilek nor Haile Selassie's tenure were notable for any women leaders, save for Empress Taitu's powerful role in a discrete period of Menilek's reign around the Battle of Adwa. Tsehai Berhane-Selassie correctly contextualizes the power dynamics of women and men as heavily influenced by the monotheistic religions that dominate Ethiopian culture, particularly Christianity and Islam.[5] Throughout much of the twentieth century, women remain strikingly absent, including during setbacks prompted by the Italian occupation as well as earlier and later efforts by Haile Selassie to consolidate his rule.

The most important period for Ethiopian women becomes the radical changes wrought by the 1974 Revolution and the socialist policies of the Derg. Women – particularly some peasant and rural women – for the first time assumed prominent roles in local organizations, including the Revolutionary Ethiopian Women's Association (REWA), which included representation in the party's politburo. In a fascinatingly triumphant and hopeful account, Rita Pankhurst recounts personal anecdotes of socialist Ethiopia as related to women, concluding that "women, especially the numerous poor women in the countryside and in the cities, had already gained much from the Revolution – much that could weight in the balance against the suffering many had endured in the turmoil of recent years."[6]

However, REWA became much like other state- and party-dominated women's association of the time across Africa in its use as a party tool rather than a radical or transformative vehicle for Ethiopian women's empowerment. In her rich ethnographic study of a village community in northern Shewa, Helen Pankhurst tells the tale of the Derg's ambiguous role in altering women's status. In particular, however, Pankhurst's work documents quite eloquently the complex and contradictory nature of Ethiopian women's statuses, especially in the northern highlands. In many respects, whether along economic, religious, or social lines, Ethiopian women have been marginalized and oppressed and yet have had creative outlets for resistance and autonomy. In Shewa and among the Amhara, for instance, this involved relative flexibility in marriage and divorce – what Helen Pankhurst calls "careering through marriage," something rarely available to other women in what is contemporary Ethiopia, or even other parts of Africa.[7]

[5] Tsehai 1997, 127.
[6] R. Pankhurst 1981, 51.
[7] H. Pankhurst 1992, 118.

The most important reforms of any for women have only come since 2000s, even if they are mainly in the legal realm. In the early 1990s, radical social reforms were made, most prominently the granting of self-determination rights, – including the right to secession – for ethnic communities (Article 39[1]). Much has been written about these innovative and controversial provisions for ethnic communities. But in addition to those provisions relating to ethnic communities, the 1995 Constitution includes bold and very specific protections for women, making Ethiopia a leader in constitutional provisions for women. Article 25 of the constitution guarantees the right to equality for all. The rather lengthy Article 35 provides various enumerated rights for women, including specifically "equal rights with men in marriage" and certain "affirmative measures." It includes language that acknowledges the "historical legacy of inequality and discrimination suffered by women in Ethiopia" and proposes measures to "provide special attention to women so as to enable them to compete and participate on the basis of equality with men in political, social and economic life as well as in public and private institutions" (Article 35[3]). Further constitutional language notes the influence of "laws, customs and practices that oppress or cause bodily or mental harm" that are prohibited, special protections in maternity leave, the right to property and land, as well as rights to family planning and full employment, pay, and promotion (Article 35[4][5][7][8]).

These constitutional provisions followed from the development in 1993 of the first National Policy on Ethiopian women, which was the first attempt to integrate gendered citizenship concerns into national-level discourses on poverty, development, and democratization. To implement this, a Women's Affairs Office in the Prime Minister's Office was created (upgraded to a ministry in 2005), and Women's Affairs Departments were established within line ministries, commissions, and agencies. In 2001, the government prepared a National Action Plan on Gender Equality to implement the national program and align it also with outcomes sought by the Millennium Development Goals related to women. Specific focus in this plan was put on poverty reduction and economic empowerment of women, education, training of women and girls, reproductive rights, health and HIV/AIDS, human rights and violence against women, leadership and decision making of women, and, finally, women and the environment. A second National Action Plan was formulated in 2006–2010 to advance similar objectives.[8]

---

[8] Sosena Demessie and Tsahai Yitbark 2008.

But the context for these dramatic policy and institutional reforms is sobering, and a brief look at the national situation is instructive. Women in Ethiopia suffer tremendous bias in the provision of services and the protection of law. They remain underrepresented in formal political and social life. Women hold 28.7 percent of seats in the House of People's Representatives and 16 percent of the seats in the House of Federation, certainly higher than in many democracies around the world, but still not close to parity level. In terms of women's leadership in other top-level government positions such as ministers of state, cabinet ministers, and party leaders, as well as in private business and professional associations, however, these figures are much lower. The numbers of women in influential and decision-making positions in the judiciary and police forces are also quite low. These questions of women's representation in a broad range of economic and political positions are significant, as multicountry regression analysis found that "powerful women" broadly conceived, not just women in formal legislative positions, "are associated with improved status" for women in regards to legal reform in particular.[9]

On other indicators of gender equity and development, Ethiopia is improving, but from a place of dramatic inequality for women and girls. For instance, gender parity in primary education is closer to being achieved, with a nationwide gross enrollment rate in primary schools for girls at 93 percent in 2009–2010 (98.7 percent for boys), but up from 53.8 percent for girls in 2002–2003 (and 74.6 percent for boys). But in light of the high attrition rate – only 18 percent of children reach grade five – few girls are advancing beyond these primary school levels. The percentage of female students in grades nine through twelve is only 39 percent and by university level, the enrollment rates for young women are 23 percent of those in government university or college.[10] Compounding the enrollment pressures, girls face significant sexual and gender harassment and violence in schools or on their way to and from school. This is evidenced by high profile cases of acid attacks on young women by their male stalkers as well as other physical violence, only recently being counteracted almost exclusively through internationally donor-funded initiatives such as girls' clubs.

The immense poverty at the national level affects women disproportionately. Poor women, both rural and urban, spend most of their time in attending to the basic needs of their family, including collecting

---

[9] Crotty 2009, 352.
[10] Ethiopia, Central Statistical Authority 2007.

water, grinding grains, preparing meals, and caring for their children. Environmental concerns such as water and fuel scarcity compound these daily tasks for women. In terms of formal and semiformal employment, women's unemployment is generously estimated at 68.5 percent, compared to male unemployment at 31.5 percent.

Finally, in health status, women also bear a disproportionate burden, particularly in light of high fertility and low health-care coverage. For instance, only 6 to 11 percent of Ethiopian women in the country give birth with the assistance of a trained birth attendant, and 25 percent of rural and 1 to 10 percent of urban women had "self-assisted" deliveries.[11] Twenty-five percent of Ethiopian women will die during pregnancy or while giving birth.[12] Other indicators are even more sobering. An analysis of the 2005 Demographic and Health Survey of Ethiopia by a local NGO also concluded that 81% of Ethiopian women believe wife beating is acceptable for at least one given reason.[13]

Both the formal legal system and the reliance on various customary laws have left the vast majority of women with little protection from certain practices of discrimination, including in land and property, in marriage and family, and in the informal market and access to resources.[14] In particular, some cultural traditions, called Harmful Traditional Practices by the Ethiopian state and civil society in Ethiopia as well as the international community, may impose a distinctly gendered burden for Ethiopian women.[15] These practices include female circumcision, early marriage, marriage by abduction, and various practices for pregnant and laboring women.[16] Thoughtful studies of cultural traditions in the highlands of

---

[11] A trained birth attendant can refer to a doctor, nurse, or trained traditional midwife, whereas most births were either self-assisted or had the help of a traditional birth attendant (TBA). The government of Ethiopia gives a figure of 11% of women with a TBA (Ethiopia, Central Statistical Authority, 2011) and UNICEF and other UN sources give a figure of 6% of women with access to a skilled birth attendent (UNICEF 2012). Either number is staggeringly low, one of the lowest in the world. The Africa regional average is 43% of births attended by skilled health personnel.

[12] Save the Children/US, 2010.

[13] Ethiopian Society of Population Studies 2008.

[14] Vaughan and Tronvoll 2003.

[15] I employ the term as used by Ethiopians, within and outside the state, not to designate my own opinion on which are "good" cultural practices and "harmful" cultural practices. Feminist scholar Sally Engle Merry notes the term is a designation rooted in part in international instruments related to women's rights such as the Convention on the Elimination of Discrimination Against Women (Merry 2006, 12).

[16] National Committee on Traditional Practices of Ethiopia (NCTPE) 1998; National Committee on Traditional Practices of Ethiopia 2003. A useful narrative descrip-

Ethiopia show evidence of women's agency in manipulating, resisting, and energizing cultural traditions, including Helen Pankhurst's study of women in northern Shewa and Olmstead's study of a local female leader in the Gamo highlands of the south.[17] Nonetheless, many of these practices impose a distinctly gendered burden of labor, social reproduction, and even violence on women and girls.

A review of the baseline survey of these practices conducted in the late 1990s points to the direct correspondence between these various practices and the cultural boundaries of particular ethnic communities. The practices are not evenly distributed among the ethnic groups of Ethiopia but are structurally tied to ethnic community identity and boundary formation and control, suggesting that social changes in these practices will be interpreted by men and women in the communities as related to their community identity as least as much as their gendered identity. For instance, while the national prevalence rate of female circumcision is as high as 73 to 90 percent, the severity of form and the age of the girl vary. It is as high as 94 percent in Afar region and as low as 46 percent in Southern Nations, Nationalities, and People's Region (SNNPR). For early marriage, the prevalence is as high as 61 percent in Amhara region and far lower in Addis Ababa and Oromiya and Afar regions. Marriage by abduction, however, is highest in SNNPR (26 percent) and lowest in Somali region and Addis Ababa.[18] This has led some to suggest that "the upsurge of ethnic consciousness after the introduction of the federal system may lead to the revival of certain traditional practices that discriminate against women, since these practices are seen as ethnic boundary markers by political or ethnic 'entrepreneurs,'"[19] although there is no evidence presented to prove that this has actually occurred.

The high prevalence rate for these practices demonstrates without a doubt the sharp limits on constitutional provisions relating to gender. This is also because constitutional protections are not enough. Legal codes must be revised, bureaucrats and public servants must be educated and incentivized to meaningfully uphold new legal provisions, and finally and most importantly, communities must be engaged in the sorts of social changes implied by provisions for the equality of women. Sally Engle Merry calls this the "process of vernacularization," in which globalized

tion of some of these practices, with case studies, is provided by Original Wolde Giorgis (2002).

[17] Helen Pankhurst 1992; Olmstead 1997.
[18] National Committee on Traditional Practices of Ethiopia (NCTPE) 1998, 2003.
[19] Vaughan and Tronvoll 2003, 67.

and state-centric principles and codes are translated in order to have meaning to local citizens.[20] This process began in Ethiopia through the work of women activists, politicians, and civil society groups to revise the various elements of the legal code that contradicted or violated the principles of the 1995 Constitution. This resulted in the passage into law in 2000 of The Revised Family Code (Proclamation 213/2000). Under the revised law, important legal changes were made, including a law prohibiting bigamy, the requirement of consent for marriage, and the stipulation that the legal age of marriage is eighteen for women and men. Further provisions include those that address distinctly Ethiopian challenges to women's equality, including a provision that violence extorted in exchange for marriage is grounds for termination of the marriage,[21] and the legal recognition of civil, religious, and customary marriages.[22]

Advocacy for the 2000 revised Family Code was nonetheless initiated and led by an important civil society organization in Ethiopia, the Ethiopian Women's Lawyers Association (EWLA), together with allies in the Women's Committee in the House of People's Representatives and the Women's Affairs Department. The revised law addressed significant biases in previous legal codes that had allowed arranged marriages and those marriages involving coercion, and that were unclear on informal and religious marriages common in much of the country, leaving women vulnerable if their marriages were contracted through these systems. The revised law also raises and equalizes the age of marriage for women and men and clearly and broadly defines domestic violence. The new law gives women rights of appeal in the decision of those who arbitrate various matters relating to family and domestic life and recognizes cohabitation as marriage under stated circumstances. Many of these provisions directly address not only legal gaps in Ethiopian law but traditional practices that impinge on women's full exercise of their other constitutionally protected rights to life, liberty, and security.

Notwithstanding the tremendous challenges to implementing these progressive provisions for women and girls, the 1995 Constitution and the Revised Family Law of 2000 do suggest a major tension inherent

---

[20] Merry 2006, 219.

[21] "Bride abduction" is a practice in specific ethnic communities of Ethiopia, although it is not widely practiced throughout the country and is certainly already part of a dialogue about changing norms of marriage even within these communities.

[22] Because many Ethiopians are married outside of the civil process, protection of the rights of women in customary and religious marriages was a valuable addition to the law. Government of Ethiopia 2000.

in Ethiopian federalism. What happens when members of an ethnic community (or their political leadership) determine that a particular practice relating to women is a constitutionally protected aspect of their national right to self-rule and cultural development? How are these two sets of rights to be adjudicated? Somewhat surprisingly, very few if any cases have arisen, even fewer than those relating to ethnic rights. As far as I know, only one case of constitutional interpretation relating to the rights of women has been taken to the House of Federation.[23] This case involved a Muslim woman who had rejected the jurisdiction of the Sharia courts, the so-called Khedija case. This did not, however, involve the assertion of ethnic group rights that we are concerned with here.

The inattention to women's issues in judicial and constitutional interpretation and application is in itself significant, as it suggests the relative importance of ethnic rights over women's rights in the current discourse about meaningful citizenship in Ethiopia. Some have argued that the legal and constitutional rhetoric notwithstanding, "state actions continue to focus on the 'woman question,' taking the lead in a paternalistic form of welfarism and suspiciously muting any call for the genuine empowerment of women."[24] I would rather challenge that it is because of a society-wide complacency about women's inequality. At least two major revolutions have been staged over the inequalities of peasants and members of oppressed ethnic nationalities, but the very idea that women and girls are equal participating citizens in social and political life has largely remained outside of national discourse on citizenship in Ethiopia. Tsehai Berhane-Selassie has argued that "stereotyped views about women's inferiority prevail, even though most men emphasize the respect they have for them."[25]

In this, the emancipatory projects of the modern period of Ethiopian history have dramatically challenged some categories of unequal citizenship and left other projects as yet mostly unfulfilled. In Ethiopia, opportunities for expanded citizenship gains for women, and the attendant benefits to their families and communities, have been mostly missed in recent decades. Although a vibrant and acrimonious debate in Ethiopia has radically altered the language and contested the practices related to ethnic group relations in the country, discussions of the democratization

---

[23] See Chapter 2 for a discussion of the House of Federation's role in constitutional interpretation. See also Tsegaye Regassa 2008.

[24] Biseswar 2008, 141.

[25] Tsehai 1997, 149.

of the home, the family, and the neighborhood remain muted, if not completely silent. Perhaps then it is not surprising that there are so few instances testing the intersection points of ethnic rights and women's rights in the country, a point that I consider next.

Possible Conflicts between Ethnic and Gendered Rights

The passage of the Revised Family Code in the House of People's Representatives in 2000 was only the first step in the process of reforming the law with respect to women's rights. The federal system allows the regional states in Ethiopia to choose to adopt the law, revise and adopt their own law, or take no action at all. The process of regional state adoption of the revised law could provide a window into the arbitration of distinct rights sets, as regional state parliaments are the constitutional guarantors of ethnic self-determination rights. In fact, most of the regional states in Ethiopia adopted the same or very similar laws with regard to the Family Code. Only in Oromiya did some hints at the possible interplay between ethnic and gendered rights crop up. The question of polygamy became a source of some debate in the regional state of Oromiya, where some political leaders in the Regional State Council, the *Chaffee*, reportedly favored the recognition of polygamous marriages in pre-adoption discussions. Women's rights advocates, particularly within the Oromiya Region's Women's Affairs Bureau, opposed the recognition of polygamous marriages. In the end, the Revised Family Code in Oromiya looks quite similar to the national code, which does not recognize polygamous marriages.[26]

Even more relevant than the outcome, at least for now, is the initial question of how a particular regional state in Ethiopia – and the larger national federal system – ought to and will in fact balance competing rights. As outlined above, the Ethiopian constitution grants ethnic communities broad and compelling rights to cultural development. These are rights that were denied by previous political regimes in modern Ethiopia. Arguably, they are central to the future unity of the country and the expansion of citizenship. In stronger language many of the state constitutions assert, on behalf of the ethnic community that predominates in their state, the power of the regional state bodies to protect and preserve these rights. For instance, the Oromiya state constitution declares that "sovereign power in the region resides in the people of the Oromo

[26] Interview #65.

Nation and the sovereignty of the people is exercised through their elected representatives and direct democratic participation." Mirroring the language and even organization of the national constitution, it states in Article 39 that "the people of the Oromo nation shall have the right to maintain their national identity, to preserve and promote their history and heritage ... and enjoy their culture"[27] What if the political leaders in the *Chaffee* had determined that the "enjoyment" of their culture included and in fact required recognition of the practice of polygamy?

Although some feminist activists might consider the decision not to recognize polygamous marriages in the Oromiya Family Code a victory, I want to suggest here that the *process* by which the law was revised represents a greater concern to both the rights of nationalities and the rights of women in Ethiopia. What is emerging in Ethiopian federalism is an increasing tendency toward centralism and ruling party dominance that has stifled debate and controversy. Although this might have seemed to protect women's rights in this case, it may not have that effect in the longer term. Deveaux makes this point forcefully in her discussion of the importance of democratic deliberation in plural societies. She argues that "when cultural communities have a central role in re-evaluating their own customs together with state bodies and civil society groups, the legitimacy of the ensuing proposals – for retaining, eliminating or reforming practices – is underscored and their practicability greatly increased."[28] In fact, failure to incorporate community norms may "leave untouched or even worsen the many forms of oppression faced by vulnerable members of cultural groups, such as women."[29]

When we look at the prevalence of various customary practices in Ethiopia that impact on women, such as domestic violence, forced marriage, bride abduction, and polygamy, it is obvious that these are widely practiced. They are defended by families and communities at the village level, most often based on values of cultural tradition and belief in their importance for health, safety, and the continuation of community norms. Although it would be misguided to say that legal changes are not important for addressing women's basic social, political, and economic equality, it is nonetheless the case in much of Ethiopia that the greater challenge is in promoting a process of community dialogue on these various practices,

---

[27] *Magalata Oromiyaa Proc. 46/2001*, 2001.
[28] Deveaux 2005, 342.
[29] Deveaux 2005, 342.

which might see the expansion of conditions for women and girls to have greater physical and emotional security.

What is needed is a way to foster the conditions under which women and men can themselves decide to stop practices that impinge on the full exercise of constitutional rights by all members. Without such a dialogue, legal reforms are of limited impact, especially in a country as poor as Ethiopia, where few of its citizens have knowledge of or access to the formal legal system. Some of the most effective interventions for women and girls in Ethiopia have occurred at the grassroots level, outside of the legal system, through community-focused discussions on social practices.[30]

The Oromiya-based NGO Hundee, for example, works with communities on poverty and development projects but incorporates a gender perspective explicitly, using traditional norms and rituals. Gender-separated workshops are held, and coordination and consultation leadership is provided by Hundee to harmonize the work of the two groups. They establish Women's Rights Defense Committees and enforce the *seera*, or traditional law of the Oromo, working through the traditional political system called the *gadaa* and through the *gadaa* elders.[31] Hundee has found that the *gadaa* has more robust and meaningful provisions for respecting women, and that the *gadaa* institutions are more effective at community enforcement than working through the formal courts or law enforcement.[32]

A local NGO in the Kembatta Tembaro zone called the Kembatti Mentti Gezzimma (KMG) of southern Ethiopia, founded by two Ethiopian women activists, has been able to do groundbreaking and culturally respectful human rights work, including work focused on abandonment of female genital mutilation/cutting (FGM/C) through a variety of local initiatives. The work of KMG demonstrates that reform for women and girls must be inclusive of women and men, it must include traditional power structures, and it will be most successful when it also integrates with antipoverty and development initiatives. The founder,

---

[30] Other examples of similar hybrid and culturally rooted reforms for women in Africa include those in Ghana (Yitah 2009), Nigeria (Mikell 2005), and South Africa (Deveaux 2005).

[31] *Seera* is a term used among many of Ethiopia's ethnic communities for their customary law, as well as the institutions associated with the law, including for the Gurage, Kambatta, Oromo, and others. See Bahru 2002. Bahru notes, without the tone of alarm sometimes used by opponents of ethnic federalism, that *seera* and other traditional systems of governance have seen an "apparent revitalization ... since 1991" (18). There is a vast literature on the *gadaa* system of the Oromo, including Asmarom Legesse (1973) and Bassi (2005).

[32] Interview, #61 2003.

Bogaletch Gebre, has asserted that public health education around issues such as HIV/AIDS and FGM/C must be based on dialogue, not laws or abstract ideas.[33] Finally, the EWLA pioneered a nationwide campaign of public education that has seen community elders come out publicly against harmful practices such as bride abduction, even exposing those who perpetrate it within the community. Other civil society organizations have accomplished dramatic reductions in bride abduction and higher levels of girls' enrollment in primary school through direct collaboration with existing community leaders and elders.[34]

Let us imagine for a moment that some members in the Oromiya *Chaffee* had persisted in their objection to a law outlawing polygamous marriages, and they had argued that Oromo cultural traditions were at stake. If they had refused to pass the revised law without debate, a genuine discussion about how to reconcile these rights could have occurred. Women activists opposed to polygamous marriages, both within the *Chaffee* and in civil society, could have presented their objections. They might have presented evidence on the impact these marriages have on women. Activists from other regional states could have been called on to present their perspectives. Is polygamy central to the Oromo culture? How widespread is it? Is it a religious or cultural tradition? What are its merits for the group – the Oromo – and for women and men? What are the objections to it – how does it impose additional burdens on women or deny them other constitutionally protected rights?[35]

Most importantly, we would have had the opportunity to hear from Oromo women who have experienced the double burden of ethnic and gendered discrimination. How central are polygamous marriages to definition of Oromo identity? Maybe women would have wished to allow polygamous marriages but want included special protections for women in these marriages. The challenge is that we do not know. It is not clear if Oromo women pushed for the prohibition on polygamous marriages, but it appears quite doubtful from the evidence. Rather, elite women from national women's organizations, together with elites within the ruling

---

[33] Shetty 2007; UNICEF 2010.

[34] Unfortunately EWLA and many other excellent civil society organizations have had to close or dramatically scale back their activities in the wake of the Charities and Societies Proclamation, as well as antiterrorism and media laws of 2009, all of which are intended to shrink nonstate involvement in many of these types of citizen-creation activities. See L. Smith, 2012; Freedom House 2011.

[35] An example of this deliberative democratic process regarding marriage law is provided for South Africa by Deveaux (2005).

party who sought to control the dialogue about women's rights, prevailed and the law was passed without discussion. Meanwhile, the prevalence of polygamy in rural parts of Ethiopia is difficult to track or challenge, but we know it continues in some communities in rather large numbers, and the formal constitutional provisions are generally irrelevant to these outcomes.

Of course, it is more complicated than saying that in this case women's rights prevailed over ethnic rights. That is the argument of those who feel that multicultural protections are not effective in promoting women's rights. By imagining what sort of interesting and meaningful debate might have occurred in this case we are reminded that these two sets of rights are not mutually exclusive and are often self-reinforcing. Feminist activists working in civil society are often too preoccupied with formal procedures and laws and neglect the tremendous importance of community norms. In fact, there may be many cultural practices of Ethiopia's ethnic groups that do a better job at protecting and promoting women's rights than the Revised Family Code or any other legal process may. Next, I present one example from Ethiopia that is meant to be illustrative of this theme rather than exhaustive of it.

Ethnic Rights as Resources for Women in Ethiopia

In an ethnographically rich discussion of the concept of *wayyuu* among the Arsi-Oromo of Bale, scholar Marit Tolo Østebø argues that these women have at their disposal a powerful weapon to protect their rights. It is a tool of their culture and part of the legal and political world of some Oromo communities but not part of formal Ethiopian law. *Wayyuu* is "a moral concept of respect and sacredness."[36] It is used to refer to something that is sacred as well as to refer to a person who should be respected or feared. Her informants in Bale tended to give long lists of persons and things that were considered *wayyuu*, including God, one's father, one's mother, one's mother's co-wives, a *hanfala* or belt that married women wear, the *sinqee* stick that a woman is given at her wedding, as well as other people, periods of time (such as pregnancy), and physical objects. Østebø concludes that *wayyuu* seems to be much more commonly applied to women and those aspects that involve the women's sphere of life. She then examines the ways in which women use these objects and their various statuses associated with *wayyuu* to influence

[36] Østebø 2007b, 35.

and even control men in their community. For instance, she asserts that "male informants clearly expressed their fear for women in general and during *ateete* mobilizations in particular, and with no doubt this is related to a strong fear for the female curse."[37] *Ateete* is a religious women-only ceremony in which "women march to a nearby riverbank where they will pray to God. This ... is done when the community faces problems, such as lack of rain, infertility, disease among humans and livestock and in times of political instability and war."[38] The *sinqee* is a stick that a woman is given at her marriage, which is used for the *ateete* mobilizations, but also when a woman has been intimidated or sexually abused, when beaten by her husband during pregnancy, or when the clan is attacked.[39]

These findings point to the significant sacred and religious role that women play in Oromo culture, and this leads Østebø to conclude that "women form a strong spiritual and religious force among the Arsi-Oromo."[40] It is a force that they are able to use to regulate and control unacceptable sexual behavior, including rape and the loss of virginity, through the use of their *wayyuu* role and their *wayyuu* objects to curse or shame a male offender. In fact, in charges of rape, a woman's word is taken over a man's word, and "if a man has been accused by a woman for rape or taking a girl's virginity, the elders in his clan will do everything possible to convince him to accept the accusation."[41]

Østebø's empirical data from some Arsi-Oromo women in Bale point to the tremendous power of culture and custom in protecting women's rights.[42] In direct contrast to the picture painted by skeptics of multiculturalism, these are women who have influence within their cultural community. They are not always victims of a privatized culture created and controlled by men who only seek to control women and succeed at it every time. This is a dynamic social context in which women and men have over centuries contested their roles and created tools of communication, contestation, and community. Norms of respect and sacredness associated with *wayyuu* can elevate and protect women. There are few

---

[37] Østebø 2007b, 36–37.
[38] Østebø 2007a, 1.
[39] Østebø 2007a, 5.
[40] Østebø 2007a, 8.
[41] Østebø 2007a, 10.
[42] It should be noted that *wayyuu* has some correspondence with related concepts among other Oromo communities, including *woyyu* and *saffuu* (Østebø 2007b, 32–33). It is also worth noting that these practices and beliefs are rapidly being lost to local communities, and their prevalence is somewhat unknown outside of specific ethnographies such as the ones noted here.

places in the world where a woman's word is believed over a man's in charges of rape or sexual assault. It would seem from an example like *wayyuu* that a group such as the Arsi-Oromo, *through* the exercise of their constitutionally protected rights to cultural development and ethnic self-rule, have a resource at their disposal. It is protected for the Oromo people by the 1995 Constitution and the Oromiya regional state constitution. Surely it would be difficult if not impossible to say that such a cultural tradition should be eliminated when it provides such a powerful resource for women. Østebø herself notes that, for various reasons, *wayyuu* is experiencing a reduction in influence among the communities with which she worked. It would be a major disservice to these women if the tools of *wayyuu* were reduced or eliminated through the destruction of the cultural traditions of the Arsi-Oromo community. In this way, multiculturalist protections of the Oromo culture provided for by the provisions in the 1995 Constitution are a *resource* for women rather than an obstacle.

I would, however, go further and assert that this is a constitutionally protected resource that could be made available to women and men in other ethnic communities in Ethiopia, in addition to the formal legal protections such as the Revised Family Code. In asserting a unique approach to the challenges of ethnic diversity, the Ethiopian constitution provides a possible treasure trove of cultural tools to complement the legal and institutional reforms that stand to protect and support women and men as much as they might impinge on them. Although I am not taking a position on the merits of the religious or social practices related to polygamy, there clearly are cultural traditions in Ethiopia and everywhere in the world that are negative for women. It is impossible to defend bride abduction or child marriage, for instance, on nearly any grounds. This is why constitutional and legal protections such as those found in the 1995 Constitution and the 2000 Family Law Code provide critical foundations for a pursuit of gender equality and human rights. If we really did an accounting, however, we might find that there are *as many* cultural traditions that protect women as those that harm or threaten them. Certainly, there are many norms, practices, and rituals in communities that could aid in the reduction of various harmful practices and support women's equal citizenship, and this not only for girls and women but for entire families and communities. By engaging cultural rights rather than banishing them, especially in a place such as Ethiopia with a rich tradition of cultural diversity, women and their allies may find a host of resources like *wayyuu* that may be better equipped to serve their needs than written law or the judicial system, for instance, which are often corrupt or politically powerless, and more often do not carry the moral weight needed to inspire actual changes in cultural practices at the community level.

Two reasonable challenges may be raised here. First, a history of ethnic oppression and marginalization, together with an underappreciation for cultural tools in general, means that there is much about these cultural norms and practices that we simply do not know. In Ethiopia, the nation-building processes described in Chapter 2 either destroyed or forced underground many cultural traditions by ethnic communities. There is a necessity, then, for a historically and empirically driven exercise of exploring the surviving traditions in Ethiopia and elsewhere. While a historical and ethnographic project is indicated, it should be one that explores what cultural norms and practices exist today in Ethiopia that may provide additional resources for women and their families. But the likelihood for such a project to be captured by patriarchal leaders and institutions is quite high, particularly in light of the general invisibility of women's meaningful citizenship in the national discourse today.

A second challenge is even more pressing, and that is the fact that these cultural resources may be unequally distributed. This is to say, whereas Arsi-Oromo women may have a set of norms, practices, and objects associated with *wayyuu*, for example, as a cultural resource that could be elevated and integrated into formal and semiformal political life in ways that provide them with additional resources for protection of their interests in family and community, it is plausible that at least some other women will not have similar tools. The empirical argument that cultures have variable resources would suggest this challenge may arise. This reality may result in two outcomes that are less than desirable: (1) women in other cultural communities may not have as many or as robust a set of cultural norms and practices at their disposal, and (2) some ethnocultural groups may perceive such a finding as an assault on their constitutionally protected rights to the exercise and development of their culture. I start with the latter possibility because it is somewhat easier to address. First, it is interesting that no prominent cases of the so-called incompatibility of ethnic rights and women's rights have arisen in Ethiopia. The refrain of liberals and critics of the ethnofederal model in general and in a place such as Ethiopia in particular is that such an institutional framework incentivizes ethnic elites to shore up community identity, and that this is often done on the "backs of women," through cultural policy and practices that distinctly impinge on women's rights. We might have expected this to have occurred in Ethiopia, and yet there is no evidence in the nearly twenty years of the federal system that this has occurred. Second, the possibility that some ethnic communities would have greater cultural resources within community traditions for women and their families than others should actually be seen as a positive situation for liberals, wherein the incentives would work in favor of ethnic communities highlighting those that help women as a way to positively distinguish their group.

But I return to the first objection, which is that women in some cultural communities may have access to more socially valuable resources in their pursuit of meaningful citizenship and equality than other women. This is a rather serious charge because we might prefer an outcome in which all women have equal access to resource sets. The response to this challenge is also twofold: first, it suggests the importance of constitutional and legal provisions as well as nationwide civil society activism on women's issues in order to provide a certain minimum set of standards with respect to women's rights. Even if a norm and associated practices such as *wayyuu* might provide some communities with "auxiliary supports,"[43] they would not be able to replace international and national norms and laws with respect to women because of the variability of cultural resources.

An additional argument is made here with respect to the variability of cultural resources across different ethnocultural groups, however, and that is that these resource sets could actually be made available to other women and ethnocultural communities as national norms are. Just as the constitutional principles and legal provisions are equally available to Wolaitta, Siltie, Oromo, Anywaa, and Amhara women in Ethiopia today – whether they choose to incorporate these provisions into their choice sets or not – so too could *wayyuu* be made available to other groups of women and other ethnocultural communities within the Ethiopian polity. It is surprisingly radical to suggest that another ethnocultural community would adopt the cultural norms or practices of a neighboring or nearby community. Yet western liberals, and elites from hegemonic groups, commonly argue that ethnocultural groups in Africa should jettison cultural traditions in favor of "universal liberal norms" of gender equality as are embodied in rewritten constitutions and legal reforms advocated and actively funded by international donor governments and organizations. There is nothing universal about these norms, and quite often the lack of

---

[43] Sklar develops the idea of "auxiliary supports" to democratization processes in Africa emanating from cultural traditions, although he does not consider the gendered implications specifically.

cultural resonance for these individualist principles is precisely why they are routinely ignored by communities and families. Conceivably in the context wherein ethnocultural identities and the attendant norms and practices are politically and socially valuable, however, such a political arrangement provides the opportunity for cultural resources to be cultivated and made available not only for members of those cultural groups but for others in society. We do not know how likely it is that women would adopt cultural practices from other ethnocultural groups, but it is at least conceptually plausible that members of one ethnocultural group in Ethiopia would find the norms and practices of another Ethiopian group to be *more* applicable to their own cultural norms and understandings than the "universalist" norms of individual equality found in the 1995 Constitution or the Revised Family Code.

Conclusion

I have argued here that although there may be contradictions between cultural rights for ethnic groups and substantive protections for women, these two sets of rights are not incompatible in the ways that liberal scholars assume or opponents of multiculturalism in Ethiopia fear. Rather, there are compelling examples of cultural traditions within ethnic communities that actually do a better job of protecting and supporting the rights of women in Ethiopia than the formal constitutional provisions relating to women's rights. Constitutional protections for ethnic groups in Ethiopia are a rich resource for gender-equality activists. If it is true that gender equality can be achieved through ethnocultural traditions in at least some cases, then women's rights are not at always odds with cultural rights but instead are supported by them.

The real challenge is that we do not yet have a full accounting of what these cultural traditions are. What is imperative, in Ethiopia and elsewhere, is an ethnographic undertaking to explore the full range of cultural traditions regulating gender and women's rights among the various ethnocultural communities. The few studies of customary law and customary legal and political institutions – such as the *yajoka qicha* and *gordanna seera* of the Gurage and other ethnic groups in Southern region, and the *seera* and *gadaa* of the Oromo, as well as the even fewer studies, such as Østebø's, of the gendered use of these tools of culture and tradition – should be followed up by comprehensive and systematic study of these traditions. The purpose should be to serve as a source for indigenous and culturally relevant legal and political traditions that support and promote women's rights. These traditions, rather than inherently inimical to women's rights in Ethiopia, are in fact a resource for women and their allies. A similar argument has been made more generally about these traditions as resources for the kind of meaningful democratization that has local resonance. Bahru asserts that although Ethiopia has a history of an authoritarian political culture, "in peripheral areas, there was an even higher degree of grassroots participation in governance, or what in contemporary parlance could be characterized as participatory democracy."[44] His work implies that the revitalization of some of these traditional institutions and legal codes could bolster democratization efforts more generally. This is equally true for women, although it is surely not straightforward.

At the same time, such possibilities for cultural and gendered rights–promotion require a political climate of open and respectful dialogue. It is clear that the question of women's rights and ethnic rights in Ethiopia is intricately connected with the question of democratization at the broader level. The exciting possibilities of federalism to reimagine an Ethiopia based not on a hegemony of certain groups, or the elites of these groups, but on mutual respect and a shared commitment to peace and economic and social development, is threatened more by increasing centralization of power and a lack of disparate voices in the public sphere than by the incompatibility of constitutional rights or the impossibility of resolving potential conflicts. These minimum conditions must be met for both women's rights and ethnocultural rights – the conditions for meaningful citizenship – to be fully realized.

As with other important categories of unequal and unrealized citizenship, Ethiopian women, including the ubiquitous Anywaa woman of the Shola market, find themselves in the position of striving for meaningful and expanded citizenship. National discourse and legal reform to realize meaningful citizenship for women came considerably later than those struggles to address other forms of unequal citizenship, particularly ethnic inequalities. But the possibilities of full and meaningful participation for women were somewhat radically introduced during the Derg regime and considerably enhanced under the federalism of the Ethiopian People's Revolutionary Democratic Front. It remains to be seen how women and their allies will be able to leverage these legal changes to overcome the daunting social inequalities in lived reality. This study has suggested strongly that achieving meaningful citizenship for women can

---

[44] Bahru 2002, 11.

be accomplished by using the tools of ethnocultural and religious group identities, not by abolishing or circumventing them, and that Ethiopian women actually have a distinctly *Ethiopian* set of tools at hand in that. It is of course a set of tools that all women and their families have – their cultural identities – that everywhere provide individual citizens with the language and practices to imagine and realize more meaningful citizenship in their country and community.

Conclusion

During a training session for high school teachers on the revised civic education curriculum in Ethiopia in 2003, I had the opportunity to discuss at some length a concept that is unique and somewhat central to the Ethiopian worldview. The teachers themselves raised the concept of *yeluññeta* and wondered how it might "obstruct democratization." *Yeluññeta* is both a cultural value and a practice in Ethiopia. It is defined as "sensitivity to opinions of others, regard for others' feelings, concern about public opinion, sense of the proprieties."[1] It refers to reserved and respectful behavior, a special sensitivity to the opinions of others – even a kind of conformity. *Yeluññeta* tells Ethiopians to defer to others when in a group, particularly older people and those in positions of authority. It can involve self-sacrifice (not eating first or taking as much food as one wants) or not giving one's opinion in certain social contexts. The teachers of civics noted that Ethiopians might at times appear passive and agreeable because *yeluññeta* would prevent them from openly disagreeing with those in positions of authority. But that does not always mean they agree or are convinced. *Yeluññeta* would inform a particular type of response that is deferential and respectful, although not at all suggesting agreement or conformity. The teachers asked how something like *yeluññeta* might impact democracy promotion, and I could substitute here citizenship expansion, if not everyone felt free to share diverse opinions and experiences.

The language of citizenship is a crucial component to citizenship-expansion projects, as I have argued throughout this book. Important

[1] Leslau 1976, 186; Kane 1990.

192

steps have been taken in recent decades to advance citizenship in Ethiopia and across sub-Saharan Africa. In Ethiopia, much later than the era of independence from European colonial powers in the rest of postcolonial Africa, formal, legal citizenship has been extended to all. Critical issues such as land ownership and ethnic equality were pushed into public discourse and onto the policy agenda, even if they remain highly contentious. Women's equality was similarly advanced through constitutional and legal reforms aimed at eliminating structural obstacles to their full and equal participation in the social, political, and economic life of the nation. Although meaningful citizenship is itself an incomplete project, and the limits of full citizenship remain contested today, there is at least a public language whereby Ethiopians can articulate identities of cultural, economic, and, especially, political value, and help reframe the vision of the Ethiopian state. The 1995 Ethiopian Constitution and the institutions of federalism, however incomplete their application has been, provide a powerful foundation on which to build an inclusive and engaged citizenry.

This book has traced an argument about citizenship creation and citizen expansion through the experience of Ethiopia. The quintessential case of a "diverse and divided society," Ethiopian federalism is neither the sole cause of conflict, nor the ultimate solution to the challenges of forging a national political culture out of unequally constituted groups of citizens. Modern Ethiopian history is full of contradictory processes when it comes to citizenship. Its internal sociocultural diversity is marked by a history of inequality intimately shaped by the colonial experience and not altogether different from other postcolonial Africa states. Both for what is unique to that history and for what is shared with those of other postcolonial African countries, Ethiopian insights into the history of citizen creation and citizenship expansion can reinvigorate the study of democratization in Africa. Citizenship reminds us that formal democracy is most centrally about making citizens in all senses of the word – legally, actively, and practically. Democratization exercises in Ethiopia and across Africa in recent decades are very much national conversations on citizenship and demand greater analytic scrutiny for their accomplishments, challenges, and potential. Just as scholars and activists asked questions about development in earlier periods, we must pay greater attention to the content of struggles for meaningful citizenship.

And yet so many Ethiopian, and African, citizens would prefer to focus on formal politics – particularly electoral politics, constitutional and legal reforms, and, especially, leadership challenges – than to analyze the concept and set of practices that I labeled here as *meaningful citizenship*. It is indeed true that the most direct experience of citizenship is through these formal dimensions of politics, whether citizenship denied or that activated through voting, standing for office or holding leaders accountable. I seek here in my concluding comments to bridge two crucial undercurrents to this study: the reality of Ethiopian politics today and the affinity between meaningful citizenship as I have described it and the political aspirations and outcomes sought by many in Africa today.

Ethiopian Understandings of Citizenship

As noted by many a thoughtful scholar of Ethiopia, the history of the country is mostly a history of the state, which is a "history [that] privileges a particular power structure and the people associated with it."[2] This accounting traces a venerable lineage of the modern state back to powerful ancient kingdoms, linking Ethiopia with traditions of monarchy, jihad, human migration, and cultural mélange that are global in nature. Yet that history does not account for all the citizens of contemporary Ethiopia, and the problem, at least from a political standpoint, is not that we do not know that these peoples have a history, but that their histories are not fully appreciated by their *fellow* Ethiopian citizens. Clapham makes the insightful point that is central here – that some people, "Amharas and Tigrayans have a *history*, whereas other peoples have only an anthropology, or at best a kind of sub-national sub-history that eventually gets subsumed within the national epic."[3]

But what does this tell us of Ethiopian history and citizenship? Let me briefly review how the history of modern Ethiopia is understood and how it relates to citizenship creation. Many Ethiopians know that the important emperors of the early modern period used their military and political skill to block European colonization and to bring important developments in education and infrastructure. As the wars of expansion and the growing of the country's borders proceeded, however, new (and old) members of the Ethiopian state were not given full citizenship rights. In particular, newly conquered peoples in the southern and western regions of modern Ethiopia increasingly bore the burden of empire, as they were forced into unequal and oppressive economic and political relations. For members of these communities, Ethiopian state expansion

---

[2] Clapham 2002, 40.
[3] Clapham 2002, 40 (emphasis in original).

meant the double burden of land alienation and ethnocultural alienation. The link between land and the question of the nationalities was forged by the Emperors Menilek and Haile Selassie, the heroes of the nationalist vision in Ethiopia.

In the wake of the 1974 Revolution and the dissolution of the monarchy, citizenship was radically introduced but stalled in its application. The Derg regime extended citizenship rights to all Ethiopians, including members of formerly oppressed ethnolinguistic groups, and critically, oversaw the dismantling of feudal land relations that were particularly onerous to members of these ethnolinguistic communities. The Derg did not truly transform citizenship in Ethiopia, however, because its violent and autocratic leadership prevented citizens from exercising their rights and duties. For the first time, Ethiopians were citizens on paper but certainly not in practice. In fact, the Derg sowed the seeds of political violence unlike any other time in modern Ethiopian history, and this legacy is the one that confronts the contemporary citizenry who are relatively easily intimidated by threats and use of violence, having lived through a period in recent history of extreme and unrelenting political violence.

More recently, Ethiopia has seen the creation of somewhat novel and distinctly African institutions under the rubric of federalism. The Ethiopian People's Revolutionary Democratic Front (EPRDF) leadership that took power from the Derg was founded on the premise of national and ethnic self-determination and communal ownership of land. The party-led transitional government enshrined these principles in a new constitution. But throughout this process, the ruling regime has demonstrated its inability and unwillingness to use citizenship as a tool for democratization. Political party domination remains a barrier to ethnic self-determination or the extension of meaningful citizenship. Although federalism has created the political space for important ethnic rejuvenation activities, such as development and promotion of ethnic nationality languages, control over these processes remains firmly in the hands of co-opted political parties and has failed to translate into political gains for the communities themselves.

At the same time, other smaller ethnolinguistic groups such as the Siltie and groups in emerging regions such as Benishangul-Gumuz have seen a tremendous flowering of ethnocultural identity, fostered by the constitution's recognition and accommodation provisions. In several important examples, the institutions of federalism have proven effective in arbitrating and even resolving ethnic conflicts, as the Siltie case demonstrates. Smaller ethnic groups have found legal and political remedy for questions of ethnic identity recognition and even language development and promotion. But the critical question is why have these institutions been so much less effective – in fact, completely ineffective – in resolving other equally contentious political conflicts, such as the question of the Oromo people's place in a democratic state?

There are two fundamental contradictions at work in Ethiopia today: one that I would argue is somewhat specific to the Ethiopian political milieu, and one that suggests a global impulse toward meaningful citizenship. The first relates to the distinctly Ethiopian traditions of hierarchy and social change. The other is glimpsed in all the myriad ways that citizens activate and contest their inclusion in the modern state – through "tea parties" and "occupy movements" and through "Arab springs" and "colored revolutions," and even over to quiet but costly brain drains and migration movements all over the world. Meaningful citizenship is a corrective to a static and state-bound definition of citizenship that neglects the fact that citizens are always in the making, always seeking to participate, contest, define, and even enforce the conditions of their citizenship. In this sense, meaningful citizenship is globally relevant, even if locally produced. Ethiopians then, like those in the rest of Africa, stand among a global community of citizens, and their beliefs, institutions, and practices of citizen creation and citizenship expansion are shared by those others.

This perspective on citizenship must be explicitly interpretive in focus, not empirical, as it is about the making *of* and the making *by* citizens. If citizenship is more than a legal status but also a practice, a thing that is *done*, then we need to better appreciate and understand these citizens-in-the-making, what they do and why they do it, or at least why they think they do. Citizenship is a powerful analytical tool with which to approach political life in Africa at this very moment precisely because the institutional reforms of the last two are closely linked with the battle over not simply "which rights" but that more fundamental "right to have rights." Like ethnicity, meaningful citizenship has also become for many Africans about the kind of quality of life and development initiatives one should expect.

Therefore, despite the limitations of institutions in bringing significant or sustained political reform or in arbitrating conflict, they can provide linguistic and procedural parameters for political competition regarding contentious issues such as ethnicity and gender equality. What we see in Ethiopia and what is happening elsewhere in sub-Saharan Africa, albeit in mostly incremental, episodic, and very grassroots ways, is the use of the language of meaningful citizenship to advance citizenship-expansion projects. Bolstering these formal institutions and grassroots efforts with informal supports will create avenues for Ethiopian citizens to activate democratic obligations from their communal identities into positive gains for the polity. The liberatory possibilities of ethnicity or gender or other types of identities and communities have not been fully appreciated or supported, certainly by national governments but also by international partners.

The Ethiopian experience with citizen creation and citizenship expansion also is instructive for the crucial reason that we have seen a significant retrenchment of citizenship gains in the country over just a short decade or so. Mainly this appears to be because of perceived weaknesses within the ruling party and the perception by political elites that their leadership was threatened. It is not necessary for me to review all the intricacies of contemporary Ethiopian politics. It is appropriate to say that the 1990s saw a markedly slow but steady political opening, mainly in the form of ethnic group organization and all sorts of what we might call community development but also in key indicators such as privatization and business development, political party mobilization, and human development improvements. The first half of the next decade (2000–2005) witnessed an incredible, although not unprecedented, burst of citizenship making and expanding. When the research for this project was completed in 2003 it was possible to ask citizens of Ethiopia any number of questions and expect to receive answers that were mostly free and unrestrained. Of course, following Ethiopian traditions of authority, many permissions and authorizations were required, but the relative open conversation at the national level led to the focus on citizenship expansion because there was so much energy around how citizens were realizing greater levels of participation and equality.

This was punctuated rather dramatically by the elections of 2005 and the period that preceded it. The energy of those years and months leading up to the May 2005 elections cannot be overstated.[4] They were perhaps quite similar to earlier epochs of Ethiopian history in their short-lived but massive citizen participation and quite unlike those earlier periods in that they were peaceful, unmediated by the military or even political elites in the way that the "revolutions" and "coups" of the late 1960s and early 1970s were, and of course not nearly as bloody as the civil wars that consumed most of the 1980s and early 1990s were. Opposition

---

[4] See the vast literature on these elections by Lyons, Arriola, Harbeson, Abbink, Clapham, Tronvoll and Aalen, Hagmann and Abbink, Pausewang, L. Smith, and others.

political parties organized, as did other crucial sets of actors, including a tremendous flourishing of private media, civil society groups, and even religious communities. In all of this, the ruling party was an active participant, particularly in preelection debates on substantive themes such as land and federalism.

It seems that the ruling party believed it would be the primary beneficiary of this political opening, perhaps as the set of actors credited with ushering in such a political sea change. There is no doubt that the EPRDF as a political party and a ruling regime did not have the necessary tools to assess public satisfaction, particularly among the youth and those of the rapidly urbanizing populace. When electoral results appeared to be so close in the parliamentary elections, and the ruling party saw how close they had come to losing their majority in Parliament, the response was swift and decisive. The brutal and thorough crackdown on political parties, but especially civil society and ethnic communities, left no doubt among Ethiopians that there was to be a return to the politics of the familiar. At least 193 citizens and security forces died, tens of thousands were arrested, and in its wake, most private media and civil society has been decimated.[5] Citizens remain, but they are chastened and far more modest in their expectations. Meaningful citizenship is most definitely not a foregone conclusion, nor a process that, once initiated, cannot be mostly reversed by powerful state elite. In the case of Ethiopia, violence at the hands of the state has mostly closed down the democratic opening, at least for the time.

What I have argued throughout this work, however, and what the evidence from the villages and towns of southern Ethiopia suggests, is that the fundamental contradiction in Ethiopian political and social life is far less a question of ruling party dominance or formal authoritarianism, despite how much that is the focus of news media, analysts, Ethiopian diaspora, and Ethiopian urban elite concerns. The contradiction is between an aspiration for equality and meaningful citizenship and a culture that values hierarchy, conformity, and structure. This is a contradiction that echoes from the halls of power in Addis Ababa down, to the homes and compounds of ordinary Ethiopians. It is also embedded in the somewhat remarkable symmetry between family life and gender relations in the most remote village hamlet outside Worabe or Welkite, Adaba or

---

[5] See the many reports cited above, as well as Aalen and Tronvoll 2008; L. Smith 2007 and forthcoming 2012; Human Rights Watch, State Department, Amnesty International, and Freedom House annual reports.

Assosa, and those in Addis Ababa's neighborhoods such as Shola. One finds an echo not only from the halls of government to community life but an echo from the homes of illiterate village families up to the homes of Addis's educated urban inhabitants. The echo is of course the sound of marriage, motherhood and fatherhood, "adopted" child worker, or maid in the family compound. It is the echo of social life at its most warm and familiar and also its most unequal and unreformed.

Throughout this text I have also argued that ethnic identities can be democracy enhancing, as they provide the foundations of citizenship and community. For many Ethiopians, membership in their ethnic community and the relative freedom under present political arrangements to develop and promote those elements of ethnic identity that are valuable to the group members has encouraged their increasing participation in Ethiopian society. It is evidenced in increasing school enrollments, greater involvement of local leaders in regional and federal government leadership, and important symbols of national identity being adapted and changed in the process of social inclusion. This highlights the democratic potential of various citizenship identities, including those that are ethnic and gendered. When activated through communal membership, ethnic associations and identifications can support democratization by providing links of recognition and inclusion. Ethiopia has a limited history of this, as Pausewang argues that the peasant associations were able to do in 1976.[6]

This process of citizenship expansion, however, is incomplete. In particular, as was shown repeatedly through this study, there are competing citizenship identities in Ethiopia. For some Ethiopians, the symbols and institutions of national identity mirror and bolster their ethnic identities in unproblematic ways. For these citizens, attempts at greater recognition and inclusion for other ethnic communities represent both a threat to old power configurations and a challenge to the fundamental notions of Ethiopian-ness. They are opposed to a more dialogic and inclusive notion of Ethiopian citizenship in part because it threatens their privileged access to a host of valuable political and economic goods, including employment and political control. But it is also because it is unfamiliar and disorienting.

For other Ethiopians, federalism, however incomplete and flawed, is the institutional process by which they are to be included within the modern state. For these groups, provisions for self-determination are fundamental

---

[6] Pausewang 1997, 201; see also Bahru and Pausewang 2002.

to their participation as Ethiopian citizens. This is particularly evident in the implementation of language policy. We have seen that there are two language policies in Ethiopia today – one that officially celebrates linguistic diversity and permits and even encourages ethnic groups to develop and promote their language, and another that is unofficial and that reinforces the dominant role of Amharic. Ethnolinguistic groups are forced to choose between ethnic development that is constitutionally protected and social, economic, and political marginalization. The inconsistent application of language policy is most notable when considering the question of a second language in Ethiopia – is it English, as the educational policy would lead us to believe, or is it Amharic, as the working language of the country?

The explanation for this is in part a reflection of the multifaceted nature of democratic development. Political institutions, including elections, power-sharing governments, and constitutions, cannot replace social discourse on contentious political issues. A constitution that enshrines ethnic equality cannot prevent individuals and even bureaucracies from undermining the practical application of these principles. If people do not participate in a dialogue about inequality and democracy, the terms of inclusion will be inherently unequal. What sorts of political institutions are most likely to support dual citizenship identities and promote a more engaged, dialogic citizenship in Africa? In Ethiopia, nominally community-based organizations with the potential for promoting ethnic ownership of political processes and local-level involvement in politics have been co-opted and abused by successive political regimes such that they are no longer effective tools of citizenship expansion.

In addition to shrinking space for political voice and participation, particularly alarming as well has been the way in which the EPRDF has "reinforced mechanisms of party control at the local level,"[7] including the massive expansion of local government offices in the *qebelle-* and *woreda*-level structures, and the recruitment of millions of new party members across the country through a nuanced mix of incentive and threat. In sum, the story of political developments in modern Ethiopia, which saw impressive gains in the late 1990s and especially the early part of the 2000s, has seen a dramatic and systematic reduction in meaningful political participation, political accountability, and political space in the past six years, with little sign of expected change. In fact, one wonders what

[7] Freedom House 2011; Aalen and Tronvoll 2009; Pausewang 1997; Bahru and Pausewang eds. 2003; Medhane and J. Young 2003.

the precipitating events for an improvement could be, with all meaningful intellectual, activist, and civil society voices in jail or in exile.

But the focus on meaningful citizenship suggests that rather than looking for reform through the formal political and social institutions, there is a need to approach questions of democratic development in alternate ways. The 2003 civic and ethical education curriculum of the Ministry of Education was an exciting if limited attempt at a new approach to teaching democratic concepts. Supporting curricular efforts such as this, which included wide-ranging discussions of citizenship, democracy, and equality, combined with alternative teaching methods and greater resources for teacher training, could go a long way in educating a new generation of Ethiopians about citizenship. Even during this exercise, however, the ruling party was bent on undermining the potential of the program for truly initiating change. For instance, the ministry refused to include a printed copy of the 1995 Constitution in textbooks. Yet the lack of popular knowledge of the constitution, beyond the distorted picture given by opposing political parties when discussing it during election periods, is a serious impediment to popular ownership of the constitutional principles. And citizens' understandings of how these formal and national-level political structures relate to how they live their lives in a day-to-day sense is completely forgotten in all of this.

One longtime scholar of Ethiopian political culture cites a small training program in Ethiopia in the mid-1990s that encouraged rural citizens to begin by asking questions about power sharing and "pluralism of opinion" in their homes and communities, before building on that at the national level.[8] Social discourse, promoted through education, the media, and community development, would encourage citizens to connect notions of democracy at the national level with social hierarchies and practices within their communities, which has the potential to democratize not only national politics but also, more crucially, ethnic and communal groups, families, and neighborhoods.

Reflecting on the concept of *yeluññeta*, which I opened this Conclusion with, relates to another cultural tradition I observed while conducting fieldwork in Ethiopia that relates to how Ethiopians express their opinions in a group. Most of my work on language policy was done through the use of focus groups. The groups were organized as dual-sex, mixed-age groups but segregated by occupation and relationship to the topic. That is to say, I had groups of parents and groups of teachers, and

---

[8] Pausewang 1997, 203.

I asked them a similar mix of opinion- and knowledge-based questions about the language policy in Ethiopia. What I observed repeatedly in both types of focus groups is that Ethiopians will not directly disagree with others. In fact, even when they are stating a divergent opinion or challenging another person's opinion or knowledge, they will often preface their remarks by a statement of agreement, before proceeding to say something that actually diverges. For example, most would say, "As he/she before me just said …" or "I agree with him/her, and …" as a sentence opener, but then go on to share a different view. It was extremely rare for a participant to open by indicating their disagreement. And although this segue was supposed to suggest agreement, respondents often had divergent opinions on the topic – some even strongly different. Yet it would be considered quite rude and perhaps controversial to transition without reference to creating consensus among fellow participants. This is in marked contrast to most western cultures, in which a high social value placed on individual opinion often leads people to start with a statement such as "I disagree …" even when they are actually agreeing, or about to simply repeat something just said by the previous speaker.

These two illustrations, one of a cultural norm and the other of a style of discussion and debate, suggest a distinctly Ethiopian way of understanding and enacting citizenship in relation to their fellows in political community. The importance of *yeluññeta* is what it can tell us about how citizen creation and, especially, citizenship expansion proceeds. It would seem that meaningful citizenship in Ethiopia will continue to be advanced through subtle, indirect, and incremental changes in the social and political milieu. Dramatic changes have occurred, usually at the hands of revolutionaries and armed militants. There have also been constitutional and legal reforms, education and personnel training and urbanization, globalization, and technological advancement. But the changes at the level of the home, family, and community that make meaningful citizenship come alive will be mostly observed and best analyzed through nuanced changes in how people communicate and relate to one another.

It is the contradiction between the lofty ideals of the 1995 Constitution for the *behereseboch* (nationalities/ethnic groups) of Ethiopia, and the way in which *zeganet* (citizenship) is directly implicated in conquest, subjugation, and subjecthood. The question for Ethiopians who long for a reformed political space is how to build *up* from that, not down. It is how to make discourse, participation, and consensus part of the building blocks of society on which semiformal and formal institutions can be built that could meaningfully democratize their political world. This must start with the family and neighborhood, which is why a consideration of women within Ethiopian life is so interesting. The general silence on questions of women's lived experience vis-à-vis the federal arrangement, or in relation to ethnic groups, political reform, poverty, and underdevelopment are indicative of the challenges therein.

In the process of writing this Conclusion I came across a rather triumphant and enthusiastic "dispatch" from Rita Pankhurst, longtime scholar of Ethiopia, on visiting Addis Ababa after the 1974 Revolution. She wrote of how her friends, city dwellers of Addis, complained to her of "absent maids and to the sight of parents unable to dispose of their young when entertaining guests"[9] because of the impact of the Revolution's compulsory literacy classes and social reforms. These reforms in the march toward meaningful citizenship in Ethiopia, which most Ethiopians would agree are essential to move their country out of the abject poverty and underdevelopment that have plagued it for so long, are still reverberating today. Today my friends and family tell of "absent maids" too, who demand too much in salary or leave for more economic opportunity in Saudi Arabia or other Gulf states, even as they themselves apply for visa lotteries to the United States or student visas to the United Kingdom or Europe.

What of these "absent maids"? How do they relate to the Anywaa woman of the Shola market? I would argue that the visual of aspiring families searching for "good household help," nannies and maids, suggests the kinds of domesticated citizenship on which I have been focused. Many Ethiopians are deeply committed to the social narratives of authority and tradition as well as the animating ideas of family and community that are embedded within those narratives and practices of authority. They will not disappear, and they should not, at least not until Ethiopians themselves decide they would like them to. But there is also a quest for something that improves life, for women and men, and for people from historically oppressed and marginalized ethnic, religious, language, and caste groups. I feel quite confident that, notwithstanding the traditions of hierarchy and social conformity, Ethiopians have an aspiration for a more equal and more meaningful citizenship. I heard it repeatedly in the narratives of history and political life in the focus group sessions in 2003, and I have seen it in evidence in small but consequential ways in markets, schools, and even homes across Ethiopia in the intervening years. The contradiction, the tension, the uneasiness of the coexistence of a dramatic

[9] R. Pankhurst 1981.

traditionalism and disciplinary authority together with a society that has seen greater social revolutions in just a couple of generations than most of the rest of Africa, let alone the world, is immense.

All of this is why a cultural tradition of discourse and deliberation should be encouraged, revived, and reinvigorated in Ethiopia. It certainly already exists, although it would not be accurate to describe it as consensual as in some other parts of sub-Saharan Africa. First, it is fairly obvious that the traditions of political authority in formal Ethiopian politics militate against any expectation of a robust and highly participatory type of political debate in the immediate future. There have been brief periods of exciting deliberative possibility – immediately after the 1974 Revolution and prior to the 2005 elections are two dramatic examples that demonstrate that Ethiopian social and political life can incorporate inclusion, participation, and social dialogue. Nevertheless, Ethiopian political and social life in both instances rapidly returned to rather familiar patterns of repression, authoritarianism, and narrowing of political space. In the recent period this is particularly evidenced by repressive legislation regarding media and civil society, periodic massive and arbitrary detention and harassment of political opposition, and, as a result of this, the relentless and highly damaging exodus of Ethiopian intellectuals, professionals, and entrepreneurs.

There is, however, another perhaps even more critical reason for looking for alternate spaces for building social discourse on citizenship within Ethiopian society, and it speaks to the competing emancipatory projects explored in this book. Because of the kinds of complex and persistent inequalities around gendered identities and the fact that these have not been treated as comprehensively or effectively as other inequalities, it would be reasonable to assert that this should be the focus of engagement and intervention moving forward. At the same time, because norms of participation and representation are rarely, if ever, discussed in the context of the Ethiopian family, home, and neighborhood to nearly the same extent provides a unique and exciting opportunity for Ethiopians to consider new spaces of citizen creation and citizenship expansion as well as new forums for engaging meaningful citizenship outside of the formalized political realms that are, for the time, mostly closed. Rather than focusing exclusively on the formal politics of elections and constitutions, perhaps there is a chance for Ethiopians and other Africans to use these well-honed tools to critique and reform the citizenship of the home and the family.

APPENDIX I

Methodology

I conducted research in Ethiopia over the course of several years. My interest in the country began while I was living in Ethiopia's southern neighbor, Kenya. While living in Kenya in 1997–1998, during that country's second multiparty election, I observed the types of violence surrounding particularly electoral politics, as well as the tremendous conversation about ethnicity that happened, both on the national stage but also over tea or dinner, in office relationships, and neighborhood life. I was intrigued by the possibility of institutional solutions to the negative consequences of the entrenchment and politicization of ethnic identities. Although Kenya itself is such a complex and fascinating place to think about these questions, work-related travel to Ethiopia suggested to me that federalism was an important and innovative experiment that was actually much more relevant to the types of questions I had. Returning to the United States for my graduate work, I turned from Kiswahili to Amharic, from unitary and nationalist rhetoric to decentralizing and ethnonationalist discourse, from Kenya to Ethiopia. Early travel in 1998 and 2001 helped me frame questions and methods for my fieldwork, which was conducted from January to December 2003.

Once in Ethiopia, I focused on language policy. Because I was interested primarily in federalism and ethnic identity, language policy provided a discrete and slightly less politically charged way to go about analyzing the elements of decentralization proposed and underway and, particularly, to begin to collect perspectives on identity politics. The first six months was mainly concentrated on elite interviews – intellectuals, politicians, government officials, international representatives, and civil society activists and practitioners. This was accomplished through snowball sampling. These were done one on one, by me, and in English. I have not included any personal names here and only indicated the interviewee by date, location of interview, and general category of occupation, in order to protect respondents' identities.[1]

Although I was initially planning to do one-on-one interviews at the local level, a crucial intervention came through a lunch conversation with a dear friend, herself a respected Ethiopian anthropologist also completing her doctoral dissertation research. She advised that focus groups would be far more effective in eliciting opinions, particularly from parents and teachers at the community level. A pilot set of focus groups and interviews was done in Wolaitta region in May 2003, and this helped me to think through not only process but also content. For instance, the school director really needed to be interviewed individually, and first. Teachers, like parents, seemed to feel more comfortable in the group setting, where one response could elicit comments from other participants. Beyond the format, we were able to reorganize the order of questions and realized we could ask more direct questions than we thought. We added an initial question about ethnicity – What makes a person Wolaitta? – before the sets of language policy questions. Not only was it possible to ask about ethnicity in this somewhat circuitous way but it gave us insights into how language identities ranked among other possible indicators of identity such as phenotype, religion, cultural practices, and so on. And by asking this question first, we had not necessarily yet indicated our interest in the topic of language policy. Finally, the rewording and asking of multiple questions all aiming at similar focal points proved a valuable way to initiate discussion. As with the elite interviews, no identifiers are used here. All that was recorded during the focus groups was gender and occupation, as well as location of the group.

I say "we" because I conducted all of these focus groups and interviews with the assistance of my husband, an Ethiopian American fluent in Amharic and on leave from his employment in the United States. I met Dawit in Minnesota, while I was in the process of applying for dissertation fieldwork support. He had left Ethiopia at age sixteen, at the height of the Derg's various military campaigns, and had only returned once in fifteen years. The chance to accompany me was an exciting opportunity for him, but it also provided me with an "insider/outsider" right alongside. Not only was he my translator and research assistant, our

---

[1] See L. Smith 2005 for more information on methodology, particularly Human Subjects Approval through the UCLA Institutional Review Board.

conversations throughout the day, on long bus rides across the country and over dinner each night, provided critical insights into the work. Although I chose the questions and set the theoretical framework, like any well-trained and capable research assistant and translator, my husband's role in the ethnographic work cannot be overstated. He was perceptive and alert to cultural cues I would easily have missed, but he also helped me think about the most basic parts of the focus group. How can we ask the school director to arrange the room for the meeting? How do we make sure that the parents and teachers who attend are randomly selected, not biased in favor of or against the language policy or federalism in general, for instance? Especially, how can we facilitate the discussion so that everyone contributes as they would like, so that not only one or two people dominate? And critically, how can we indicate our concern with an equal number of women participants and encourage their participation? The success of a focus group conversation in a remote school classroom in a hamlet of Ethiopia depends on the balance of physical environment, social interaction, and, most particularly, the control and presence of a figure of authority. One must come with enough documentation to indicate that one has permission to operate but not so much that free conversation cannot ensue. Striking that balance is probably the most challenging aspect of ethnographic research of this kind, at least in Ethiopia.

Did Dawit's presence and my identity as a white American woman married to an Ethiopian man, a citizen of the United States, change the research dynamic? Undoubtedly it did. We introduced ourselves at the start of every interview as husband and wife, explaining that the research was for my doctoral dissertation, and that Dawit lived in America with me, but that our family was also here in the country. We did not deceive our respondents into thinking that we were professional colleagues. In fact, we honestly explained our great commitment to development and peace in Ethiopia, something that Ethiopians would most definitely expect of diaspora returnees but not necessarily of a typical foreign researcher. This seemed to gain us a bit of access and trust. There were often inquiries about my ability to cook Ethiopian food or my crude attempts at Amharic or Afaan Oromo. Questions about where we were living, where Dawit's family was from, and of course, how many children we had, were quite common. I will leave it to Ethiopians and my readers to decide if this enhanced the findings or not. Like all aspects of conducting political ethnography, my identity and Dawit's identity and presence, our working team, had an impact on each focus group and interview.

School-based interviews and focus groups were conducted from May through November 2003. We visited twenty schools in three regional states of Ethiopia. In between that time, I continued elite interviews. I also volunteered for some time as a trainer of trainers for the newly revised civic and ethical education curriculum. This opportunity to train high school teachers from across Ethiopia was another tremendously valuable research opportunity because I learned through them the specific challenges of teaching topics such as democracy, the 1995 Constitution, and human rights. Those high school teachers are on the front lines of citizen making in Ethiopia. They are undertrained, underpaid, and underappreciated. Yet the work they do is crucial in molding Ethiopian citizens with new ideas of meaningful citizenship and equality, built on top of centuries of hierarchy and conformity. It is a work of monumental significance. And they are passionate and capable professionals, quite impressive in their reflective worldview and humble in their assessment of their capabilities.

The fieldwork was mainly completed by the end of 2003, and the writing followed, including transcribing and translating some of the focus group sessions. Assistance was provided by a well-trained Afaan Oromo translator in the Minneapolis area. Further conversations, follow-up field trips, and many conferences have all contributed to my analytical concern with citizenship. I did not know this would be the "way out" of the research, so to speak. At the end of 2003, I had a meeting with an esteemed Oromo intellectual, and over a steaming cup of coffee at a café near Addis Ababa University, he reminded me that I had the interviews, the field notes, the images. Now I had to "find the door out" of all I had seen and heard. As I wrote in the cold Minnesota winter the following year, the door out was by way of the citizen. I kept returning again and again to a concern with those parents and teachers out in the towns and villages, people for whom parliaments and elections and party politics seem to matter little. What matters is how to acquire the resources for themselves and their children to survive, and yes, to thrive. A resigned but hopeful air permeated the field notes and pictures on my desk. A slow and patient approach, for sure, but one that was not dejected, not uninformed, not unengaged. Ethiopian citizens, the peasantry especially, has suffered and struggled for a long time. They live mostly in tremendous poverty and great physical uncertainty. But they reinvent and reenergize their lives each day, through family, through coffee and food, through creativity in song and poem and crafts. People warmly welcomed us, patiently answered our questions, and accepted our interest in staying with the work of "development" in Ethiopia, as they are also committed to it.

I have tried to resist the danger of poorly matched comparison – to other parts of Africa even – but especially to my own home context of the United States. Still, I recently taught a lovely historical text on the women's movement in the United States by historian Stephanie Coontz and was struck by several similarities. First, the women's movement in the United States was often led by elite women but as it democratized, incorporating the concerns and demands of black women, Latina women, lesbian women, poor women, and so on, it contributed to the democratization of the larger society. Second, these changes occurred at a very slow pace in the life of a given family or community. Coontz has spoken of the prospects for her mother and grandmother as vastly different from her own. Of course, my eighteen-year-old female students live in a world strikingly different from the one in which Coontz went to college. My reply to those who challenge my approach to citizenship, especially the meaningful participatory citizenship of women, because it requires great patience and time is: You are right. It will be a slow process. What fieldwork in Ethiopia has given me, however, is a great optimism for the creativity and persistence, even at a slow slog, that human beings are capable of. Ethiopian parents, male and female alike, evidenced a commitment to a more equal society for their children, and they are creating it each day in home and community. The citizenship of this book cannot come from the constitution or an election or even a coalition of political or economic elites. It must be built up by families.

From the standpoint of methodology, the work never ended. I have returned to Ethiopia for other endeavors almost every year since, sometimes for a few weeks, sometimes a few months. There have been trips to Bonga, Tepi, Bench Maji, Robe, and Jimma, as well as lots of stays in the Shola market. Ethiopia moves on, making more citizens, and of course, like many women, I have born one of these future citizens too. The concerns of a more equal citizenship, a meaningful citizenship, provide the impetus to all this work.

APPENDIX II

Questionnaire for Parents and Community Members (English)

<u>Background information</u>

Focus Group #:

Date/Time (start and end):

Facilitator (name and title):

Translator (name and title):

Other government/nongovernment personnel present (those who are not respondents):

Region:

Zone:

Woreda:

Town/Village name (PA/Qebelle):

Urban, semi-urban, rural, or remote rural:

Location of focus group (give as many details as necessary):

Number of adults present (over age 18):

Number of each gender present (or approximate):

Interview Questions

What is your age?

Are you married?

How many people were born in this town?

What grade level did you finish in school?

Can you read and write in Amharic?

Can you read and write in English?

Do you or anyone in your family have a job?

What is your ethnic group?

How many people here are of another ethnicity? Which ethnicities?

What makes a person Oromo/Amhara/Gurage/Siltie/Wolaitta/Berta/Gumuz/Shinasha?

What is your mother tongue?

Can you speak another language besides your mother tongue?

Which ones?

Can you also read and write in your mother tongue?

Do you have children?

How many children do you have?

What do you think of your children's school? Are you happy with it?

What language(s) are they taught in?

At what grade levels?

Are you happy with the language policy in your children's school?

Do you know when the decision was made for children to be taught in your mother tongue?

Previously, did they learn in a different language?

If so, which language?

Were you involved at all in meetings regarding this decision?

If yes, who told you about the meeting – the school, the Qebelle, the Woreda or Zonal Council, or someone you know? Do you remember when they were held and who led the meetings?

Who made the decision for children in your area to learn in this language?

Government in Addis Ababa_____
Government in regional capital_____
Local people from this area_____
Other_____(identify)

In your opinion, do you think learning in your mother tongue is important for developing your child's culture and history?

Why or why not?

Do you think it helps your child to learn and understand better than learning in other language?

Why or why not?

Do you think that learning in your mother tongue affects national unity?

Why or why not?

Do your children have access to written materials (besides school texts) in your mother tongue?

Newspapers____ Children's books _____ Other _____

Are there any radio programs in your mother tongue?

Do you listen to them?

Do you know if there are any other children at this school that do not speak your mother tongue?

Do most of the teachers at this school speak the language of the people from this area?

Do you think that the teachers at your child's school are properly trained in your local language?

If you had a choice to send your child to another government (public) school which taught in a different language, would you send them?

Why or why not?

Compared to the past, is the way education is given now better or worse?

Why or why not?

Please list in order of importance the languages you would most prefer your children be taught in:

1. _____

2. _____

3. _____

Specific Questions for Siltie and Gurage Regions

[For Siltie respondents]: Did you vote in the referendum two years ago about separating the Siltie from the Gurage?

[For Siltie respondents]: Who told you to vote?

[For Siltie respondents]: Why did you vote?

[For Siltie respondents]: Are you happy with the decision made by the Siltie people to become their own zone?

[For Siltie respondents]: Why or why not?

[For Gurage respondents]: Did you hear about the referendum two years ago to separate the Siltie from the Gurage?

[For Gurage respondents]: What do you think of the vote by the Siltie to separate?

APPENDIX III

Questionnaire for School Directors

<u>Background information</u>

Focus Group #: _____

Date/Time (start and end): _____

Facilitator (name and title): _____

Translator (name and title): _____

Other government/nongovernment personnel present (those who are not respondents):

_____

Region: _____

Zone: _____

Woreda: _____

Town/Village name (PA/Qebelle): _____

Urban, semi-urban, rural, or remote rural: _____

Location of focus group (give as many details as necessary): _____

Number of adults present (over age 18): _____

Number of each gender present (or approximate): _____

Interview Questions

A. Basic Information on the School
What is the enrollment at your school?

What percent of the students are female?

How many teachers are on staff here? How many are female?

What percent have the proper qualifications (i.e. Certificate for First Cycle and Diploma for Second Cycle)?

What are the facilities here, including number of classrooms?

How many shifts do you have?

Do you have a laboratory?

Do you have a library?

B. Personal Experience
How long have you been a school director?

How long were you a teacher?

Where were you a teacher?

C. Language Policy
Who made the decision regarding the language policy in your area? When was this?

How do the parents feel about the language policy in this school? Explain.

How do the teachers feel about the language policy? Explain.

How is the quality of the teaching materials (textbooks and teacher's guides) in the local language?

How is the quality of teacher training in the local language?

How is the student performance as related to the use of the local language (better or not)? Explain (also give drop-out rates, repetition rates, and exam scores, if available).

How does teaching in the local language affect performance of the students?

Do you think that learning in a local language is important for developing a child's culture, history, and customs?

Do you think that learning in a local language affects national unity of Ethiopia?

Do most of the children in your school have access to other written materials in the local language, including dictionaries?

What makes a person Oromo/Amhara/Gurage/Siltie/Woalitta/Berta/Gumuz/Shinasha?

D. General Educational Issues in Ethiopia

What are the general issues your school faces?

How would you relate the relationship of this school to the village or area that it serves? Is the community supportive and interested in the education of your children?

Are there any other questions which I did not ask or information you would like to add?

APPENDIX IV

Questionnaire for Teachers

<u>Background information</u>

Focus Group #: _____

Date/Time (start and end): _____

Facilitator (name and title): _____

Translator (name and title): _____

Other government/nongovernment personnel present (those who are not respondents):

_____

Region: _____

Zone: _____

Woreda: _____

Town/Village name (PA/Qebelle): _____

Urban, semi-urban, rural, or remote rural: _____

Location of focus group (give as many details as necessary):

_____

Number of adults present (over age 18): _____

Number of each gender present (or approximate): _____

Interview Questions

What grade level do you teach?

What subject do you teach?

How long have you been teaching at this school?

Have you ever taught at any other school?

Where and when?

Where did you do your training?

Teacher Training Institute or Teacher Training College?

For how long?

When?

Do you have a Certificate, Diploma, or Degree?

What is your first language?

What other languages do you speak?

What language(s) were you taught in school?

What language are your classes taught in?

Did you receive training in this language?

If yes, when was this and for how long?

What language do most children in your classes speak at home?

Do you know if there are any other children in your class or at this school that do not speak the nationality language of this area?

Do you think most parents in this area are happy with the language policy in the schools?

Do you think that if most parents had a choice to send their child to another school which taught a different language, would they send them?

Why or why not?

Do you think learning in a local language is important for developing a child's culture, customs, and history?

Do you think it helps children learn more or less than learning in other language?

Why or why not?

Who made the decision for children in your area to learn in this language?

Government in Addis Ababa ____ Government in regional capital___
Local people ___ Other_____ (identify)

Do you think that learning in your nationality language affects the national unity of Ethiopia?

Do most of the children in your class have access to written materials in the nationality language?

Newspapers____ Children's books _____ Other_____

Are the textbooks and teacher's guides that you use to teach various subjects in the nationality language adequate? Please explain.

When did you start teaching in the nationality language in this area?

How would you rate the relationship between this village/area and this primary school? Is the community supportive and interested in the education of children? Please explain.

What makes a person Oromo/Amhara/Gurage/Siltie/Wolaitta/Berta/Gumuz/Shinasha?

Bibliography

Aalen, Lovise. "Ethnic Federalism in a Dominant Party State: The Ethiopian Experience, 1991–2000." MA thesis, University of Bergen, Norway, 2001.

Aalen, Lovise and Kjetil Tronvoll. "The 2008 Ethiopian Local Elections: The Return of Electoral Authoritarianism." *African Affairs* 108, 430, 2009.

Abbink, Jon. "Breaking and Making the State: The Dynamics of Ethnic Democracy in Ethiopia." *Journal of Contemporary African Studies* 13, 1995.

Abraham Hussein and Habtamu Wondimu. *The Culture and History of the Siltie-Speaking People of Azernet Berbere* (in Amharic). Addis Ababa: Bole Publishers, 1991.

Adams, B.A. "A Tagmemic Analysis of the Wolaitta Language." Ph.D. dissertation, University of London, 1983.

Advocates for Human Rights. "Human Rights in Ethiopia: Through the Eyes of the Oromo Diaspora." December 2009.

Ake, Claude. *The Feasibility of Democracy in Africa*. Dakar: Codesria, 2000.

Alemseged Abbay. "Diversity and State-Building in Ethiopia." *African Affairs* 103, 2004.

Aminzade, R. "From Race to Citizenship: The Indigenization Debate in Post-Socialist Tanzania." *Studies in Comparative International Development* 38, 1, 2003.

Anderson, Benedict R. *Imagined Communities: Reflections on the Origin and Spread of Nationalism*. Rev. and extended ed. London and New York: Verso, 1991.

Arendt, Hannah. *The Origins of Totalitarianism*. NY: The World Publishing Company. 1951.

Asafa Jalata. *Oromia and Ethiopia: State Formation and Ethnonational Conflict, 1868–1992*. Boulder, CO: Lynne Rienner Publishers, 1993.

Asfaw Girma-Selassie, David L. Appleyard, and Edward Ullendorff. *The Amharic Letters of Emperor Theodore of Ethiopia to Queen Victoria and Her Special Envoy*. Preserved in the India Office Library and the Public Record Office, Oriental documents; 2. Oxford and New York: Published for the British Academy by the Oxford University Press, 1979.

Asmarom Legesse. *Gada: Three Approaches to the Study of African Society*. New York: Free Press, 1973.

Asnake Kefale Adegehe. "Federalism and Ethnic Conflict in Ethiopia: A Comparative Study of the Somali and Benishangul-Gumuz Regions." Ph.D. dissertation, Leiden University, 2009.

Assefa Fisseha. "Theory versus Practice in the implementation of Ethiopia's ethnic federalism" in *Ethnic Federalism: The Ethiopian Experience in Comparative Perspective* edited by David Turton, Athens: Ohio University Press, 2006.

Assefa Tolera. "Ethnic Integration and Conflict: The Case of Indigenous Oromo and Amhara Settlers in Aaroo Addis Alem, Kiramu Area, Northeastern Wallaga." MA thesis, Addis Ababa University, 1995.

Bahru Zewde. *A History of Modern Ethiopia, 1855–1974*. Athens: Ohio University Press, 1991.

Pioneers of Change in Ethiopia: The Reformist Intellectuals of the Early Twentieth Century. Athens: Ohio University Press, 2002.

"Systems of Local Governance among the Gurage: The *Yajoka Qicha* and the *Gordana Sera*." In *Ethiopia: The Challenge of Democracy from Below*, edited by Bahru Zewde and Siegfried Pausewang. Uppsala, Sweden: Nordiska Afrikainstitutet, 2003.

Bahru Zewde, ed. *Society, State, and Identity in Africa History*. Addis Ababa: Forum for Social Studies, 2008.

Bahru Zewde and Siegfried Pausewang, eds. *Ethiopia: The Challenge of Democracy from Below*. Uppsala, Sweden: Nordiska Afrikainstitutet, 2003.

Balsvik, Randi Rønning. *Haile Sellassie's Students: The Intellectual and Social Background to Revolution, 1952–1977*. East Lansing: African Studies Center, Michigan State University in cooperation with the Norwegian Council of Science and the Humanities, 1985.

The Quest for Expression: The State and the University under Three Regimes, 1952–2005. Addis Ababa: Addis Ababa University Press, 2007.

Bamgbose, Ayo. *Mother Tongue Education: The West African Experience*. London: Hodder and Stoughton, 1976.

Barkan, Joel D. "The Many Faces of Africa: Democracy across a Varied Continent." *Harvard International Review* 24, 2, 2002.

Barnes, Cedric. "Ethiopia: A Sociopolitical Assessment." Report of the UNHCR Status Determination and Protection Information Section, May 2006.

Barry, Brian M. *Culture and Equality: An Egalitarian Critique of Multiculturalism*. Cambridge, MA: Harvard University Press, 2001.

Bassi, Marco. *Decisions in the Shade: Political and Juridical Processes among the Oromo-Borana*. Trenton, NJ: Red Sea Press, 2005.

Baxter, P.T.W., Jan Hultin, and Alessandro Triulzi. *Being and Becoming Oromo: Historical and Anthropological Enquiries*. Lawrenceville, NJ: Red Sea Press, 1996.

Baylis, Elena A. "Beyond Rights: Legal Process and Ethnic Conflicts." *Michigan Journal of International Law* 25, 2004.

Beiner, Ronald. *Theorizing Citizenship*. SUNY Series in Political Theory: Contemporary Issues. Albany: State University of New York Press, 1995.

Belete Bizuneh. "Women in Ethiopian History: Bibliographic Review." *Northeast African Studies* 8, 3, 2001.

Bender, M. Lionel. "Ethiopian Language Policy, 1974–1981." *Anthropological Linguistics* 27, 1985.

Bender, M. Lionel, J.D. Bowen, R.L. Cooper, and C.A. Ferguson, eds. *Language in Ethiopia*. London: Oxford University Press, 1976.

Benhabib, Seyla. "'Nous' Et 'Les Autres': The Politics of Complex Cultural Dialogue in a Global Civilization." In *Multicultural Questions*, edited by Christian Joppke and Steven Lukes. New York: Oxford University Press, 1999.

Berhanu Bibiso. "Production Practices in Wolaitta of South-West Ethiopia: The Case of Damot-Woyde." MA thesis, Addis Ababa University, 1995.

Berman, Bruce, Dickson Eyoh, and Will Kymlicka, eds. *Ethnicity and Democracy in Africa*. Athens: Ohio University Press, 2004.

Biseswar, Indrawatie. "Problems of Feminist Leadership among Educated Women in Ethiopia: Taking Stock in the Third Millennium." *Journal of Developing Societies* 24, 2, 2008.

Boothe, Ken and Roland Walker. "Mother Tongue Education in Ethiopia: From Policy to Implementation." *Language Problems and Language Planning* 21, 1, 1997.

Bosniak, Linda. "Persons and Citizens in Constitutional Thought." *I-Con* 8, 1, 2010.

Bratton, Michael and Nic van de Walle. *Democratic Experiments in Africa: Regime Transitions in Comparative Perspective*. New York: Cambridge University Press, 1997.

Bratton, Michael, Robert Mattes, and E. Gyimah-Boadi, eds. *Public Opinion, Market Reform, and Democracy in Africa*, New York: Cambridge University Press, 2005.

Brautigam, Deborah. "The 'Mauritius Miracles': Democracy, Institutions, and Economic Policy." In *State, Conflict, and Democracy in Africa*, edited by Richard Joseph. Boulder, CO: Lynne Rienner Publishers, 1999.

Brietzke, Paul. "Law and Rural Development in Ethiopia." *African Studies Review* 18, 2, 1975.

Brubaker, Rogers. *Citizenship and Nationhood in France and Germany*. Cambridge, MA: Harvard University Press, 1992.

Carmichael, Tim. "Approaching Ethiopian History: Addis Ababa and Local Governance in Harar, c. 1900–1950." Ph.D. dissertation, Michigan State University, 2001.

Chernetsov, Sevir B. "On the Origins of the Amhara." *St. Petersburg Journal of African Studies* 1, 1, 1993.

Clapham, Christopher. *Haile Selassie's Government*. New York: Praeger, 1969.

   Transformation and Continuity in Revolutionary Ethiopia. Cambridge: Cambridge University Press, 1988.

   "Rewriting Ethiopian History." *Annales d'Ethiopie* 28, 2002.

   "Post-War Ethiopia: The Trajectories of Crisis." *Review of African Political Economy* 36, 120, 2009.

Cohen, Gideon. "Identity and Opportunity: The Implications of Using Local Languages in the Primary Education of SNNPR, Ethiopia." Ph.D. dissertation, London, SOAS, 2000.

Collier, Paul. *Breaking the Conflict Trap: Civil War and Development Policy.* Washington, DC: World Bank, 2003.

Coontz, Stephanie. *A Strange Stirring: The "Feminine Mystique" and American Women at the Dawn of the 1960s.* New York: Basic Books, 2011.

Cooper, Robert L. "Government Language Policy." In *Language in Ethiopia,* edited by M. Lionel Bender, J.D. Bowen, R.L. Cooper, and C.A. Ferguson. London: Oxford University Press, 1976.

Cornell, Svante E. "Autonomy as a Source of Conflict: Caucasian Conflicts in Theoretical Perspective." *World Politics* 54, 2, 2002.

Crawford, Gordon and Christof Hartmann, eds. *Decentralisation in Africa: A Pathway Out of Poverty and Conflict?* Amsterdam: Amsterdam University Press, 2008.

Crotty, Patricia McGee. "Family Law in Sub-Saharan Africa." *Journal of Women, Politics & Policy* 30, 4, 2009.

Crummey, Donald. "Society and Ethnicity in the Politics of Christian Ethiopia during the Zamana Mesafent." *The International Journal of African Historical Studies* 8, 2, 1975.

"Abyssinian Feudalism." *Past & Present* 89, 1980.

"Society, State, and Nationality in the Recent Historiography of Ethiopia." *The Journal of African History* 31, 1, 1990.

Land and Society in the Christian Kingdom of Ethiopia, from the Thirteenth to the Twentieth Century. Urbana: University of Illinois Press, 2000.

Daniel Aberra. "Language (Wo-Ga-Go-Da) Caused Conflict in North Omo Zone: A Lesson toward Future Policy Implementations." In *OSSREA Workshop on Conflict in the Horn: Prevention and Resolution.* Addis Ababa: OSSREA, n.d.

Deckha, Maneesha. "Is Culture Taboo? Feminism, Intersectionality, and Culture Talk in Law." *Canadian Journal of Women & the Law* 16, 1, 2004.

Dereje Feyissa. "The Experience of Gambella Regional State." In *Ethnic Federalism: The Ethiopian Experience in Comparative Perspective,* edited by David Turton. Athens: Ohio University Press, 2006.

"The Ethnic Self and the National Other: Anywaa Identity Politics in Reference to the Ethiopian State System." In *Society, State, and Identity in African History,* edited by Bahru Zewde. Addis Ababa: Forum for Social Studies, 2008.

Deveaux, Monique. "A Deliberative Approach to Conflicts of Culture." In *Minorities within Minorities: Equality, Rights, and Diversity,* edited by Avigail Eisenberg and Jeff Spinner-Halev. New York: Cambridge University Press, 2005.

Diamond, Larry Jay and Marc F. Plattner, eds. *The Global Resurgence of Democracy,* 2nd ed. Baltimore, MD: Johns Hopkins University Press, 1996.

Donham, Donald L., and Wendy James, eds. *The Southern Marches of Imperial Ethiopia: Essays in History and Social Anthropology.* Athens: Ohio University Press, 2002.

Donham, Donald L. "Old Abyssinia and the new Ethiopian empire: themes in social history," in Donham and James *The southern Marches of Imperial Ethiopia: Essay sin History and Social Anthropology* Athens: Ohio University Press, 2002.

Doorenspleet, Renske. "Political Parties, Party Systems, and Democracy in Sub-Saharan Africa." In *African Political Parties: Evolution, Institutionalism, and Governance*, edited by M.A. Mohamed Salih. London: Pluto, 2003.

Edwards, Jon R. "Slavery, the Slave Trade and Economic Reorganization of Ethiopia 1916–1935", *African Economic History*, 11, 1982.

Eide, Oeyvind. *Revolution and Religion in Ethiopia: A Study of Church and Politics with Special Reference to the Ethiopian Evangelical Church Mekane Yesus, 1974–1985*. Studia missionalia Upsaliensia, 66. Uppsala: Uppsala University, 1996.

Eisenberg, Avigail and Jeff Spinner-Halev, eds. *Minorities within Minorities: Equality, Rights, and Diversity*. New York: Cambridge University Press, 2005.

Ekeh, Peter. "Colonialism and the Two Publics in Africa: A Theoretical Statement." *Comparative Studies in Society and History* 17, 1, 1975.

"Individuals' Basic Security Needs and the Limits of Democratization in Africa." In *Democracy and Ethnicity in Africa*, edited by Bruce Berman, et al., Athens, OH: Ohio University Press, 2004.

Elaigwu, J. Isawa. "Nation-Building and Changing Political Structures." In *Africa since 1935*, edited by Ali Al Amin Mazrui, Christophe Wondji, and UNESCO. International Scientific Committee for the Drafting of a General History of Africa. Berkeley: University of California Press, 1993.

Emebet Mulugeta. "Trajectory of the Institute of Gender Studies at Addis Ababa University, Ethiopia." *Feminist Africa* 9, 2009.

Englebert, Pierre. *Africa: Unity, Sovereignty, and Sorrow*. Boulder, CO: Lynne Rienner Publishers, 2009.

Ethiopian Human Rights Council. *Compiled Reports of EHRCO*. Addis Ababa: EHRCO, 2003a.

Compiled Reports of EHRCO. Addis Ababa: EHRCO, April 2003b.

"*An Ethnic Conflict Flared Up in West Harrarghe Zone, 71st Special Report.*" Addis Ababa: Ethiopian Human Rights Council, 2003c.

"Human Rights Violations Occurred during clashes between students and security forces in Oromia Region, 76th Special report", Addis Ababa: Ethiopian Human Rights Council, 2004.

Ethiopian Society of Population Studies. "Gender Inequality and Women's Employment: In-depth analysis of the Ethiopian Demographic and Health Survey 2005," October 2008.

Etzioni, Amitai. *The Essential Communitarian Reader*. Lanham, MD: Rowman & Littlefield, 1998.

Etzioni, Amitai, D. Volmert, and E. Rothschild. *The Communitarian Reader: Beyond the Essentials*. Lanham, MD: Rowman & Littlefield, 2004

Ezekiel Gebissa. "The Italian Invasion, the Ethiopian Empire, and Oromo Nationalism: The Significance of the Western Oromo Confederation of 1936." *Northeast African Studies* 9, 3, 2002a.

"Introduction: Rending Audible the Voices of the Powerless." *Northeast African Studies* 9, 3, 2002b.

Leaf of Allah: Khat and Agricultural Transformation in Harerge Ethiopia, 1875–1991. Athens: Ohio University Press, 2004.

Ezekiel Gebissa, ed. *Contested Terrain, Essays on Oromo Studies, Ethiopianist Discourse, and Politically Engaged Scholarship*. Trenton, NJ: Red Sea Press, 2009.

Fekadu Gadamu. "Ethnic Associations in Ethiopia and the Maintenance of Urban-Rural Relationships, with Special Reference to the Alemgana-Walamo Road Construction." Ph.D. Dissertation, London: University of London, 1972.

Fishman, Joshua A. *Language and Ethnicity in Minority Sociolinguistic Perspective*. Philadelphia: Multilingual Matters, Ltd., 1989.

   Handbook of Language and Ethnic Identity. New York: Oxford University Press, 1999.

Fisseha Mekonnen. "Some Socio-Psychological Implications of the Trend Towards Promoting the Languages of Ethiopia." In *Ethiopia in Broader Perspective: Papers of the XIIIth International Conference of Ethiopian Studies*. Kyoto, Japan: Shokado Book Sellers, 1997.

Freedom House. "Freedom in the World: Ethiopia, 2011," online at http://www. freedomhouse.org/report/freedom-world/2011/ethiopia.

Gabreyesus Hailemariam. *The Gurague and Their Culture*. Los Angeles: Vantage Press, 1991.

Gebru Tareke. *Ethiopia: Power and Protest: Peasant Revolts in the Twentieth Century*. African Studies Series, 71. New York: Cambridge University Press, 1991.

   The Ethiopian Revolution: War in the Horn of Africa. New Haven, CT: Yale University Press, 2009.

Gershman, Carl and Maina Kiai. "Out of Africa." *The New Republic*, February 4, 2009.

Geschiere, Peter. *The Perils of Belonging: Autochthony, Citizenship, and Exclusion in Africa and Europe*. Chicago: University of Chicago Press, 2009.

Girma-Selassie Asfaw, David Appleyard, eds. with Edward Ullendorff, *The Amharic Letters of EmperorTheodore of Ethiopia to Queen Victoria and her Special Envoy Preserved in the India Office Library*, Oxford: Oxford University Press, 1979.

Girmay Berhe Tsadik. "Implementation of Decentralization of Educational Management at Woreda Level in Tigray and Amhara National Regional States in Ethiopia." MA thesis, Addis Ababa University, 1998.

Glickman, Harvey. *Ethnic Conflict and Democratization in Africa*. Atlanta: African Studies Assoc. Press, 1995.

Gray, John. *Liberalism*. 2nd ed. Minneapolis: University of Minnesota Press, 1995.

Greenfield, Richard. *Ethiopia: A New Political History*. New York: F.A. Praeger, 1965.

Gurr, Ted Robert. *Minorities at Risk: A Global View of Ethnopolitical Conflicts*. Washington, DC: United States Institute of Peace Press, 1993.

Habtamu Wondimu. "Psychological Modernity and Attitudes to Social Change in Ethiopian Young Adults: The Role of Ethnic Identity and Stereotypes." In *NIRP Research for Policy Series* 9. Amsterdam: The Netherlands-Israel Development Research Program, 2001.

Habyarimana, James, Macartan Humphreys, Daniel N. Posner and Jeremy M Weinstein. *Coethnicity: Diversity and the Dilemmas of Collective Action.* NY: Russell Sage Foundation, 2009.

Hale, Henry. "Divided We Stand: Institutional Sources of Ethnofederal State Survival and Collapse." *World Politics* 56, 2, 2004.

Halisi, C.R.D. *Black Political Thought in the Making of South African Democracy.* Bloomington: Indiana University Press, 1999.

Halisi, C.R.D., P.J. Kaiser, and S.N. Ndegwa. "Rethinking Citizenship in Africa: Guest Editors' Introduction: The Multiple Meanings of Citizenship – Rights, Identity, and Social Justice in Africa." *Africa Today* 45, ¾, 1998.

Harbeson, John W. *The Ethiopian Transformation: The Quest for the Post-Imperial State.* Boulder, CO: Westview Press, 1988.

"Rethinking Democratic Transitions: Lessons from Eastern and Southern Africa." In *State, Conflict, and Democracy in Africa*, edited by Richard Joseph. Boulder, CO: Lynne Rienner Publishers, 1999.

"Ethiopia's Extended Transition." *Journal of Democracy* 16, 4, 2005.

Heater, D.B. *What Is Citizenship?* Malden, MA: Polity Press, 1999.

Heran Sereke-Brhan. "'Like Adding Water to Milk': Marriage and Politics in Nineteenth-Century Ethiopia." *International Journal of African Historical Studies* 38, 1, 2005.

Herbst, John. "The Role of Citizenship Laws in Multiethnic Societies: Evidence from Africa." In *State, Conflict, and Democracy in Africa*, edited by Richard Joseph. Boulder, CO: Lynne Rienner Publishers, 1999.

Herr, Ranjoo Seodu. "A Third World Feminist Defense of Multiculturalism." *Social Theory and Practice* 30, 1, 2004.

Hoben, Allan. *Land Tenure among the Amhara of Ethiopia: The Dynamics of Cognatic Descent.* Monographs in Ethiopian Land Tenure, No. 4. Chicago: University of Chicago Press, 1973.

Hoben, Susan J. "The Language of Education in Ethiopia: Empowerment or Imposition?" In *New Trends in Ethiopian Studies, Papers of the 12th International Conference of Ethiopian Studies.* East Lansing: Michigan State University, 1994.

Holcomb, Bonnie K. and Sisai Ibssa. *The Invention of Ethiopia.* Trenton, NJ: Red Sea Press, 1990.

Horowitz, Donald L. *Ethnic Groups in Conflict.* Berkeley: University of California Press, 1985.

A Democratic South Africa? Constitutional Engineering in a Divided Society. Perspectives on Southern Africa. 46. Berkeley: University of California Press, 1991.

Hudson, Grover. "Gurage Studies: Collected Articles by Wolf Leslau." *Journal of the American Oriental Society* 114, 4, 1994.

"Linguistic Analysis of the 1994 Ethiopian Census." *Northeast African Studies* 6, 3, 2003.

"Languages of Ethiopia and Languages of the 1994 Ethiopian Census." *Aethiopica: International Journal of Ethiopian and Eritrean Studies* 7, 2004.

Human Rights Watch. "Ethiopia: Lessons in Repression: Violations of Academic Freedom in Ethiopia," 15, 2, 2003.

Suppressing Dissent: Human Rights Abuses and Political Repression in Ethiopia's Oromia Region. New York: Human Rights Watch, vol. 17, no. 7(1), 2005a.

"Targeting the Anuak: Human Rights Violations and Crimes against Humanity in Ethiopia's Gambella Region," vol. 17, no. 3(a). New York: Human Rights Watch, 2005b.

Huntington, Samuel P. *Who are we? The challenges to America's national identity*. NY: Simon & Schuster, 2004.

Ihonvbere, Julius Omozuanvbo and John Mukum Mbaku. *Political Liberalization and Democratication in Africa: lessons from country experiences*. Westport, Conn: Praeger, 2003.

Immergut, Ellen M. "The Theoretical Core of the New Institutionalism." *Politics & Society* 26, 1, 1998.

Isin, Engin F. and Greg M. Nielsen, eds. *Acts of Citizenship*. New York: Palgrave Macmillan, 2008.

Jain, Pratibha. "Balancing Minority Rights and Gender Justice: The Impact of Protecting Multiculturalism on Women's Rights in India." *Berkeley Journal of International Law* 23, 201, 2005.

Johnson, Douglas H. "On the Nilotic Frontier: Imperial Ethiopia in the Southern Sudan, 1898–1936." In Donham, Donald L., and Wendy James, eds. *The Southern Marches of Imperial Ethiopia: Essays in History and Social Anthropology*, Athens: Ohio University Press 1986.

Joireman, Sandra Fullerton. "Opposition Politics and Ethnicity in Ethiopia: We Will All Go Down Together." *The Journal of Modern African Studies* 35, 3, 1997.

Joseph, Richard, ed. *State, Conflict, and Democracy in Africa*. Boulder, CO: Lynne Rienner Publishers, 1999.

Kane, Thomas Leiper. *Amharic-English Dictionary*. Wiesbaden: O. Harrassowitz, 1990.

Keller, Edmond J. *Revolutionary Ethiopia: From Empire to People's Republic*. Bloomington: Indiana University Press, 1988.

"Drought, War, and the Politics of Famine in Ethiopia and Eritrea." *The Journal of Modern African Studies* 30, 4, 1992.

"The Ethnogenesis of the Oromo Nation and Its Implications for Politics in Ethiopia." *The Journal of Modern African Studies* 33, 4, 1995.

"Making and Remaking State and Nation in Ethiopia." In *Borders, Nationalism, and the African State*, edited by Ricardo Rene Larémont. Boulder, CO: Lynne Rienner Publishers, 2005.

Keller, Edmond J. and Lahra Smith. "Obstacles to Implementing Territorial Decentralization: The First Decade of Ethiopian Federalism." In *Sustainable Peace: Power and Democracy after Civil Wars*, edited by Philip Roeder and Donald Rothchild. Ithaca, NY: Cornell University Press, 2005.

Kidane Mengisteab. "New Approaches to State Building in Africa: The Case of Ethiopia's Ethnic Based Federalism." *African Studies Review* 40, 3, 1997.

Kymlicka, Will. *Multicultural Citizenship: A Liberal Theory of Minority Rights*. New York: Oxford University Press, 1995.

Kymlicka, Will. *Can liberal pluralism be exported? Western political theory and ethnic relations in Eastern Europe*. NY: Oxford University Press, 2001.

Kymlicka, Will and Alan Patten, eds. *Language Rights and Political Theory*. Oxford and New York: Oxford University Press, 2003.

Laitin, David D. *Language Repertoires and State Construction in Africa*. Cambridge Studies in Comparative Politics. New York: Cambridge University Press, 1992.

Laitin, David D. and R. Reich. "A Liberal Democratic Approach to Language Justice." In *Language Rights and Political Theory*, edited by Kymlicka and Patten. NY: Oxford University Press. 2003.

Laitin, David D. and Said S. Samatar. *Somalia: Nation in Search of a State*. Profiles: Nations of Contemporary Africa. Boulder, CO: Westview Press, 1987.

Lake, David A. and Donald S. Rothchild. *The International Spread of Ethnic Conflict: Fear, Diffusion, and Escalation*. Princeton, NJ: Princeton University Press, 1998.

Laponce, J. and B. Saint-Jacques. "Introduction: Institutions as Problem-Solvers." *International Political Science Review* 18, 3, 1997.

Larémont, Rene Ricardo. *Borders, Nationalism, and the African State*. Boulder, CO: Lynne Rienner Publishers, 2005.

Leenco Lata. *The Ethiopian State at the Crossroads: Decolonization and Democratization or Disintegration?* Lawrenceville, NJ: Red Sea Press, 1999.

Lefort, René. "Powers – *Mengist* – and Peasants in Rural Ethiopia: The May 2005 Elections." *Journal of Modern African Studies* 45, 2, 2007.

"Ethiopia's Election: All Losers." *Open Democracy*, 2010.

Leslau, Wolf. *Concise Amharic Dictionary: Amharic-English: English-Amharic*. Wiesbaden: O. Harrassowitz, 1976.

Levine, Donald Nathan. *Greater Ethiopia: The Evolution of a Multiethnic Society*. 2nd ed. Chicago: University of Chicago Press, 2000.

"Oromo Narratives." *Journal of Oromo Studies* 14, 2, 2007.

Lewis, Karoki. "Celebrations at Lalibela." BBC slideshow. January 2009. http://news.bbc.co.uk/2/hi/7860753.stm.

Lijphart, Arend. *Democracy in Plural Societies: A Comparative Exploration*. New Haven, CT: Yale University Press, 1977.

"The Wave of Power-Sharing Democracy." In *The Architecture of Democracy: Constitutional Design, Conflict Management, and Democracy*, edited by Andrew Reynolds. New York: Oxford University Press, 2002.

Lindberg, Staffan I. *Democracy and Elections in Africa*. Baltimore, MD: Johns Hopkins University Press, 2006.

Lonsdale, John. "Moral and Political Argument in Kenya." In *Ethnicity and Democracy in Africa*, edited by Bruce Berman et al. *Ethnicity and Democracy in Africa*, Athens: Ohio University Press, 2004.

MacIntyre, A.C. *After Virtue: A Study in Moral Theory*. Notre Dame, IN: University of Notre Dame Press, 1981.

Mamdani, Mahmood. *Citizen and Subject: Contemporary Africa and the Legacy of Late Colonialism*. London: James Currey, 1996.

Manby, Bronwen. *Struggles for Citizenship in Africa*. New York: Zed Books, 2009.

Mannathoko, Changu. "Feminist Theories and the Study of Gender Issues in Southern Africa." In *Gender in Southern Africa: Conceptual and Theoretical Issues*, edited by Ruth Meena. Harare, Zimbabwe: SAPES Books, 1992.

Manning, Carrie. "Assessing African Party Systems after the Third Wave." *Party Politics* 11, 6, 2005.

Marcus, Harold G. *The Life and Times of Menilek II: Ethiopia 1844–1913.* Oxford Studies in African Affairs. Oxford: Clarendon Press, 1975.

A History of Ethiopia. Berkeley: University of California Press, 1994.

Markakis, John. "The Politics of Identity: The Case of the Gurage in Ethiopia." In *Ethnicity and the State in Eastern Africa*, edited by M.A. Mohamed Salih and J. Markakis. Uppsala, Sweden: Nordiska Afrikainstitutet, 1998.

"Ethnic Conflict in Pre-Federal Ethiopia." In *1st National Conference on Federalism, Conflict, and Peace Building.* Addis Ababa: Addis Ababa University, 2003.

Ethiopia: The Last Two Frontiers. Suffolk: James Currey, 2011.

Markakis, John and Asmelash Beyene. "Representative Institutions in Ethiopia." *The Journal of Modern African Studies* 5, 2, 1967.

Marshall, T.H. and T. Bottomore. *Citizenship and Social Class.* Concord, MA: Pluto Press, 1991.

Martiniello, Marco. "Citizenship." In *A Companion to Racial and Ethnic Studies*, edited by David Theo Goldberg and John Solomos. Malden, MA: Blackwell, 2002.

Mattes, Robert. "Understanding Identity in Africa: A first cut." Afrobarometer Working paper No. 38, 2004.

May, Stephen, ed. *Language and Minority Rights: Ethnicity, Nationalism, and the Politics of Language.* Language in Social Life Series. New York: Longman, 2001.

May, Stephen. "Misconceiving Minority Language Rights: Implications for Liberal Political Theory." In *Language Rights and Political Theory*, edited by Will Kymlicka and Alan Patten. New York: Oxford University Press, 2003.

McCann, James. *From Poverty to Famine in Northeast Ethiopia: A Rural History, 1900–1935.* University of Pennsylvania Press Publications in Ethnohistory. Philadelphia: University of Pennsylvania Press, 1987.

Orality, State Literacy, and Political Culture in Ethiopia: Translating the Ras Kassa Registers. Boston: Boston University, African Humanities Program, African Studies Center, 1991.

People of the Plow: An Agricultural History of Ethiopia, 1800–1990. Madison: University of Wisconsin Press, 1995.

McNabb, Christine. "Language Policy and Language Practice: Implementation Dilemmas in Ethiopia." Ph.D. dissertation, Institute of International Education, Stockholm, Sweden, 1989.

"Language Policy and Language Practice: Implementing Multilingual Literacy Education in Ethiopia." *African Studies Review* 33, 3, 1990.

Medhane Tadesse and John Young. "TPLF: Reform or Decline?" *Review of African Political Economy* 97, 2003.

Mekuria Bulcha. "The Survival and Reconstruction of Oromo National Identity." In *Being and Becoming Oromo: Historical and Anthropological Enquiries*, edited by Jan Hultin, Alessandro Triulzi and P.T.W. Baxter. Lawrenceville, NJ: Red Sea Press, 1996.

"The Politics of Linguistic Homogenization in Ethiopia and the Conflict over the Status of *Afaan Oromoo*." *African Affairs* 96, 1997.

The Making of the Oromo Diaspora: A Historical Sociology of Forced Migration. Minneapolis: Kirk House Publishers, 2002.

Mengistu Dessalegn. "A Study of the Initial Preparation of Textbooks in Sidamigna." Senior essay, Addis Ababa University, 1995.

Merera Gudina. *Ethiopia: Competing Ethnic Nationalisms and the Quest for Democracy, 1960–2000*. Addis Ababa: Shaker Publishers, 2003.

Merkel, Wolfgang. "Embedded and Defective Democracies." *Democratization* 11, 5, 2004.

Merry, Sally Engle. *Human Rights and Gender Violence: Translating International Law into Local Justice*. Chicago: University of Chicago Press, 2006.

Mesfin Molla. "The Attitude of Parents, Students, and Teachers in Using Hadigna as a Moi in Primary Schools of Hadiya Zone." Senior essay, Addis Ababa University, 2001.

Mikell, Gwendolyn. "Introduction." In *African Feminism: The Politics of Survival in Sub-Saharan Africa*. Edited by Gwendolyn Mikell, Philadelphia: University of Pennsylvania Press, 1997.

"Working from Within: Nigerian Women and Conflict Resolution" *Georgetown Journal of International Affairs*, 6, 2, 2005.

Mill, John Stuart. *Considerations on Representative Government*, edited by H. Acton. London: J.M. Dent, 1972.

Ministry of Education, Transitional Government of Ethiopia. "National Education and Training Policy (NETP)." Unpublished report. Addis Ababa: Ministry of Education, 1994.

Mo Ibrahim Foundation. "Press Release", October 3, 2010. http://www.moibrahimfoundation.org/en/pressrelease/media-centre/press-releases/overall-governance-performance-scores-in-africa-driven-by-gains-in-economic-and-human-development-bu.html

Mohammed Hassen. *The Oromo of Ethiopia: A History, 1570–1860*. New York: Cambridge University Press, 1990.

"Matcha-Tulama Association, 1963–1967 and the Development of Oromo Nationalism." In *The Search for Freedom and Democracy: Oromo Nationalism and Ethiopian Discourse*, edited by Asafa Jalata. Lawrenceville, NJ: Red Sea Press, 1998.

Mulugeta Seyoum. "The Development of the National Language in Ethiopia: A Study of Language Use and Policy." Ph.D. dissertation, Georgetown University, 1984.

Mutua, Makau. *Kenya's Quest for Democracy: Taming the Leviathan*. Boulder: Lynne Rienner Publishers, 2008.

National Committee on Traditional Practices of Ethiopia (NCTPE). "Baseline Survey on Harmful Traditional Practices in Ethiopia," 1998.

Unpublished paper presented at the workshop on Communication, Information, and Better Practices to Policymakers, August 2003.

Ndegwa, Stephen N. "Citizenship and Ethnicity: An Examination of Two Transition Moments in Kenyan Politics." *American Political Science Review* 91, 3, 1997.

A Decade of Democracy in Africa. Boston: Brill, 2001.

Norris, Pippa. "Choosing Electoral Systems: Proportional, Majoritarian, and Mixed Systems." *International Political Science Review* 18, 3, 1997.

North, Douglass Cecil. *Institutions, Institutional Change, and Economic Performance: The Political Economy of Institutions and Decisions.* Cambridge and New York: Cambridge University Press, 1990.

Okin, Susan Moller, Joshua Cohen, Matthew Howard, and Martha Craven Nussbaum. *Is Multiculturalism Bad for Women?* Princeton, NJ: Princeton University Press, 1999.

Oldfield, A. *Citizenship and Community: Civic Republicanism and the Modern World.* New York: Routledge, 1990.

Olmstead, Judith V. *Woman between Two Worlds: Portrait of an Ethiopian Rural Leader.* Urbana: University of Illinois Press, 1997.

Olukoshi, Adebayo O., Liisa Laakso, and Nordiska Afrikainstitutet. *Challenges to the Nation-State in Africa.* Uppsala, Sweden: Nordiska Afrikainstitutet, in cooperation with the Institute of Development Studies, University of Helsinki, 1996.

Original Wolde Giorgis. "Democratisation and Gender." In *Ethiopia: the Challenge of Democracy from Below,* edited by Bahru Zewde and Siegfried Pausewang. Uppsala, Sweden: Nordiska Afrikainstitutet, 2002.

Osaghae, Eghosa E. "Political Transitions and Ethnic Conflict in Africa." *Journal of Third World Studies* 21, 1, 2004.

Østebø, Marit Tolo. "*Wayyuu* – Women's Rights and Respect among the Arsi-Oromo." Draft paper presented at the 16th International Conference of Ethiopian Studies, Trondheim, Norway, July 2007a.

"Respected Women: A Study of Wayyuu and Its Implications for Women's Sexual Rights among the Arsi Oromo of Ethiopia." MA thesis, University of Bergin, 2007b.

Østebø, Terje. *Localising Salafism: Religious Change among Oromo Muslims in Bale, Ethiopia.* Boston: Brill, 2012.

Ottaway, Marina. "Ethnic Politics in Africa: Change and Continuity." In *State, Conflict, and Democracy in Africa,* edited by Richard Joseph, Boulder, CO: Lynne Rienner Publishers, 1999.

Ottaway, Marina and David Ottaway. *Ethiopia: Empire in Revolution.* New York: Africana Pub. Co., 1978.

Page, Melvin, Stephanie F. Beswick, Tim Carmichael, and Jay Spaulding, eds. *Personality and Political Culture in Modern Africa: Studies Presented to Professor Harold G. Marcus.* Boston: African Studies Center, Boston University, 1998.

Pankhurst, Alula and Damen Haile Mariam. "The *Iddir* in Ethiopia: Historical Development, Social Function, and Potential Role in HIV/AIDS Prevention and Control." *Northeast African Studies* 7, 2, 2000.

Pankhurst, Helen. *Gender, Development, and Identity: An Ethiopian Study.* London: Zed Books, 1992.

Pankhurst, Richard. *Language and Education in Ethiopia: Historical Background to the Post-War Period.* Addis Ababa: Haile Selassie I University, 1969.

A Social History of Ethiopia: The Northern and Central Highlands from Early Medieval Times to the Rise of Emperor Téwodros II. First American ed. Trenton, NJ: Red Sea Press, 1992.

Pankhurst, Rita. "Correspondent's Report: Women in Ethiopia Today." *Africa Today* 28, 1, 1981.

Parekh, Bhikhu C. *Rethinking Multiculturalism: Cultural Diversity and Political Theory.* Cambridge, MA: Harvard University Press, 2000.

Patten, Alan. "Political Theory and Language Policy." *Political Theory* 29, 5, 2001.

Pausewang, Siegfried. "Democratic Dialogue and Local Tradition." In *Ethiopia in Broader Perspective, Vol. II.* Kyoto: Shokado, 1997.

"Internal Politics." Unpublished paper, 2005.

Pausewang, Siegfried, ed. "Exploring New Political Alternatives for the Oromo in Ethiopia: Report from the Oromo Workshop and Its After-Effects." Bergen, Norway: Chr. Michelsen Institute, 2009.

Pausewang, Siegfried, Kjetil Tronvoll, and Lovise Aalen, eds. *Ethiopia since the Derg: A Decade of Democratic Pretension and Performance,* New York: Zed Books, 2002.

Perham, Margery Freda. *The Government of Ethiopia.* Evanston, IL: Northwestern University Press, 1969.

Pocock, J.G.A. "The Ideal of Citizenship since Classical Times." In *Theorizing Citizenship,* edited by Ronald Beiner. Albany: State University of New York Press, 1995.

Poluha, Eva. "Ethnicity and Democracy – A Viable Alliance?" In *Ethnicity and the State in Eastern Africa,* edited by M.A. Mohamed Salih and John Markakis. Uppsala, Sweden: Nordiska Afrikainstitutet, 1998.

Powell, Eve M. Troutt. *A Different Shade of Colonialism: Egypt, Great Britain, and the Mastery of the Sudan.* Berkeley: University of California Press, 2003.

Putnam, Robert. *Bowling Alone: The Collapse and Revival of American Community.* New York: Simon & Schuster, 2001.

Rawls, John. *A Theory of Justice.* Cambridge, MA: Belknap Press, 1971.

Raz, Joseph. "How Perfect should one be? And Whose Culture Is?" In *Is Multiculturalism Bad for Women?* Susan Moller Okin. Princeton, NJ: Princeton University Press, 1999.

Réaume, Denise G. "Beyond Personality: The Territorial and Personal Principles of Language Policy Reconsidered." In *Language Rights and Political Theory,* edited by Will Kymlicka and Alan Patten. New York: Oxford University Press, 2003.

Reid, Richard. *Frontiers of Violence in North-East Africa: Genealogies of Conflict since c. 1800.* Oxford: Oxford University Press, 2011.

Reilly, Ben and Andrew Reynolds, *Electoral Systems and Conflict in Divided Societies, Papers on International Conflict Resolution, No. 2.* Washington, DC: National Academy Press, 1999.

Reynolds, Andrew, ed. *The Architecture of Democracy: Constitutional Design, Conflict Management, and Democracy*. Oxford Studies in Democratization. New York: Oxford University Press, 2002.

Robins, Steven, Andrea Cornwall, and Bettina von Lieres. 2008. "Rethinking 'Citizenship' in the Postcolony." *Third World Quarterly* 29, 6, 2008.

Roeder, Philip G. and Donald S. Rothchild. *Sustainable Peace: Power and Democracy after Civil Wars*. Ithaca, NY: Cornell University Press, 2005.

Rothchild, Donald S., and Victor A. Olorunsola. *State versus Ethnic Claims: African Policy Dilemmas*. Westview Special Studies on Africa. Boulder, CO: Westview Press, 1983.

Roy-Campbell, Zaline M. *Empowerment through Language: The African Experience – Tanzania and Beyond*. Trenton, NJ and Asmara, Eritrea: Africa World Press, 2001.

Ruth Iyob. *The Eritrean Struggle for Independence: Domination, Resistance, Nationalism, 1941–1993*. Cambridge and New York: Cambridge University Press, 1995.

Samatar, Abdi Ismail. "Ethiopian Federalism: Autonomy versus Control in the Somali Region." *Third World Quarterly* 25, 6, 2004.

Sanchez, Janet Hoard. "Political Incorporation in Ethiopia, 1875–1900: The Gurage, Jimma, and Limmu-Enarea." MA thesis, California State University, 1974.

Sandel, M.J. *Liberalism and the Limits of Justice*. New York: Cambridge University Press, 1982.

Sartori, Giovanni. *Comparative Constitutional Engineering: An Inquiry into Structures, Incentives, and Outcomes*. New York: New York University Press, 1994.

Save the Children/US. "Women on the Front Lines of Health care: State of the World's Mothers 2010," May 2010.

Scarritt, James R. and Shaheen Mozaffar. "The Specification of Ethnic Cleavages and Ethnopolitics Groups for the Analysis of Democratic Competition in Contemporary Africa." *Nationalism and Ethnic Politics* 5, 1999.

Semir Yusuf. "The Politics of *Historying*: A Postmodern Commentary on Bahru Zewde's *History of Modern Ethiopia*." *African Journal of Political Science and International Relations* 3, 9, 2009.

Shachar, Ayelet. *Multicultural Jurisdictions: Cultural Differences and Women's Rights, Contemporary Political Theory*. Cambridge and New York: Cambridge University Press, 2001.

The Birthright Lottery: Citizenship and Global Inequality. Cambridge, MA: Harvard University Press, 2009.

Shack, William. *The Gurage: A People of the Ensete Culture*. London: Oxford University Press, 1966.

The Central Ethiopians: Amhara, Tigrigna, and Related Peoples. Ethnographic Survey of Africa, Part IV. London: International African Institute, 1974.

Sherif Leri. "A History of the Silti Community in Addis Ababa: A Study in Rural-Urban Migration." Senior thesis, Addis Ababa University, 1985.

Shinn, David H. "Ethiopia: The Oromo and the Oromo Liberation Front." Unpublished paper, 2004.

Silte People's Democracy Union Party. "Party Statement." 2002.

Sisk, Timothy D. *Democratization in South Africa: The Elusive Social Contract.* Princeton, NJ: Princeton University Press, 1995.

Power Sharing and International Mediation in Ethnic Conflicts. Perspectives Series. Washington, DC: United States Institute of Peace Press, 1996.

Sklar, R.L. "African Politics: The Next Generation." In *State, Conflict, and Democracy in Africa*, edited by Richard Joseph. Boulder: Lynne Rienner Publishers, 1999.

Skutnabb-Kangas, Tove. *Multilingualism for All.* European Studies on Multilingualism, 4. Lisse, the Netherlands: Swets & Zeitlinger, 1995.

Skutnabb-Kangas, Tove and Robert Phillipson. *Rights to Language: Equity, Power, and Education: Celebrating the 60th Birthday of Tove Skutnabb-Kangas.* Mahwah, N.: L. Erlbaum Associates, 2000.

Smith, Lahra. "Voting for a Nationality: Ethnic Identity, Political Institutions, and Citizenship in Ethiopia." Ph.D. dissertation, University of California, Los Angeles, 2005.

"Voting for an Ethnic Identity: Procedural and Institutional Responses to Ethnic Conflict in Ethiopia." *Journal of Modern African Studies* 45, 4, 2007.

"The Politics of Contemporary Language Policy in Ethiopia." *Journal of Developing Societies* 24, 2, 2008.

"Explaining Violence after Recent Elections in Ethiopia and Kenya." *Democratization* 16, 5, 2009.

"A Disturbance or a Massacre? The Consequences of Electoral Violence in Ethiopia." In *Voting in Fear: Electoral Violence in sub-Saharan Africa*, edited by Dorina Bekoe. Washington, DC: United States Institute of Peace Press, 2012.

Smith, R.M. "The 'American Creed' and American Identity: The Limits of Liberal Citizenship in the United States." *Western Political Science Quarterly* 41, 1988.

Solomon Lemma. "Survey Study of Teachers and Parents Attitude toward Using Wolaitta Language as a Medium of Instruction in Primary Schools in Wolaitta." Senior essay, Addis Ababa University, 1995.

Song, Sarah. *Justice, Gender, and the Politics of Multiculturalism.* New York: Cambridge University Press, 2007.

Sorenson, John. *Imagining Ethiopia: Struggles for History and Identity in the Horn of Africa.* New Brunswick, NJ: Rutgers University Press, 1993.

Sosena Demessie and Tsahai Yibark. "A Review of National Policy on Ethiopian Women." In *Digest of Ethiopia's National Policies, Strategies, and Programs*, edited by Taye Assefa. Addis Ababa: Forum for Social Studies, 2008.

Spears, Ian. "Africa: The Limits of Power-Sharing." *Journal of Democracy* 13, 3, 2002.

Stepan, Alfred C. *Arguing Comparative Politics.* New York: Oxford University Press, 2001.

Taylor, Charles. *Philosophical Arguments.* Cambridge, MA: Harvard University Press, 1995.

Taylor, Charles, Amy Gutmann, and Charles Taylor. *Multiculturalism: Examining the Politics of Recognition.* Princeton, NJ: Princeton University Press, 1994.

Teferra Haile-Selassie. *The Ethiopian Revolution, 1974–91: From a Monarchical Autocracy to a Military Oligarchy.* New York: Kegan Paul International, 1997.

Teshale Tibebu. *The Making of Modern Ethiopia: 1896–1974.* Lawrenceville, NJ: The Red Sea Press, 1995.

"Review of *Prowess, Piety, and Politics: The Chronicles of Abeto Iyasu and Empress Zewditu of Ethiopia (1909–1930)* by Gebre-Igziabiher Elyas and Reidulf K. Molvaer." *The International Journal of African Historical Studies* 30, 1, 1997.

Teshome G. Wagaw. "Education and Language Policy in a Divided Ethiopia: Reversing the Quest of the Centuries and Pressing toward the Uncharted Future." In *Ethiopia in Broader Perspective, Vol. III.* Kyoto: Shokado, 1997.

"Conflict of Ethnic Identity and the Language of Education Policy in Contemporary Ethiopia." *Northeast African Studies* 6, 3, 1999.

Tibebe Eshete. "A Reassessment of Lij Iyasu's Political Career with Particular Emphasis upon His Fall." In *Personality and Political Culture in Modern Africa: Studies Presented to Professor Harold G. Marcus,* edited by Melvin E. Page et al. Boston: African Studies Center, Boston University, 1998.

Tiffen, Mary. "Transition in Sub-Saharan Africa: Agriculture, Urbanization, and Income Growth." *World Development* 31, 8, 2003.

Tilly, Charles. "Citizenship, identity and social history," *International Review of Social history* 41, 3, 1995.

Tollefson, James W. and Amy Tsui. *Medium of Instruction Policies: Which Agenda? Whose Agenda?* Mahwah, NJ: L. Erlbaum Publishers, 2004.

Trimingham, J. Spencer. *Islam in Ethiopia.* London: Frank Cass, 1965.

Tronvoll, Kjetil. *War and the Politics of Identity in Ethiopia: Making Enemies and Allies in the Horn of Africa.* Suffolk, UK: James Currey, 2009.

Tsegaye Regassa. "Federalism, Democracy, and Governance." Unpublished paper, 2002.

"Regulating Local-State Behavior: Towards Entrenching Constitutionalism at the Sub-National level in Ethiopia." Unpublished paper, June 2008.

"Sub-National Constitutions in Ethiopia: Towards Entrenching Constitutionalism at State Level." *Mizan Law Review,* 3, 1, 2009.

Tsehai Berhane-Selassie. "Ethiopian Rural Women and the State." In *African Feminism: The Politics of Survival in Sub-Saharan Africa,* edited by Gwendolyn Mikell, Philadelphia: University of Pennsylvania Press, 1997.

"Ethiopia." In *The Greenwood Encyclopedia of Women's Issues Worldwide,* vol. 6, edited by Lynn Walter et al. Westwood, CT: Greenwood Press, 2003.

Tully, James. *Strange Multiplicity: Constitutionalism in an Age of Diversity.* New York: Cambridge University Press, 1995.

"The Challenge of Reimagining Citizenship and Belonging in Multicultural and Multinational Societies." In *The Demands of Citizenship,* edited by Catriona McKinnon and Iain Hampsher-Monk. New York: Continuum, 2000.

UNICEF Country Statistics: Ethiopia. http://www.unicef.org/infobycountry/ethiopia_statistics.html, September 2012.

UNICEF Innocenti Research Center. "The Dynamics of Social Change: Towards the Abandonment of Female Genital Mutilation/Cutting in Five African Countries." Florence, Italy: UNICEF, 2010.

USAID/Ethiopia. *Ethiopia Education Sector Review*, Part II, June 1996.

U.S. Department of State. "Ethiopia: Country Reports on Human Rights Practices," edited by Human Rights and Labor Bureau of Democracy, 2000.

——— "Ethiopia: Country Reports on Human Rights Practices," edited by Human Rights and Labor Bureau of Democracy, 2004.

Vaughan, Sarah. *Ethnicity and Power in Ethiopia*, Ph.D. Dissertation, University of Edinburgh, Scotland, 2003.

——— "Responses to Ethnic Federalism in Ethiopia's Southern Region." In *Ethnic Federalism: The Ethiopian Experience in Comparative Perspective*, edited by D. Turton. Athens: Ohio University Press, 2006.

Vaughan, Sarah and Kjetil Tronvoll. "Ethiopia: Structures and Relations of Power." In *Background Documents: Country Strategy*. SIDA studies no. 10, March 2003.

Volpp, Leti. "Feminism versus Multiculturalism." *Columbia Law Review* 101, 5, 2001.

Walzer, Michael. *Spheres of Justice: A Defence of Pluralism and Equality*. New York: Basic Books, 1983.

Wamwere, Koigi. *Negative Ethnicity: From Bias to Genocide*. New York: Seven Stories Press, 2003.

Whitaker, Beth. "Citizens and Foreigners: Democratization and the Politics of Exclusion in Africa." *African Studies Review* 48, 1, 2005.

Wing, Susanna D. *Constructing Democracy in Transitioning Societies in Africa: Constitutionalism and Deliberation in Mali*. New York: Palgrave Macmillan, 2008.

Woldemariam, Mesfin. "Where Will the Present Path Take Us?" *Vision 2020: Whither Ethiopia?* Addis Ababa: Ethiopian Economic Association, 2003.

Woods, Dwayne. "The Tragedy of the Cocoa Pod: Rent-seeking, Land and Ethnic Conflict in Ivory Coast." *The Journal of Modern African Studies*, 41, 4, December 2003.

Woodward, Peter and Murray Forsyth. *Conflict and Peace in the Horn of Africa: federalism and its alternatives*. Brookfield, VY: Dartmouth Publishing Co. 1994.

Worku Nida. *Jabidu: YaGurage Hizb Bahilena Tarik*. Addis Ababa: Bole Printing Press, 1991.

——— "Gurage Urban Migration and the Dynamics of Cultural Life in the Village." In *Essays on Gurage Language and Culture*, Grover Hudson, ed. Wiesbaden: Harrasowitz Verlg, 1996.

——— "*Fanonet*: Ethnohistorical Notes on the Gurage Urban Migration in Ethiopia." *Ufahamu: Journal of the African Activist Association* 28, 2–3, 2000.

Wunsch, James S., and Dele Olowu, eds. *The Failure of the Centralized State: Institutions and Self-Governance in Africa*. Boulder: Westview Press, 1990.

Yanow, Dvora. *How Does a Policy Mean? Interpreting Policy and Organizational Actions.* Washington, DC: Georgetown University Press, 1996.

Yitah, Helen. "'Fighting with proverbs': Kasena Women's (Re)Definition of Female Personhood through Proverbial Jesting," *Research in African Literatures*, 40, 3, 2009.

Young, Crawford. *The Rising Tide of Cultural Pluralism: The Nation-State at Bay?* Madison: University of Wisconsin Press, 1993.

    The African Colonial State in Comparative Perspective. New Haven, CT: Yale University Press, 1994.

Young, Iris Marion. *Justice and the Politics of Difference.* Princeton, NJ: Princeton University Press, 1990.

Young, John. "Along Ethiopia's Western Frontier: Gambella and Benishangul in Transition." *The Journal of Modern African Studies* 37, 1999.

Zerihun Kebede. "Problems of Using Hadiyegna as a Medium of Instruction in Primary Schools in Lemmo Woreda." Senior essay, Addis Ababa University, 2001.

Zuern, Elke. 2009. "Democratization as Liberation: Competing African Perspectives on Democracy." *Democratization* 16, 3, 2009.

Government and Political Party Documents

Benishangul-Gumuz Regional Education Bureau (REB). "Education Statistics Annual Abstract," edited by Education Management Information Systems, 2000.

EPRDF (Ethiopian People's Revolutionary Democratic Front). "Concluding Local Elections." Unpublished, n.d.a.

    "Constitutional Right – The Question of Identity." Unpublished, n.d.b.

    "EPRDF's Five-Year Program of Development, Peace and Democracy." Unpublished, 2000.

Ethiopia. "Constitution of the Democratic Republic of Ethiopia." 1995.

Ethiopia, Central Statistical Authority. "The 1984 Population and Housing Census of Ethiopia: Analytical Report at National Level," edited by Office of the Population and Housing Census Commission. Central Statistical Authority, 1991.

    Central Statistical Authority. "1994 Population and Housing Census of Ethiopia." 1996.

    "The 1994 Population and Housing Census of Ethiopia, Results for Oromiya Region, Vol. I, Parts I & II," edited by Office of Population and Housing Census Commission. Addis Ababa: Central Statistical Authority, 1996.

    "The 1994 Population and Housing Census of Ethiopia, Results for Southern Nations, Nationalities, and People's Region, Vol. II Analytical Report," edited by Office of Population and Housing Census Commission. Addis Ababa: Central Statistical Authority, 1998.

    "The 1994 Population and Housing Census of Ethiopia: Results at Country Level, Vol. I: Statistical Report," edited by Office of Population and Housing Census Commission. Addis Ababa: Central Statistical Authority, 1998.

"The 1994 Population and Housing Census of Ethiopia, Results at Country Level, Vol. II: Analytical Report," edited by Office of Population and Housing Census Commission. Addis Ababa: Central Statistical Authority, 1999.

"The 2007 Population and Housing Census of Ethiopia," edited by Office of Population and Housing Census Commission. Addis Ababa: Central Statistical Authority, online at http://www.csa.gov.et/, 2007.

"Ethiopia 2011 Demographic and Health Survey." Addis Ababa: Central Statistical Authority, 2011.

Ethiopia, Institute for the Study of Ethiopian Nationalities (ISEN). "Excerpts from Documents of the Founding Congress of WPE on the People's Democratic State and the Nationalities Question." 1984.

A Brief Almanac of Ethiopian Nationalities (Amharic), 1986. This is all I have. It was a government document, not officially "published" but available at Addis Ababa University in Amharic.

Ethiopia, Ministry of Education. "Education Sector Development Program Action Plan." 1999a.

"Indicators of the Ethiopian Education System." 1999b.

"Education Sector Development Program Report." 2000.

"Education Sector Development Programme (ESDP) Consolidated National Performance Report: 1999/00." 2001a.

"Ethiopia Education Sector Development Programme (ESDP) Mid-Term Review Mission, 1." 2001b.

"Indicators of the Ethiopian Education System." edited by EMIS, 2003.

Civic and Ethical Educational Student's Textbook, Grade 9. Addis Ababa, Ethiopia: Ministry of Education, September 2003.

Ethiopia, Negarit Gazeta. "Proclamation to Provide for the Establishment of National/Regional Self-Governments: Proc.7/1992." Addis Ababa, 1992.

"Constitution of the Federal Democratic Republic of Ethiopia, Proc. No. 1/1995." Addis Ababa, 1995a.

"Proclamation to Make the Electoral Law of Ethiopia Conform with the Constitution of The Federal Democratic Republic of Ethiopia, Proc. 111/1995." Addis Ababa, 1995b.

"The Revised Family Code Proclamation of 2000, Proc. No. 213/2000." Addis Ababa, 2000.

"Reorganization of the Executive Organs of the Federal Democratic Republic of Ethiopia, Proc. 256/2001." Addis Ababa, 2001.

Ethiopia, The National Literacy Campaign Coordinating Committee. "Every Ethiopian Will be Literate and Will Remain Literate," Addis Ababa, May 1981.

Transitional Government of Ethiopia. "National Education and Training Policy (NETP)." Addis Ababa: Ministry of Education, 1994.

House of Federation. "Bahrewerq Mesmes People Case – House of Federation." Unpublished, Addis Ababa, 2000a (Mo08/93).

"Benishangul-Gumuz Language Case #1 Dissenting Opinion – House of Federation." Unpublished, Addis Ababa, 2000b.

"Benishangul-Gumuz Language Case #2 Letter from the Regional President – House of Federation." Unpublished, Addis Ababa, 2000c.

"Benishangul-Gumuz Language Case #3 Recommendation of the CCI and HOF." Unpublished, Addis Ababa, 2000d.

"Denta Budem Kinchichila People's Case, House of Federation (CCI) and Dissenting Opinion." Unpublished, Addis Ababa, 2000e (DDB/08/72/93).

House of Federation, Parliament of Ethiopia. "Siltie Identity Determination Case, HTMF 15/4013/1." Addis Ababa. Unpublished, 2001.

Magalata Oromiyaa Proc. 46/2001. "Revised Constitution of 2001 of the Oromia Region." 2001.

SNNPR Regional Education Bureau (REB). "Educational Statistics Annual Abstract, SNNPR," edited by Program Plan, Project and Information Service. Addis Ababa, 2001–2002.

Newspaper Articles

Abera Degefa, "Language in Ethiopia." *The Reporter,* June 11, 2003.

Addis Tribune. "NEB Says *Siltes* Vote for Independent Nationality." *Addis Tribune,* April 13, 2001.

Beshir Gedda. "The Question of Ethnicity in Ethiopia." *Addis Tribune,* October 6, 2001.

Delsol, Colette, "Interview with Dawud Ibsa Ayanna." *Les Nouvelles,* March 29, 2006.

Independent Online. "Ethiopian Court Jails Five for 'Massacre.'" April 2, 2005, online at www.iol.co.za.

Jewell, James. "Culture Allies: Ethiopian Government Donates Land for Hundreds of Congregations." *Christianity Today,* May 17, 2005.

Kelyesus Bekele. "The So-Called Independent Newspapers disseminate False Reports on the Conflict in Gambella." *The Reporter,* June 23, 2004.

Melaku Demissie. "Scholar Recommends English as Federal Working Language." *The Reporter,* June 11, 2003.

Reuters. "Ethiopia Clashes Kill Six in Dispute over Boundary." February 23, 2005.

Samuel Assefa. "Two Concepts of Sovereignty." *Addis Tribune,* March 24, 2000.

Shetty, Priya. "Bogaletch Gebre: Ending Female Genital Mutilation in Ethiopia." *The Lancet* 369, 957, 2071, June 2007.

Tedla Desta. "Over 5 Mln. Children with No Access to Education." *The Daily Monitor,* December 12, 2004.

United Nations Office for the Coordination of Humanitarian Affairs, Integrated Regional Information Networks (IRIN). "At Least 15 Killed in Awasa Riots." May 27, 2002.

"Uneasy Calm Restored in Awasa." June 25, 2002.

"Focus on Gambella Violence." January 8, 2004a.

"Renewed Fighting Reported in the West." February 9, 2004b.

"Soldiers to Be Tried over Gambella Killings." March 18, 2005.

Visafric. "Riots, Deaths over New Language in Ethiopia." November 9, 1999, online at www.visafric.com.

Wainaina, Binyavanga. "No Country for Old Hatreds." *New York Times,* January 6, 2008.

Wiren, Robert. "Interview with Bulcha Demeksa." *Les Nouvelles,* April 14, 2005.

World Organization against Torture. "Ethiopia: 'From Today Forward There Will Be No Anuak': the Attempted Elimination of the Anuak People." Press Release, April 13, 2004.

Interviews

Interview #9: Academic, Addis Ababa, January 2003.

Interview #13: Academic, Addis Ababa, January 2003.

Interview #17: NGO Representative, Addis Ababa, February 2003.

Interview #23: Official, House of Federation, Addis Ababa, February 2003.

Interview #27: NGO Representative, Addis Ababa, March 2003.

Interview #28: NGO Representative, Addis Ababa, March 2003.

Interview #35: Academic, Addis Ababa, April 2003.

Interview #41: Official, Oromiya Regional Education Bureau (REB), Addis Ababa/Finfinee, May 2003.

Interview #42: Academic, Addis Ababa, May 2003.

Interview #43: Official, Wolaitta Zone Education Office (ZEO), Soddo, June 2003.

Interview #46: Official, Southern Nations, Nationalities and People's Regional Education Bureau (REB), Awassa, June 2003.

Interview #48: NGO Representative, Soddo, June 2003.

Interview #50: Technical Expert, Oromiya Regional Education Bureau (REB), Addis Ababa/Finfinee, July 2003.

Interview #51: Technical Expert, Oromiya Regional Education Bureau (REB), Addis Ababa/Finfinee, July 2003.

Interview #52: Technical Expert, Oromiya Regional Education Bureau (REB), Addis Ababa/Finfinee, July 2003.

Interview #54: Official, Southern Nations, Nationalities, and People's (SNNPR) Regional Bureau of Education (REB), Awassa, June 2003.

Interview #58: Official, Gurage Zone Education Office (ZEO), Welkite, September 2003.

Interview #61: Head, Local/Regional NGO, Addis Ababa, September 2003.

Interview #64: Academic, Addis Ababa, September 2003.

Interview #65: NGO representative, Addis Ababa, October 2003.

Interview #66: Official, Siltie Zone Education Office (ZEO), Worabe, October 2003.

Interview #67: Official, Siltie Zone Education Office (ZEO), Worabe, October 2003.

Interview #71: Official, Benishangul Gumuz Information Bureau, Assosa, October 2003.

Interview #76: Official, Bale Zone Education Office (ZEO), Robe, October 2003.

Interview #85: Member of Parliament, Addis Ababa, November 2003.

Interview #87: Official, Oromiya Regional Education Bureau (REB), Addis Ababa/Finfinee, May 2003.

Interview #88: Academic, Addis Ababa, December 2003.

Interview #90: Representative, Siltie People's Democratic Unity Party (SPDUP), Addis Ababa, December 2003.

Index

BOOKS IN THIS SERIES